DICTIONARY OF BASIC BIBLICAL HEBREW

SHLOMO KARNI

DICTIONARY OF BASIC BIBLICAL HEBREW

carta
JERUSALEM

Shlomo Karni

Dictionary of Basic Biblical Hebrew

Arrangement: Tamara Shauli
Cover design: Tsahi Ben-Ami

Carta, Jerusalem
18 Ha'uman Street, P.O. Box 2500, Jerusalem 91024
E-mail: cartaben@netvision.net.il
Website: http://holyland-jerusalem.com

ISBN 965-220-498-6

Printed in Israel

IN LOVING MEMORY OF MY PARENTS
ITZHAK AND CHANA PROMNICKI

לעילוי נשמות הורַי

יצחק שמואל וחנה פרומניצקי

FOREWORD

This dictionary is intended for English speakers with a basic knowledge of Hebrew and a keen desire to read the Bible in its original language. Such users may be religious school students and teachers, universities and colleges with Hebrew/Bible programs, seminary students and teachers, rabbis, priests, ministers, and other students of Scripture.

In line with the declared objectives, this dictionary relates to most of the Pentateuch, Joshua, Judges, Samuel (I, II), Kings (I, II), Ruth and Esther, as well as parts of Ezra, Nehemiah and Chronicles (I, II).

My compilation was done with careful methodology. Over the past twenty-seven years of teaching Biblical Hebrew, I had asked each student to keep a running list of words that he/she/we used in class. The compilation of all these lists, some 1,600, form the basis for the dictionary. I discovered, much to my delight, that a beautiful pattern had emerged: almost every entry appears an average of six times in the Hebrew Bible.

In compiling the English translation of the entries, I consulted the Jewish Publication Society (JPS), the King James Version (KJV), the Revised Standard Version (RSV), the Jerusalem Bible and the Oxford edition of the Bible.

Dictionary of Basic Biblical Hebrew consists of two parts:

Dictionary of some 6,400 entries of the most common words in the Hebrew Bible (*Tanach*). Entries are based and explained on the concept of the *root* and *patterns* of a word.

For instance, the entry נִפְקַד is found under "נ", and is cross-referenced with פקד, where it is listed among other verbal stems of that root. Similarly, a common name like חַוָּה is translated as "Eve" and its root is cited as חיה ("live"), so as to explain the textual "because" in "because she was the mother of all the living" (Genesis 3:20).

Grammar: introduction to basic grammar and syntax with topics such as prefixes and suffixes; nouns; gender; number; adjectives; tenses; verbs and stems. Explanations are simple and easily understood. Terms used are those approved by The Academy of the Hebrew Language. Typical among these is: וָו הַהִפּוּךְ, translated as "ו marking the future," or "ו marking the past," rather than descriptions such as "w*aw* conversive" or "inversion *waw.*"

Existing Hebrew-English dictionaries such as Megiddo and Ben-Yehuda, are general in nature *Dictionary of Basic Biblical Hebrew* concentrates on the treasures of Biblical words and cross-references approaches to roots

Another feature is the section which eases the reader into the structure of Biblical Hebrew.

Dictionary of Basic Biblical Hebrew is thus the ideal stepping stone to more elaborate works such as those of Klein, Brown-Driver-Briggs, Mandelkern, Koehler & Baumgartner or Even-Shoshan.

Shlomo Karni

CONTENTS

FORMAT OF ENTRIES

Noun:
singular, singular construct-; plural, plural construct-;
(Alternate patterns are given, sometimes in parentheses.)

Examples:

1. n.m. ; **בַּיִת, בֵּית-** ; **בָּתִּים, בָּתֵּי**
   a. house, home
   b. household, family
   c. holder
   d. tribe, people
   e. within מִבַּיִת

2. n.f. ; **יָד, יַד-** ; **יָדַיִם, יְדֵי-** ; **יָדוֹת, יְדוֹת-**
   a. hand
   b. handle
   c. portion, share
   d. area
   e. monument

Note: In many cases, as here, there are two forms of the plural.

Adjective:
masculine, masculine construct-; feminine, feminine construct-; masculine plural, masculine plural construct-; feminine plural, feminine plural construct-;

Example:
adj. ; **יָפֶה, יְפֵה-** ; **יָפָה, יְפַת-** ; **יָפוֹת, יְפוֹת-**
beautiful, handsome

Note: Here, the m.pl. is not given, since it is not used in the Bible within the scope of this dictionary.

Verb:
Unvowelled root letters v. פעל
The seven verbal stems with their associated numbers 1), 2),..., 7). Listed in the third person, m.s., ("he") in the past tense. Not all verbs have all seven stems. The seven stems are:
1) קַל (פָּעַל) 2) נִפְעַל 3) פִּעֵל 4) פֻּעַל 5) הִתְפַּעֵל 6) הִפְעִיל 7) הָפְעַל

Root:

The root accompanies an entry, to provide a better understanding and as a cross-reference to be looked up.

Note: In some cases the root given is based on the interpretation of the word as it appears in the Bible, rather than its etymology (e.g., בָּבֶל root בלל, rather than the Akkadian bab'il, 'the gate of (the God) 'il').

Example:

מֹאזְנַיִם, מֹאזְנֵי- ; n.m.pl.

scales; balance (root: אזן)

For the convenience of the reader, the Hebrew alphabet and the list of the seven verbal stems appear at the bottom of alternate pages in the dictionary.

ABBREVIATIONS

adj.	adjective
adv.	adverb
conj.	conjunction
f.	feminine
inter.	interjection
m.	masculine
n.	noun
num.	number,numerical
pl.	plural
prep.	preposition
pron.	pronoun
pr.n.	proper noun, personal name
s.	singular

HEBREW-ENGLISH DICTIONARY OF THE BIBLE

This dictionary, in line with common usage, reads from left to right. Each page, however, is arranged in Hebrew sequence with the right column to be read first. ➤

א

אָב, אַב-, אֲבִי-; אָבוֹת, אֲבוֹת- n.m.
a. father
b. elder
c. founder
d. leader
e. parents אָבוֹת
f. family בֵּית-אָב

אבד v.
1) אָבַד be destroyed; be lost
3) אִבֵּד destroy
6) הֶאֱבִיד destroy

אֲבֵדָה, אֲבֵדַת- n.f. loss; lost item

אֲבַדּוֹן n.m.
a. destruction
b. death
c. tomb (root: אבד)

אבה v.
1) אָבָה want; desire

אָבִיב n.m.
a. wheat (unripened)
b. Abib, name of a month

אֶבְיוֹן, אֶבְיוֹן-; אֶבְיוֹנִים, אֶבְיוֹנֵי-;
n.m. poor, needy

אֲבִימֶלֶךְ pr.n.m. Abimelech
("king's father") (roots: אָב, מֶלֶךְ)

אַבִּיר, אַבִּיר-; אַבִּירִים, אַבִּירֵי-;
n., adj., m.
a. strong; brave
b. bull
c. horse; horseman (?)

אָבִיר, אֲבִיר- n.m. Strong One, attribute of God

אבל v.
1) אָבַל
a. dry up, wither
b. mourn, be sad
5) הִתְאַבֵּל be in mourning
6) הֶאֱבִיל
a. dry up
b. destroy

אָבֵל, אֲבֵל-; אֲבֵלִים, אֲבֵלֵי-;
n., adj., m. sad, in mourning

אֵבֶל, אֵבֶל- n.m. mourning

אֲבָל adv., conj.
a. but
b. indeed

אֶבֶן, אֶבֶן-; אֲבָנִים, אַבְנֵי-; n.f.
a. stone, rock
b. ancient weight

אַבְנֵט, אַבְנֵט-; אַבְנֵטִים n.m.
sash; wide belt worn by the priest

אַבְנֵר pr.n.m. Abner ("father of Ner")
(roots: אָב, נֵר)

אָבָק, אֲבַק- n.m. dust

אַבְרָהָם pr.n.m. Abraham
(see following entry)

אַבְרָם pr.n.m. Abram ("lofty leader")
(roots: אָב, רָם)
Abraham's original name

אַבְשָׁלוֹם pr.n.m. Absalom
("father of peace")
(roots: אָב, שָׁלוֹם)

אֲגַם, אֲגַם-; אֲגַמִּים, אַגְמֵי-; n.m.
a. lake
b. thicket; reed

אַגְמוֹן n.m. reed

אֲגַף; אֲגַפִּים n.m. battalion

אִגֶּרֶת, אִגֶּרֶת- ; אִגְּרוֹת, אִגְּרוֹת- ; n.f.
letter, message

אֱדוֹם pr.n.m. Edom (root: אָדֹם)

אָדוֹן, אֲדוֹן- ; אֲדוֹנִים, אֲדוֹנֵי- ; n.m.
a. ruler; master; owner
b. honorary title of God (root: דין?)

אַדִּיר, אַדִּיר- ; אַדִּירִים, אַדִּירֵי- ; adj., n.m.
a. great
b. mighty
c. a powerful person

אדם v.
1) אָדַם be red
4) מְאָדָּם painted red (present tense)
5) הִתְאַדֵּם glow red
6) הֶאְדִּים become red

אָדֹם adj. m. red

אָדָם pr.n.m., n.m.
a. Adam (root: אֲדָמָה)
b. human being; mortal
c. mankind
d. man בֶּן-אָדָם (roots: בֵּן, אָדָם)

אֲדַמְדַּם ; אֲדַמְדֶּמֶת ; אֲדַמְדַּמּוֹת adj.
reddish

אֲדָמָה, אַדְמַת- ; אֲדָמוֹת, אַדְמוֹת- ; n.f.
a. land
b. field
c. dirt
d. country

אֶדֶן, אֶדֶן- ; אֲדָנִים, אַדְנֵי- ; n.m.
basis, foundation

אֲדֹנָי pr.n.m. one of God's names ("my Lord") (root: אָדוֹן)

אֲדֹנִיָּהוּ pr.n.m. Adonijah ("my master is God") (root: אָדוֹן, יָהּ)

אַדֶּרֶת, אַדֶּרֶת- ; n.f. leather coat

אהב v.
1) אָהַב
a. love
b. like
c. enjoy
3) אִהֵב desire; lust

אַהֲבָה, אַהֲבַת- ; n.f.
a. love
b. friendship

אֲהָהּ interj. ah; alas

אֹהֶל, אֹהֶל- ; אֹהָלִים, אָהֳלֵי- ; n.m.
a. tent
b. cover
c. residence; home

אַהֲרֹן pr.n.m. Aaron

אוֹ conj.
a. or
b. and if
c. or else
d. otherwise

אוֹב, אוֹב- ; אוֹבוֹת, אוֹבוֹת- ; n.m.
a. ghost; spirit
b. spell
c. person who conjures spirits

אוֹדוֹת n.f.pl. deeds, acts
Used only with עַל: concerning, regarding, on account of עַל אוֹדוֹת

אוה v.
3) אִוָּה desire; wish; want
5) הִתְאַוָּה covet; desire

אַוָּה, אַוַּת- ; n.f. desire

אוֹי interj. alas; woe to...

אוֹיֵב, אוֹיֵב- ; אוֹיְבִים, אוֹיְבֵי- ; n.m.
enemy; adversary (root: איב)

אֱוִיל ; אֱוִילִים adj., n.m.
a. boor
b. fool

אוּלַי conj. perhaps

1) קַל (פָּעַל) 2) נִפְעַל 3) פִּעֵל 4) פֻּעַל 5) הִתְפַּעֵל 6) הִפְעִיל 7) הָפְעַל

אוּלָם conj. however; but

אוּלָם, אוּלָם-; אוּלָמִים, אוּלַמֵּי-; n.m.
a. hall
b. portico; porch

אִוֶּלֶת, אִוֶּלֶת-; n.f. foolishness; boorishness; stupidity

אָוֶן, אוֹן n.m.
a. lie
b. delusion; nothingness
c. evil thoughts

אוֹן; אוֹנִים n.m., pr.n.
a. strength
b. mourning
c. On (pr.n.)

אוֹפֶה n.m. baker
(root: אפה)

אוֹפַן (אוֹפָן), אוֹפַן-; אוֹפַנִּים, אוֹפַנֵּי-;
wheel n.m.

אוץ v.
1) אָץ hurry; rush
6) הֵאִיץ press; urge

אוֹצָר, אוֹצַר-; אוֹצָרוֹת, אוֹצְרוֹת-;
n.m.
a. treasure
b. collection
c. storehouse

אור v.
1) אוֹר become light; shine
2) נָאוֹר become light; shine
6) הֵאִיר shine on; give light

אוֹר, אוֹר-; אוֹרִים n.m.
light; brightness; glow

אוּר, אוּר-; אוּרִים n.m. fire

אוֹרֵג; אוֹרְגִים n.m. weaver

אוּרִיָּה pr.n.m. Uriah
("God's fire") (roots: אוּר, יָהּ)

אוּרִים n.m.pl.
(usually together with תֻּמִּים)
the oracles worn by the High Priest on his breastplate

אוֹת, אוֹת-; אוֹתוֹת, אוֹתוֹת-; n.m.f.
a. sign, mark
b. symbol
c. miracle

אוֹתִי, אוֹתְךָ, אוֹתָךְ, אוֹתוֹ, אוֹתָהּ, אוֹתָנוּ, אֶתְכֶם, אֶתְכֶן, אוֹתָם, אוֹתָן
declension of אֵת as a direct object: me, you (m.s.), you (f.s.), him, her, us, you (m.pl.), you (f.pl.), them (m.), them (f.)

אָז adv.
a. then
b. in the past

אֵזוֹב n.m. hyssop

אֵזוֹר, אֵזוֹר-; n.m.
a. loincloth
b. girdle

אַזְכָּרָה n.f. burned offering
(root: זכר)

אזן v.
6) הֶאֱזִין listen; hear

אֹזֶן, אֹזֶן-; אָזְנַיִם, אָזְנֵי-; n.f. ear

אזר v.
1) אָזַר a. gird
b. strengthen
3) אִזֵּר a. gird
b. strengthen
5) הִתְאַזֵּר strengthen oneself

אֶזְרָח, אֶזְרַח-; n.m. citizen; resident

אָח, אֲחִי-; אַחִים, אֲחֵי-; n.m.
a. brother
b. relative
c. friend

אָח n.f. oven; brazier

אַחְאָב pr.n.m. Ahab
("father's brother") (roots: אָח, אָב)

אֶחָד, אַחַד- ; **אֲחָדִים** adj., n.m.
a. one
b. united
c. someone
d. none
e. (pl.) a few

אָחוֹר, אֲחוֹרֵי- ; n.m., adv. a. back
b. backwards
c. yet (in the future)

אָחוֹת, אֲחוֹת- ; **אַחְיוֹת-** ; n.f.
a. sister
b. darling; beloved woman

אחז v.
1) אָחַז a. hold; grab; grip
b. shut
2) נֶאֱחַז be caught; be held
2) נֹאחַז settle in the land

אֲחֻזָּה, אֲחֻזַּת- ; n.f. possession;
holding (root: אחז)

אֲחַזְיָהוּ pr.n.m. Ahaziah
("God's possession") (roots: אחז, יהו)

אַחַר adv., prep. a. after
b. later
c. behind

אחר v.
3) אֵחַר a. be late; tarry
b. delay

אַחֵר ; **אַחֶרֶת** ; **אֲחֵרִים** ; **אֲחֵרוֹת** adj.
a. different
b. other; another
c. strange

אַחֲרוֹן ; **אַחֲרוֹנָה** ; **אַחֲרוֹנִים** adj.
a. last; final
b. the one behind

אַחֲרֵי- ; adv., prep. pl. of אַחַר

אַחֲרֵי-כֵן adv. afterwards; then

אַחֲרִית, אַחֲרִית- ; n.f.
a. end (of place or time)
b. conclusion
c. remainder

אֲחֹרַנִּית adv. backwards

אַחַת n., adj.f. a. one
b. single

אטם v.
1) אָטַם shut; close

אִי, אִי- ; **אִיִּים, אִיֵּי-** ; n.m. a. island
b. (pl.) lands overseas
c. jackal
d. alas (interj.)

אֵי adv. where?
which? אֵי-זֶה
from where? אֵי-מִזֶּה

אֵיבָה, אֵיבַת- ; n.f. hatred

אֵיד, אֵיד- ; n.m. calamity; misfortune

אַיֵּה adv. where?

אִיּוֹב pr.n.m. Job

אִיזֶבֶל pr.n.f. Jezebel

אֵיךְ adv. a. how
b. (exclamation of sorrow)

אֵיכָה adv. a. see אֵיךְ
b. the Book of Lamentations

אַיִל, אֵיל- ; **אֵילִים, אֵילֵי-** ; n.m.
a. ram
b. notable; leader
c. main pillar or post

אַיָּל ; **אַיָּלִים** n.m. deer

אַיָּלָה (אַיֶּלֶת) ; אַיָּלוֹת n.f. doe

אֵילָם ; אֵילַמּוֹת n.m. hall; vestibule

אֵימָה, אֵימַת- ; אֵימִים (אֵימוֹת) n.f.
fear; terror

אַיִן, אֵין- ; n.m. negating word:
a. nothing
b. not existing
c. no, not
d. impossible
e. from where? מֵאַיִן

אֵינֶנִּי, אֵינְךָ, אֵינֶנּוּ, אֵינֶנָּה, אֵינֶנּוּ,
אֵינְכֶם, אֵינָם declension of אֵין
I am not, you are not,...

אֵיפָה, אֵיפַת- ; n.f.
unit of dry measure, approximately one bushel

אֵיפֹה adv. where?

אִישׁ, אִישׁ- ; אֲנָשִׁים (אִישִׁים),
אַנְשֵׁי- ; n.m. a. man
b. someone
c. husband
d. no one
e. member of a tribe or of a people
f. anyone

אֵיתָן ; אֵיתָנִים n., adj., m. a. strength
b. strong
c. Ethan (pr.n.m.)

אַךְ conj. a. only
b. but
c. however
d. indeed
e. just as...

אַכְזָרִי adj. m. cruel

אכל v.
1) אָכַל a. eat
b. destroy
2) נֶאֱכַל be consumed
4) אֻכַּל be destroyed
6) הֶאֱכִיל feed

אֹכֶל n.m. food

אָכְלָה n.f. food

אָכֵן adv. indeed

אִכָּר ; אִכָּרִים n.m. farmer

אַל- (negating word) no; do not...; not

אֵל n.m. a. God
b. god
c. (abbreviation of אֵלֶּה, adj.) these
d. in my power לְאֵל יָדִי

אֶל prep. a. to; towards
b. of; about

אלה v.
1) אָלָה a. swear
b. curse
6) הֶאֱלָה cause to swear

אָלָה, אָלַת- ; אָלוֹת, אָלוֹת- ; n.f.
a. curse
b. sworn pact

אֵלָה ; אֵלִים n.f. terebinth (tree)

אֵלֶּה pr. these

אֱלֹהִים, אֱלֹהֵי- ; n.m.pl. a. God
(usually singular)
b. gods
c. angels
d. judges

אֱלוֹהַּ n.m. a. God
b. god; deity

אַלּוֹן ; אַלּוֹנִים, אַלּוֹנֵי- ; n.m. oak tree

אַלּוּף, אַלּוּף- ; אַלּוּפִים, אַלּוּפֵי- ; n.m.
a. leader
b. intimate friend

אֵלַי, אֵלֶיךָ, אֵלַיִךְ, אֵלָיו, אֵלֶיהָ, אֵלֵינוּ, אֲלֵיכֶם, אֲלֵיהֶם declension of אֶל
to me, to you (m.s.), to you (f.s.), to him, to her, to us, to you (m.pl.), to them (m.pl.)

אֵלִיָּהוּ (אֵלִיָּה) pr.n.m. Elijah
("my god is God") (roots: אֵלִי, יָהּ)

אֱלִיל ; אֱלִילִים, אֱלִילֵי- ; n.m.
a. idol; false god
b. quack; deceit

אֱלִיעֶזֶר pr.n.m. Eliezer
("my God is help") (roots: אֵלִי, עזר)

אֱלִישָׁע pr.n.m. Elisha
("God will save") (roots: אֵל, ישע)

אלם v.
2) נֶאֱלַם be silenced

אִלֵּם ; אִלְּמִים adj.m. mute

אֲלֻמָּה ; אֲלֻמּוֹת n.f. sheaf

אַלְמָנָה ; אַלְמָנוֹת n.f. widow

אֶלְעָזָר pr.n.m. Elazar
("God has helped") (roots: אֵל, עזר)

אֶלֶף ; אֲלָפִים, אַלְפֵי- ; adj., n.m.
a. thousand
b. cattle
c. clan; family

אֵם, אֵם- ; אִמּוֹת, אִמּוֹת- ; n.f. mother

אִם conj.
a. if
b. except
c. but
d. whether
e. when

אָמָה, אֲמַת- ; אֲמָהוֹת, אַמְהוֹת- ; n.f.
maidservant

אַמָּה, אַמַּת- ; אַמּוֹת n.f. cubit

אֵמוּן ; אֱמוּנִים, אֱמוּנֵי- ; n.m. a. trust
b. honesty

אֱמוּנָה, אֱמוּנַת- ; אֱמוּנוֹת n.f.
a. steadiness
b. stability
c. justice
d. faith

אַמִּיץ adj.m. a. strong
b. brave

אמל v.
4) אֻמְלַל a. dry up; wither
b. be weak, oppressed

אמן v.
1) אָמַן raise; bring up
2) נֶאֱמַן be steady
6) הֶאֱמִין trust, believe in

אָמֵן n.m., adv. a. truth
b. so be it; amen
c. verily; truly

אָמְנָם, אֻמְנָם conj. indeed

אמץ v.
1) אָמַץ be strong
3) אִמֵּץ strengthen
5) הִתְאַמֵּץ try; strive

אמר v.
1) אָמַר say; command
לֵאמֹר to wit, that is, as follows
2) נֶאֱמַר be said, be spoken

אֹמֶר, אֹמֶר- ; אֲמָרִים, אִמְרֵי- ; n.m.
saying, utterance

אִמְרָה, אִמְרַת- ; אֲמָרוֹת, אִמְרוֹת- ;
n.f. saying, utterance
(root: אמר)

אֱמֹרִי pr.n.m. Emorite
(ancient nation in Canaan)

אֱמֶת, אֱמֶת- ; n.f. truth

אַמְתַּחַת, אַמְתַּחַת- ; **אַמְתְּחוֹת-** ; n.f.
bag

אָן, אָנָה adv. a. where to?
b. until when?
c. here and there

אָנָּא, אָנָּה conj. please

אנה v.
1) אָנָה mourn
3) אִנָּה cause
4) אֻנָּה happen
5) הִתְאַנָּה seek a pretext, bait

אָנוּשׁ ; **אֲנוּשָׁה** adj. mortal; incurable

אֱנוֹשׁ n.m. a. man
b. Enos (pr.n.m.)

אנח v.
2) נֶאֱנַח moan, groan

אֲנָחָה ; **אֲנָחוֹת, אַנְחוֹת-** ; n.f. moan

אֲנַחְנוּ pr. we

אֲנִי pr. a. I
b. me

אֳנִי n.m. fleet

אֳנִיָּה, אֳנִיַּת- ; **אֳנִיּוֹת, אֳנִיּוֹת-** ; n.f.
ship, boat

אָנֹכִי pr. I

אנף v.
1) אָנַף be angry
5) הִתְאַנֵּף be angry

אֲנָשִׁים n.m.pl. see אִישׁ

אָסוֹן n.m. calamity, accident

אָסִיר, אַסִּיר ; **אֲסִירִים, אֲסִירֵי-** ;
n.m. prisoner (root: אסר)

אסף v.
1) אָסַף a. collect, gather
b. remove
2) נֶאֱסַף a. be gathered
b. be destroyed
3) אִסֵּף gather
4) אֻסַּף be gathered
5) הִתְאַסֵּף a. gather
b. congregate

אסר v.
1) אָסַר a. tie; harness
b. vow
2) נֶאֱסַר be tied

אִסָּר (אֱסָר) n.m. vow; oath

אַף, אַף- ; **אַפַּיִם, אַפֵּי-** ; n.m. a. nose
b. anger
c. face (pl.)

אַף conj. a. also
b. even though אַף כִּי
c. much less אַף כִּי

אפה v.
1) אָפָה bake
2) נֶאֱפָה be baked

אֵפוֹ, אֵפוֹא adv. then; therefore; so

אֵפוֹד n.m. a. ephod
(a garment worn by the High Priest)
b. mantle
c. a vessel for worship service

אָפִיק, אֲפִיק- ; **אֲפִיקִים, אֲפִיקֵי-** ;
n.m. a. riverbed
b. river

אֹפֶל n.m. darkness

אֲפֵלָה ; אֲפֵלוֹת n.f. darkness

אפס v.
1) אָפֵס cease; come to an end

אֶפֶס ; אַפְסֵי- n.m., conj. ;
a. nil; nothing
b. end
c. however

אפף v.
1) אָפַף surround

אפק v.
5) הִתְאַפֵּק hold back; control oneself

אֵפֶר, אֵפֶר- n.m. ; ashes

אֶפְרַיִם pr.n.m. Ephraim ("fertile")
(root: פרה)

אֶצְבַּע, אֶצְבַּע- ; אֶצְבָּעוֹת, אֶצְבְּעוֹת- ;
n.f.
a. finger
b. toe

אצל v.
1) אָצַל
a. bestow
b. set aside

אֵצֶל adv. near; by; at

אצר v.
1) אָצַר amass; store up

ארב v.
1) אָרַב ambush; lie in wait

אַרְבֶּה n.m. locust

אֲרֻבָּה ; אֲרֻבּוֹת, אֲרוּבּוֹת- ; n.f.
a. opening in the sky for rain (metaphor)
b. chimney
c. eye socket

אַרְבַּע n., adj., f. four

אַרְבָּעָה, אַרְבַּעַת- ; n., adj., m. four

אַרְבָּעִים n., adj., m., f. forty

אַרְגָּמָן n.m. purple cloth; purple thread

אֲרוּכָה, אֲרוּכַת- ; n.f. healing; cure

אֲרוֹן (אָרוֹן) ; אֲרוֹן- ; n.m.
a. the Holy Ark
b. box
c. coffin

אֶרֶז, אֶרֶז- ; אֲרָזִים, אַרְזֵי- ; n.m.
cedar tree

אֹרַח, אֹרַח- ; אֳרָחוֹת, אָרְחוֹת- ; n.m.f.
a. way
b. manner

אֲרֻחָה, אֲרֻחַת- ; n.f. meal

אֲרִי (אַרְיֵה) ; אֲרָיוֹת n.m. lion

אֲרִיאֵל n.m.
a. hero
b. the altar in the Temple
c. name for Jerusalem ("God's lion")
(roots: אֲרִי, אֵל)
d. Ariel ("God's lion"), pr.n.m.

ארך v.
1) אָרַךְ be long; extend
6) הֶאֱרִיךְ
a. make longer
b. be long

אָרֹךְ, אֶרֶךְ- ; adj.m. long

אֹרֶךְ, אֹרֶךְ- ; n.m. length

אֲרָם pr.n. Mesopotamia (country f.)
(people m., pl.) - today's Iraq
(also followed by "two rivers" נַהֲרַיִם)

אַרְמוֹן, אַרְמוֹן- ; אַרְמְנוֹת, אַרְמְנוֹת- ;
n.m. castle; palace

אֲרַמִּי adj.m. Aramean, Mesopotamian

אֶרֶץ, אֶרֶץ- ; אֲרָצוֹת, אַרְצוֹת- ; n.f.
a. country
b. land
c. field

ארר v.
1) אָרַר a. curse
b. swear
3) אֵרַר a. curse
b. swear

ארש v.
3) אֵרַשׂ betroth; engage to marry

אֵשׁ n.f., m. a. fire
b. wrath

אֲשֵׁדָה ; אֲשֵׁדוֹת, אַשְׁדוֹת- ; n.f.
slope of a mountain

אִשֶּׁה, אִשֵּׁה- ; אִשִּׁים, אִשֵּׁי- ; n.m.
burnt offering

אִשָּׁה, אֵשֶׁת- ; נָשִׁים, נְשֵׁי- ; n.f.
a. woman
b. wife

אָשׁוּר, אֲשׁוּר- ; אֲשׁוּרִים n.m. step

אַשּׁוּר pr.n. Assyria; Assyrian

אֲשִׁישָׁה ; אֲשִׁישׁוֹת, אֲשִׁישֵׁי- ; n.f.
a. raisin cake (?)
b. wine bottle (?)

אֶשְׁכּוֹל, אֶשְׁכּוֹל- ; אַשְׁכְּלוֹת, אֶשְׁכְּלוֹת- ; n.m.
a. cluster (of grapes)
b. Eshkol pr.n.

אשם v.
1) אָשַׁם be guilty

אָשָׁם ; אֲשָׁמִים n.m. a. sin
b. guilt offering at the Temple

אַשְׁמָה, אַשְׁמַת- ; אֲשָׁמוֹת, אַשְׁמוֹת- ; n.f.
a. sin
b. guilt

אַשְׁפָּה, אַשְׁפַּת- ; אַשְׁפּוֹת, אַשְׁפּוֹת- ; n.f.
a. quiver (for arrows)
b. garbage heap

אשר v.
3) אִשֵּׁר a. guide
b. praise

אָשֵׁר pr.n.m. Asher ("fortune")
(root: אשר)

אֲשֶׁר pr., conj. a. which; that; who
b. because
c. in order that
d. like; as
e. if
f. wherever בַּאֲשֶׁר
g. like; since; when כַּאֲשֶׁר
h. to whatever; to whomever לַאֲשֶׁר
i. from what; from whom מֵאֲשֶׁר

אֲשֵׁרָה ; אֲשֵׁרוֹת, אֲשֵׁרִים n.f.
a. pole; sacred post
b. Canaanite goddess, mate of Baal

אַשְׁרֵי conj. a. happy is...
b. happy are...

אֵשֶׁת n.f. see אִשָּׁה

אַתְּ pr., f., m., s. you (as subject)
(see also אַתָּה)

אֵת, אֶת- ; prep.
a. (precedes a definite direct object - see "Grammar" section 15.9).
It declines as:
אוֹתִי, אוֹתְךָ, ..., אוֹתָנוּ, אֶתְכֶם, ...
b. in
c. with
d. before; in front of
It declines as:
אִתִּי, אִתְּךָ, אִתָּךְ, ..., אִתָּנוּ, ...

אתה v.

1) אָתָה come; arrive

6) הֵתָה (הֶאֱתָה) bring

אַתָּה ; אַתְּ ; אַתֶּם ; אַתֵּן (אַתֵּנָה) pr.
(as subject) you (m.s.); you (f.s.); you (m.pl.); you (f.pl.)

אָתוֹן, אֲתוֹן- ; **אֲתוֹנוֹת** n.f.
she-ass, female donkey

אִתִּי, אִתְּךָ, אִתָּךְ, ...
with me, with you, ... (see אֵת above)

אַתֶּם pr.m.pl. you (as subject)
(see also אַתָּה above)

אֶתְמוֹל adv. yesterday

אַתֵּן, אַתֵּנָה pr.f.pl. you (as subject)
(see also אַתָּה above)

אֶתְנַן, אֶתְנַן- ; **אֶתְנַנִּים, אֶתְנַנֵּי-** ; n.m.
fee (of a whore)

ב

בְּ, בַּ, בָּ, בֶּ, בֵּ, בּ prep., conj.
a. in
b. at
c. on
d. among
e. for
f. with
g. by (see also "Grammar", section 6.1). The declension is:
בִּי, בְּךָ, בָּךְ, בּוֹ, בָּהּ, בָּנוּ, בָּכֶם, בָּכֶן, בָּהֶם
(בָּם), בָּהֶן (בָּהֵן, בָּהֵנָּה)

בְּאֵר, בְּאֵר- ; בְּאֵרוֹת, בְּאֵרוֹת- ; n.f.
a. water well
b. ditch

בֹּאר (בּוֹר) ; בֹּארוֹת n.m.
pit; cistern

בְּאֵר-שֶׁבַע pr.n.f.
Beersheba
("seven wells", or "well of oath")
(roots: בְּאֵר, שבע)

באש v.
stink 1) בָּאַשׁ
turn foul; rot 6) הִבְאִישׁ

בַּאֲשֶׁר conj., adv.
a. because
b. where
c. wherever

בָּבֶל pr.n.f.
Babel
(root: בלל)

בגד v.
betray 1) בָּגַד

בֶּגֶד, בֶּגֶד- ; בְּגָדִים, בִּגְדֵי- ; n.m.
a. clothing; cover
b. betrayal

בִּגְלַל prep.
a. for the sake of
b. on account of

בַּד (בָּד) ; בַּדִּים, בַּדֵּי- ; n.m.
a. pole; handle (for carrying)
b. branch of a vine
c. bone
d. linen; cloth
e. alone; separately לְבַד
f. in addition לְבַד מִ-
g. in addition מִלְּבַד

בָּדָד adv.
alone; separately

בְּדִיל n.m.
tin

בדל v.
be separated 2) נִבְדַּל
separate; distinguish 6) הִבְדִּיל

בֶּדֶק, בֶּדֶק- ; n.m.
damage, crack in a structure

בהל v.
panic, be scared 2) נִבְהַל
a. scare 3) בִּהֵל
b. speed up
be rushed 4) בֹּהַל
a. scare 6) הִבְהִיל
b. rush

בְּהֵמָה, בֶּהֱמַת- ; בְּהֵמוֹת, בַּהֲמוֹת- ; n.f.
a. cattle
b. domesticated beasts

בֹּהֶן, בֹּהֶן- ; בְּהוֹנוֹת, בְּהוֹנוֹת- ; n.m.
a. thumb
b. big toe

בַּהֶרֶת ; בֶּהָרוֹת n.f.
skin discoloration

בוא v.
a. come; arrive 1) בָּא
b. approach

c. happen
d. set (the sun)
6) הֵבִיא bring; cause to arrive
7) הוּבָא be brought; be given

בוז v.
1) בָּז despise; scorn

בּוּז, בּוּז- ; n.m. scorn;
derision (root: בוז)

בּוּל n.m. a. piece; block
b. harvest
c. ancient Hebrew month pr.n.

בוס v.
1) בָּס tramp; step on
3) בּוֹסֵס tramp; step on
5) הִתְבּוֹסֵס wallow in; roll in

בּוֹסֵס (בוס) v. tramp; step on

בּוּץ n.m. fine linen

בּוֹר, בּוֹר- ; בּוֹרוֹת, בּוֹרוֹת- ; n.m.
a. ditch
b. pit
c. prison
d. grave

בוש v.
1) בּוֹשׁ a. be ashamed
b. dry up
3) בּוֹשֵׁשׁ tarry; be late
5) הִתְבּוֹשֵׁשׁ be ashamed
6) הֵבִישׁ a. bring shame on
b. cancel

בַּז n.m. loot; spoil; booty;
(root: בזז)

בזה v.
1) בָּזָה mock; flout
2) נִבְזֶה be despised

בִּזָּה n.f. loot; spoil (root: בזז)

בזז v.
1) בָּזַז loot; plunder
2) נָבוֹז be looted
4) בֻּזַּז be looted

בָּחוּר ; בַּחוּרִים, בַּחוּרֵי- ; n.m.
young man; lad

בָּחוּר adj.m. a. chosen
b. best (root: בחר)

בָּחִיר, בְּחִיר- ; בְּחִירִים, בְּחִירֵי- ;
adj.m. chosen by God (root: בחר)

בחן v.
1) בָּחַן test; try; examine
2) נִבְחַן be tested

בחר v.
1) בָּחַר a. choose
b. prefer
בָּחוּר a. chosen
b. best
2) נִבְחַר be chosen

בטח v.
1) בָּטַח a. rely; trust
b. be calm
6) הִבְטִיחַ promise; assure

בֶּטַח adv. safely; securely
safely; securely לָבֶטַח

בֶּטֶן, בֶּטֶן- ; n.f. a. stomach
b. womb

בִּי conj. please

בִּי, בְּךָ, בָּךְ, בּוֹ, בָּהּ, בָּנוּ, בָּכֶם, בָּכֶן, בָּם, בָּהֶן
declension of ב
in me, in you,...
See also "Grammar", section 6.1

בֵּין, בֵּינוֹת prep. among; between

בין v.
1) בָּן understand
2) נָבוֹן be wise
5) הִתְבּוֹנֵן watch; pay attention
6) הֵבִין understand; perceive

בִּינָה, בִּינַת- ; n.f. a. wisdom
b. understanding (root: בין)

בֵּיצָה ; בֵּיצִים, בֵּיצֵי- ; n.f. egg

בִּירָה n.f. a. fortified city
b. fortress

בַּיִת, בֵּית- ; בָּתִּים, בָּתֵּי- ; n.m.
a. house
b. home
c. household; family
d. holder
e. tribe; people
f. within מִבַּיִת

בֵּית-אֵל pr.n. Bethel
("house of God") (roots: בַּיִת, אֵל)

בֵּית-לֶחֶם pr.n. Bethlehem
("house of food") (roots: בַּיִת, לֶחֶם)

בָּכָא ; בְּכָאִים n.m. balsam tree (?)

בכה v.
1) בָּכָה weep
3) בִּכָּה mourn

בְּכוֹר, בְּכוֹר- ; בְּכוֹרִים, בְּכוֹרוֹת, בְּכוֹרוֹת- ; n.m. firstborn male

בִּכּוּרִים, בִּכּוּרֵי- ; n.m.pl. first fruits

בְּכִי, בְּכִי- ; n.m. crying; mourning
(root: בכה)

בְּכִירָה n.f. firstborn female

בְּכֹרָה n.f. birthright of the firstborn

בַּל- (prefix) no; non; not

בלה v.
1) בָּלָה be worn out; wither
3) בִּלָּה destroy

בָּלֶה ; בָּלָה ; בָּלִים ; בָּלוֹת adj.
worn out

בַּלָּהָה ; בַּלָּהוֹת, בַּלְהוֹת- ; n.f. terror; fear

בְּלִי adv. a. without
b. not (verbs)
c. for lack of מִבְּלִי
d. without בִּבְלִי

בְּלִיַּעַל n.m. evil

בלל v.
1) בָּלַל a. mix with liquid
b. confuse
5) הִתְבּוֹלֵל be mixed; be assimilated

בלע v.
1) בָּלַע swallow
3) בִּלַּע destroy; damage

בִּלְעֲדֵי prep. a. except
b. without

בִּלְתִּי conj. a. no; not
b. except
c. for lack of

בְּמִדְבַּר "in the desert of ..."
- the Book of Numbers

בָּמָה ; בָּמוֹת, בָּמוֹת-, בָּמֳתֵי- ; n.f.
a. shrine
b. back
c. body

בְּמוֹ prep. poetic form of בְּ

בֵּן, בֶּן- ; בָּנִים, בְּנֵי- ; n.m. a. son

b. child
c. member (of a tribe, a family, etc.)
d. (with a number) ...years old

בנה v.
1) בָּנָה build; establish
2) נִבְנָה be built; be established

בִּנְיָמִין pr.n.m. Benjamin
("son of the right hand")
(roots: בֵּן, יָמִין)

בִּנְיָן n.m. building; structure
(root: בנה)

בַּעֲבוּר prep. a. for; on account of; for the sake of
b. in order that; so that

בְּעַד prep. a. through; by way of
b. for; because of
c. over
d. up (against)

בְּעִיר n.m. cattle

בעל v.
1) בָּעַל a. possess; own
b. espouse; marry
בְּעוּלָה married woman

בַּעַל, בַּעַל-; בְּעָלִים, בַּעֲלֵי-; n.m.
a. husband
b. master; owner
c. possessor of...

בַּעַל pr.n.m. Baal ("master"),
Canaanite god (root: בַּעַל)

בער v.
1) בָּעַר a. burn
b. be ignorant
2) נִבְעַר be ignorant
3) בִּעֵר a. ignite
b. destroy
6) הִבְעִיר a. ignite
b. destroy

בעת v.
2) נִבְעַת be scared
3) בִּעֵת scare

בָּצִיר n.m. vintage, grape harvest
(root: בצר)

בצע v.
1) בָּצַע a. be greedy
b. rob
c. break
3) בִּצַּע a. break
b. carry out

בֶּצַע, בֶּצַע-; a. riches; earnings
b. ill-gotten gain

בָּצֵק n.m. dough

בצר v.
1) בצר glean
בצור, בצורה, בצורים, בצורות fortified, walled (city)
2) נבצר be prevented
3) בצר fortify

בקע v.
1) בקע a. rip open
b. break into
2) נבקע burst apart; break open
3) בקע split
6) הבקיע breach (walls of a city)

בקעה, בקעת-; בקעות; n.f. valley; plain

בקק v.
1) בקק destroy
2) נבק be destroyed

בקר v.
3) בקר a. examine
b. seek
c. visit

בָּקָר, בְּקַר- ; **בְּקָרִים** n.m. cattle

בֹּקֶר ; **בְּקָרִים** n.m. morning

בקש v.
3) בִּקֵּשׁ a. search; seek
b. demand; ask
c. wish

בַּקָּשָׁה n.f. request; desire

בַּר (בָּר) n.m. grain (of cereal plants)

בַּר ; **בָּרָה** ; **בָּרֵי-** ; adj. pure; clean

בֹּר n.m. purity

ברא v.
1) בָּרָא create
2) נִבְרָא be created
3) בֵּרֵא cut down trees
6) הִבְרִיא feed; fatten

בְּרֵאשִׁית "In the beginning of...", or "Initially" - the Book of Genesis (root: רֹאשׁ)

בָּרָד n.m. hail

ברה v.
1) בָּרָה a. eat
b. choose
6) הִבְרָה feed

בָּרוּךְ, בְּרוּךְ- ; **בְּרוּכִים, בְּרוּכֵי-** adj.
a. praised
b. blessed (root: v. ברך)

בָּרוּךְ pr.n.m. Baruch ("blessed") (root: ברך)

בְּרוֹשׁ ; **בְּרוֹשִׁים** n.m. cypress tree

בַּרְזֶל n.m. a. iron
b. hardness (symbolically)

ברח v.
1) בָּרַח run away; escape
6) הִבְרִיחַ cause to flee

בָּרִיא ; **בְּרִיאָה** ; **בְּרִיאִים** ; **בְּרִיאוֹת** ; adj.
fat

בְּרִיחַ, בְּרִיחַ- ; **בְּרִיחִים, בְּרִיחֵי-** ; n.m.
bar (to close a gate)

בְּרִית, בְּרִית- ; n.f. covenant

ברך v.
1) בָּרַךְ a. kneel
b. bless
3) בֵּרֵךְ a. bless
b. curse (euphemism)
4) בֹּרַךְ be blessed
5) הִתְבָּרֵךְ bless oneself
6) הִבְרִיךְ cause to kneel

בֶּרֶךְ, בֶּרֶךְ- ; **בִּרְכַּיִם, בִּרְכֵּי-** ; n.f. knee

בְּרָכָה, בִּרְכַּת- ; **בְּרָכוֹת, בִּרְכוֹת-** ; n.f.
a. blessing
b. gift (root: ברך)

בְּרֵכָה, בְּרֵכַת- ; **בְּרֵכוֹת, בְּרֵכוֹת-** ; n.f.
pond; pool

בָּרָק, בְּרַק- ; **בְּרָקִים** n.m. a. lightning
b. glitter

ברר v.
1) בָּרַר select
2) נָבַר be purified
3) בֵּרֵר purify
5) הִתְבָּרֵר a. be pure
b. act purely
6) הֵבֵר purify

בשל v.
1) בָּשַׁל a. ripen
b. cook
3) בִּשֵּׁל cook
4) בֻּשַּׁל be cooked

6) הִבְשִׁיל cause to ripen

בֹּשֶׂם ; בְּשָׂמִים n.m.
a. spice
b. aromatic herb

בשׂר v.
3) בִּשֵּׂר
a. inform
b. herald; announce

בָּשָׂר, בְּשַׂר- ; בְּשָׂרִים n.m.
a. flesh
b. body
c. living creature

בֹּשֶׁת, בָּשְׁת- ; n.f.
shame; infamy (root: בוש)

בַּת, בַּת- ; בָּנוֹת, בְּנוֹת- ; n.f.
a. daughter
b. woman
c. (with a number) ...years old
d. settlement around a large city
e. the population of... (city, country)

בַּת ; בַּתִּים n.f. unit of liquid measure
(equivalent to אֵיפָה)

בַּת יַעֲנָה ; בְּנוֹת יַעֲנָה ; n.f. ostrich
(also יָעֵן)

בְּתוּלָה, בְּתוּלַת- ; בְּתוּלוֹת, בְּתוּלוֹת- ;
a. maiden; virgin n.f.
b. the residents of ... בְּתוּלַת בַּת

בְּתוּלִים, בְּתוּלֵי- ; n.m.pl. virginity

1) קַל (פָּעַל) 2) נִפְעַל 3) פִּעֵל 4) פֻּעַל 5) הִתְפַּעֵל 6) הִפְעִיל 7) הֻפְעַל

גאה v.

1) גָּאָה a. triumph
b. rise
c. grow

גֵּאֶה ; גֵּאִים, גְּאֵי- adj.m. proud

גַּאֲוָה, גַּאֲוַת- ; n.f. a. pride
b. arrogance (root: גאה)

גָּאוֹן, גְּאוֹן- ; n.m. a. pride
b. arrogance
c. glory; majesty (root: גאה)
d. jungle

גֵּאוּת, גֵּאוּת- ; n.f. a. pride
b. glory
c. rising (root: גאה)

גאל v.

1) גָּאַל a. save; redeem; deliver
b. defile
2) נִגְאַל a. be saved; be delivered
b. be defiled
3) גֵּאַל defile
4) גֹּאַל be defiled
5) הִתְגָּאֵל defile oneself
6) הִגְאִיל defile

גְּאֻלָּה, גְּאֻלַּת- n.f. deliverance; redemption (root: גאל)

גַּב, גַּב- ; גַּבִּים, גַּבֵּי- ; n.m. a. back
b. top part
c. hill

גבה v.

1) גָּבַהּ a. rise
b. be haughty
6) הִגְבִּיהַּ raise; elevate

גָּבֹהַּ, גְּבַה- ; adj.m. tall; high (root: גבה)

גֹּבַהּ ; גְּבָהִים, גָּבְהֵי- ; n.m. a. height
b. pride; haughtiness (root: גבה)

גְּבוּל, גְּבוּל- ; גְּבוּלִים, גְּבוּלֵי- ; n.m.
a. border
b. area (root:גבל)

גְּבוּלָה ; גְּבוּלוֹת, גְּבוּלוֹת- ; n.f.
border (root: גבל)

גִּבּוֹר, גִּבּוֹר- ; גִּבּוֹרִים, גִּבּוֹרֵי- ; n.,
a. man of power adj., m.
b. brave (root: גבר)

גְּבוּרָה, גְּבוּרַת- ; גְּבוּרוֹת n.f.
strength; might; power (root: גבר)

גָּבִיעַ, גְּבִיעַ- ; גְּבִיעִים, גְּבִיעֵי- ; n.m.
a. goblet; cup
b. decoration shaped like a blossom

גְּבִירָה, גְּבֶרֶת- ; n.f.
a. mistress of the house
b. lady
c. king's mother or wife

גבל v.

1) גָּבַל a. set a border
6) הִגְבִּיל b. border; set bounds

גִּבְעָה, גִּבְעַת- ; גְּבָעוֹת, גִּבְעוֹת- ; n.f.
hill

גבר v.

1) גָּבַר prevail; overpower
3) גִּבֵּר strengthen
5) הִתְגַּבֵּר prevail
6) הִגְבִּיר strengthen

גֶּבֶר ; גְּבָרִים n.m. man (root: גבר)

גָּג, גַּג- ; גַּגּוֹת, גַּגּוֹת- ; n.m. roof

גַּד n.m. luck

גָּד pr.n.m. Gad ("luck") (root: גַּד)

גדד v.
5) הִתְגּוֹדֵד a. gash one's flesh
b. assemble in groups

גְּדוּד, גְּדוּד- ; גְּדוּדִים, גְּדוּדֵי- ; n.m.
regiment; military troop

גָּדוֹל ; גְּדוֹלָה ; גְּדוֹלִים ; גְּדוֹלוֹת adj.
a. big; large
b. strong
c. important
d. adult; grownup (root: גדל)

גְּדִי, גְּדִי- ; גְּדָיִים, גְּדָיֵי- ; n.m. kid
(a young goat)

גדל v.
1) גָּדַל grow; increase
3) גִּדֵּל a. raise
b. exalt; praise
5) הִתְגַּדֵּל brag
6) הִגְדִּיל a. make large
b. exceed
c. brag
d. use deceit
e. jeer

גֹּדֶל, גֹּדֶל- ; n.m. a. greatness
b. majesty (root: גדל)

גְּדֻלָּה, גְּדֻלַּת- ; גְּדֻלּוֹת n.f. a. honor
b. great deeds (pl.) (root: גדל)

גדע v.
1) גָּדַע a. break
b. cut
2) נִגְדַּע be broken
3) גִּדַּע demolish

גדף v.
3) גִּדֵּף curse

גדר v.
1) גָּדַר fence in

גָּדֵר, גֶּדֶר- ; גְּדֵרִים n.f. fence; hedge

גְּדֵרָה ; גְּדֵרוֹת, גִּדְרוֹת- ; n.f.
fence; sheepfold (root: גדר)

גֵּו (גַּו) n.m. a. body
b. back

גּוֹאֵל, גּוֹאֵל- ; גּוֹאֲלִים n.m.
a. family relative
b. redeemer; savior (root: גאל)

גּוֹי ; גּוֹיִם, גּוֹיֵי- ; n.m. nation; people

גְּוִיָּה, גְּוִיַּת- ; גְּוִיּוֹת, גְּוִיּוֹת- ; n.f.
a. cadaver; dead body
b. body

גּוֹלָה n.f. a. exile
b. people in exile (root: גלה)

גוע v.
1) גָּוַע die; expire

גור v.
1) גָּר a. reside; sojourn
b. be fearful
c. harm; attack
5) הִתְגּוֹרֵר reside

גּוּר ; גּוּרִים, גּוּרֵי- ; n.m. cub (animal)

גּוֹרָל, גּוֹרַל- ; גּוֹרָלוֹת n.m. a. lot
(object for deciding a choice by chance)
b. decision so made
c. allotted portion

גִּזָּה, גִּזַּת- ; n.f. fleece of wool

גזז v.
1) גָּזַז shear; cut
2) נָגֹז be cut off

גָּזִית n.f. hewn stones

גזל v.
1) גָּזַל a. rob
b. subvert
c. defraud

גָּזֵל, גֵּזֶל- ; n.m. robbery
(root: גזל)

גְּזֵלָה, גְּזֵלַת- ; n.f. a. robbery
b. item robbed (root: גזל)

גזר v.
1) גָּזַר a. cut
b. split
2) נִגְזַר a. be cut
b. be decreed

גִּזְרָה n.f. a. vacant place
b. terrace (?)

גַּחֶלֶת ; גֶּחָלִים, גַּחֲלֵי- ; n.f. hot coal

גַּי (גַּיְא), גֵּי- ; גֵּאָיוֹת n.m.f. valley

גִּיד, גִּיד- ; גִּידִים, גִּדֵי- ; n.m.
sinew; tendon

גיח v.
1) גָּח rush out

גיל v.
1) גָּל rejoice

גִּיל n.m. a. joy
b. a person's age

גַּל, גַּל- ; גַּלִּים, גַּלֵּי- ; n.m.
a. mound; pile
b. wave (of water)
c. fountain

גַּלְגַּל ; גַּלְגַּלִּים n.m. wheel (root: גלל)

גֻּלְגֹּלֶת ; גֻּלְגְּלוֹת- ; n.f. a. skull
b. head

גלה v.
1) גָּלָה a. reveal; show
b. go into exile
2) נִגְלָה a. be revealed
b. be exiled
3) גִּלָּה a. show
b. uncover
6) הִגְלָה exile
7) הָגְלָה be exiled

גֻּלָּה, גֻּלַּת- ; גֻּלּוֹת, גֻּלֹּת- ; n.f. a. bowl
b. round protrusion
c. water well

גִּלּוּלִים, גִּלּוּלֵי- ; n.m.pl. fetishes;
idols

גָּלוּת, גָּלוּת- ; n.f. a. exile
b. people in exile (root: גלה)

גלח v.
3) גִּלַּח shave
4) גֻּלַּח be shaved
5) הִתְגַּלָּח shave oneself

גְּלִילָה ; גְּלִילוֹת- ; n.f. district; region

גלל v.
1) גָּלַל roll; move

גָּלָל ; גְּלָלִים, גֶּלְלֵי- ; n.m. dung

גַּם conj. a. also; too
b. (for emphasis, between two nouns or verbs)
c. even though
d. is it not הֲגַם

גְּמוּל, גְּמוּל- ; גְּמוּלִים, גְּמוּלֵי- ; n.m.
a. reward
b. consequence (root: גמל)

גמל v.
1) גָּמַל a. wean (a baby)
b. reward; repay
c. sprout
2) נִגְמַל be weaned

גָּמָל ; גְּמַלִּים, גְּמַלֵּי- ; n.m. camel

גמר v.
1) גָּמַר finish

גַּן, גַּן- ; גַּנִּים, גַּנֵּי- ; n.m. garden; grove

גנב v.
1) גָּנַב steal
2) נִגְנַב be stolen
3) גִּנֵּב steal often
4) גֻּנַּב be stolen
5) הִתְגַּנֵּב sneak into

גַּנָּב ; גַּנָּבִים n.m. thief; robber

גַּנָּה ; גַּנּוֹת n.f. garden; grove

גנן v.
1) גָּנַן protect; shelter
6) הֵגֵן protect; shield

געל v.
1) גָּעַל reject; spurn
2) נִגְעַל be defiled

גער v.
1) גָּעַר scold; rebuke

גְּעָרָה, גַּעֲרַת- ; n.f. a. rebuke; reprimand
b. shout (root: גער)

געש v.
1) גָּעַשׁ tremble; shake
5) הִתְגָּעֵשׁ tremble; shake

גֶּפֶן, גֶּפֶן- ; גְּפָנִים n.f. grapevine

גָּפְרִית n.f. sulphur

גֵּר, גֵּר- ; גֵּרִים, גֵּרֵי- ; n.m.
a. temporary resident
b. stranger

גרה v.
3) גֵּרָה incite; provoke
5) הִתְגָּרָה a. harass
b. wage war

גֵּרָה n.f. a. cud
b. ancient coin (1/20 of a שֶׁקֶל)

גָּרוֹן n.m. throat

גֶּרֶם, גֶּרֶם- ; גְּרָמִים n.m. bone

גֹּרֶן, גֹּרֶן- ; גֳּרָנוֹת, גָּרְנוֹת- ; n.f.
a. threshing floor
b. barn

גרע v.
1) גָּרַע diminish; take away
2) נִגְרַע be diminished; be reduced
3) גֵּרַע reduce

גרר v.
1) גָּרַר a. drag
b. chew the cud
4) גֹּרַר be cut
5) הִתְגּוֹרֵר whirl

גרש v.
1) גָּרַשׁ chase; drive out
2) נִגְרַשׁ be driven out
3) גֵּרַשׁ evict; drive out; expel
4) גֹּרַשׁ be evicted

גַּשׁ, גֶּשׁ, גְּשָׁה v. imperative of v. נגש

גֶּשֶׁם, גֶּשֶׁם- ; גְּשָׁמִים, גִּשְׁמֵי- ; n.m.
rain

גֶּשֶׁת v. infinitive of v. נגש

גַּת ; גִּתּוֹת ; n.f. winepress

ד

דאג v.
1) דָּאַג a. worry
b. fear

דְּאָגָה n.f. a. worry
b. fear (root: דאג)

דֹּב ; דֻּבִּים n.m.f. bear

דִּבָּה, דִּבַּת- n.f. slander; defamation

דְּבוֹרָה ; דְּבוֹרִים n.f. a. bee
b. Deborah ("bee") pr.n.f.

דְּבִיר ; דְּבִיר- n.m.
inner sanctuary of the Temple;
Holy of Holies

דְּבֵלָה, דְּבֶלֶת- ; דְּבֵלִים n.f.
pressed fig cake

דבק v.
1) דָּבַק adhere to; cleave to
6) הִדְבִּיק catch up with; close in on

דבר v.
1) דָּבַר a. speak
b. say
c. tell
2) נִדְבַּר talk with
3) דִּבֵּר a. speak
b. say
c. destroy
4) דֻּבַּר be spoken
5) הִדַּבֵּר be spoken
6) הִדְבִּיר conquer

דָּבָר, דְּבַר- ; דְּבָרִים, דִּבְרֵי- n.m.
a. saying
b. word
c. utterance
d. matter
e. item
f. thing

דִּבְרֵי הַיָּמִים n.m. pl.
The Books of Chronicles
("the words of the days", or "the
matters of the days") (roots: דָּבָר, יוֹם)

דְּבָרִים n.m.pl.
the Book of Deuteronomy ("words")
(root: דָּבָר)

דֶּבֶר n.m. plague; pestilence

דְּבַשׁ n.m. honey

דָּג ; דָּגִים, דְּגֵי- n.m. fish

דָּגָה, דְּגַת- n.f. fish (collectively)

דֶּגֶל, דֶּגֶל- ; דִּגְלֵי- n.m. flag;
standard

דָּגָן, דְּגַן- n.m. grain; cereal plants

דּוֹב see דֹּב

דּוֹד, דּוֹד- ; דּוֹדִים n.m. a. uncle
b. beloved
c. lovemaking דּוֹדִים

דָּוִד (דָּוִיד) pr.n.m. David ("beloved")
(root: דוד ?)

דּוּד, דְּוָדִים n.m. a. kettle
b. container
c. mandrake herb דּוּדָאִים

דוה v.
1) דָּוָה be ill

דּוֹר, דּוֹר- ; דּוֹרִים, דּוֹרוֹת ; n.m.
a. generation
b. forever
(in combinations like לְדוֹר דּוֹר, etc.)

דושׁ v.
1) דָּשׁ a. crush
b. thresh
2) נָדוֹשׁ be crushed
7) הוּדַשׁ be crushed

דחה v.
1) דָּחָה a. push
b. repel

דַּי, דֵּי- ; n.m. a. limit
b. quantity
c. sufficiently (before a noun)
d. whenever מִדֵּי

דין v.
1) דָּן a. judge
b. rule

דִּין, דִּין- ; דִּינִים, דִּינֵי- ; n.m.
a. legal case
b. dispute

דָּיֵק n.m. siege wall; mound

דכא v.
3) דִּכָּא oppress; crush
4) דֻּכָּא be oppressed

דכה v.
1) דָּכָה be oppressed
2) נִדְכָּה be oppressed
3) דִּכָּה oppress

דַּל ; דַּלִּים ; n.m. poor man

דלג v.
1) דָּלַג skip; jump
3) דִּלֵּג skip; jump

דלה v.
1) דָּלָה draw water (from a well)
3) דִּלָּה raise

דַּלָּה, דַּלַּת- ; דַּלּוֹת ; n.f.
a. warp thread in a loom
b. the poor (collectively)
c. hair

דָּלִית ; דָּלִיּוֹת ; n.f. twig

דלל v.
1) דָּלַל a. become poor
b. become weak

דלק v.
1) דָּלַק a. burn
b. pursue
6) הִדְלִיק ignite

דֶּלֶת ; דְּלָתַיִם, דַּלְתֵי- ; דְּלָתוֹת, דַּלְתוֹת- ; n.f. door

דָּם, דַּם- ; דָּמִים, דְּמֵי- ; n.m. blood

דמה v.
1) דָּמָה a. resemble
b. cease
2) נִדְמָה a. resemble
b. be lost; perish
3) דִּמָּה a. compare
b. describe
c. think

דְּמוּת, דְּמוּת- ; n.f. a. image
b. shape

דמם v.
1) דָּמַם a. be silent
b. cease; stop
2) נָדַם be destroyed

דֹּמֶן n.m. dung

דִּמְעָה, דִּמְעַת- ; דְּמָעוֹת ; n.f.
teardrop

דָּן pr.n.m. Dan
("judge") (root: דין)

דָּנִיֵּאל pr.n.m. Daniel
("my judge is God") (roots: דין, אֵל)

דעך v.
1) דָּעַךְ be extinguished

דַּעַת, דַּעַת- ; n.f. a. knowledge
b. wisdom (root: ידע)

דַּק, דַּקָּה, דַּקִּים, דַּקּוֹת adj. a. fine
b. thin

דקק v.
1) דַּק (דָּקַק) grind to a powder
6) הֵדֵק grind to a powder

דקר v.
1) דָּקַר stab
2) נִדְקַר be stabbed
4) דֻּקַּר be stabbed

דָּרוֹם n.m. south

דְּרוֹר n.m.f. a. freedom (m.)
b. spice (m.)
c. swallow (f.)

דרך v.
1) דָּרַךְ a. step; tread
b. bend (a bow)
6) הִדְרִיךְ a. lead
b. makc walk

דֶּרֶךְ, דֶּרֶךְ- ; דְּרָכִים, דַּרְכֵי- ; n.m.f.
a. road; way; path
b. manner (root: דרך)

דרש v.
1) דָּרַשׁ a. inquire
b. demand
c. search
d. ask
e. claim
2) נִדְרַשׁ be sought out

דֶּשֶׁא n.m. a. green grass
b. vegetation

דשן v.
1) דָּשַׁן become fat
3) דִּשֵּׁן a. fatten
b. remove ashes
4) דֻּשַּׁן become fat

דֶּשֶׁן n.m.
a. fatness; fat
b. ashes of the altar

דָּת, דַּת- ; דָּתֵי- n.f. a. law
b. rule

ה

הַ-, הָ-, הֶ- article
a. the
b. which; that
See also "Grammar", section 5.1

הֲ-, הַ-, הֶ-
interrogative prefix indicating a question

הֶאֱבִיד אבד v.
destroy

הֶאֱבִיל אבל v.
a. dry
b. destroy

הֶאְדִּים אדם v.
become red

הֶאֱזִין אזן v.
listen; hear

הֶאָח interj.
aha!; for joy!

הֵאִיץ אוץ v.
press; urge

הֵאִיר אור v.
give light; shine on

הֶאֱכִיל אכל v.
feed

הֶאֱלָה אלה v.
cause to swear

הֶאֱמִין אמן v.
trust; believe in

הֶאֱרִיךְ ארך v.
extend; make longer

הַב (הָבָה), הָבִי, הָבוּ יהב v.
a. give!
b. let us...

הִבְדִּיל בדל v.
a. separate
b. distinguish

הִבְהִיל בהל v.
a. scare
b. rush

הִבְטִיחַ בטח v.
promise

הֵבִיא בוא v.
a. bring
b. cause to arrive

הִבִּיט נבט v.
look; gaze

הֵבִין בין v.
understand; perceive

הִבִּיעַ נבע v.
say; utter

הֵבִישׁ בוש v.
a. bring shame on ...
b. cancel

הבל v.
1) הָבַל
a. be deluded
b. be vain
6) הֶהְבִּיל
delude

הֶבֶל, הֲבֵל-; הֲבָלִים, הַבְלֵי- n.m.
a. futility
b. vanity

הֶבֶל pr.n.m.
Abel (root: הֶבֶל ?)

הִבְעִיר בער v.
ignite

הִבְקִיעַ בקע v.
breach (the walls of a city)

הֵבֵר ברר v.
purify

הִבְשִׁיל בשל v.
cause to ripen

הִגְאִיל גאל v.
defile

הִגְבִּיל גבל v.
border

הִגְבִּיר גבר v.
strengthen

הֻגַּד נגד v.
be told

1) קַל (פָּעַל) 2) נִפְעַל 3) פִּעֵל 4) פֻּעַל 5) הִתְפַּעֵל 6) הִפְעִיל 7) הָפְעַל

הִגְדִּיל גדל v. — a. make large; b. exceed; c. brag; d. deceive; e. jeer

הגה v.
1) הָגָה — a. think; b. speak; c. make sounds (dove, lion); d. remove

הִגִּיד נגד v. — tell

הִגִּיעַ נגע v. — a. make touch; b. reach

הִגִּיר נגר v. — pour

הִגִּישׁ נגש v. — a. bring near; b. offer

הִגְלָה גלה v. — exile

הָגְלָה גלה v. — be exiled

הִדְבִּיק דבק v. — catch up with; close in on

הִדְבִּיר דבר v. — conquer

הִדֻּבַּר דבר v. — be spoken

הִדִּיחַ נדח v. — a. exile; b. push away

הִדְלִיק דלק v. — inflame

הֲדֹם, הֲדֹם- ; n.m. — footstool

הֲדַס ; הֲדַסִּים ; n.m. — myrtle

הדף v.
1) הָדַף — repel; push

הֵדֵק דקק v. — grind to a powder

הדר v.
1) הָדַר — honor; respect

הָדָר, הֲדַר- ; n.m. — glory; majesty

הֲדָרָה, הַדְרַת- ; n.f. — glory; majesty

הִדְרִיךְ דרך v. — lead

הֶהְבִּיל הבל v. — delude

הָהֵם adj., pron.m.pl. — those (see also הֵם)

הוּא pron.m.s. — a. he; b. it; c. that; d. which

הִוא — see הִיא

הוֹאִיל יאל v. — venture; undertake

הוּבָא בוא v. — a. be brought; b. be given

הוֹבִיל יבל v. — a. lead; b. bring

הוֹבִישׁ יבש v. — cause to dry

הוּבַל יבל v. — a. be lead; b. be brought

הוֹגָה יגה v. — a. oppress; b. afflict

הוֹגִיעַ יגע v. — tire

הוֹד, הוֹד- ; n.m. — glory; majesty

הוֹדָה ידה v. — a. praise; b. confess

הוֹדִיעַ ידע v. — inform; tell

הוֹדַע ידע .v		be known
הוּדַשׁ דוש .v		be crushed
הָוָה, הָוָא היה .v		is (rare)
הַוָּה, הַוַּת-; הַוּוֹת .n.f		evil
הוֹחִיל יחל .v		a. await b. hope
הוּטַל טול .v		be thrown
הוֹי .interj		a. alas; ah b. ho
הוּכַח יכח .v		be punished
הוֹכִיחַ יכח .v		a. reprove; judge b. decree
הוּכַן כון .v		be established
הוֹלִיד ילד .v		beget
הוֹלִיךְ ילך .v		a. lead b. carry
הוֹלֵל הלל .v		make a fool of
הוֹלֵלוּת .n.f		foolishness (root: הלל)
הום .v		
	1) הָם	a. cause panic b. roar
	2) נֵהוֹם	buzz with excitement
הוּמַת מות .v		be killed
הוֹן, הוֹן-; .n.m		wealth; property; riches
הוֹנָה ינה .v		a. do wrong b. oppress
הוּנַח נוח .v		a. be placed b. be calmed
הוּסַב סבב .v		be surrounded
הוּסַד יסד .v		be founded
הוֹסִיף יסף .v		a. continue b. increase
הוּסַר סור .v		be removed
הוּעַד יעד .v		be directed
הוּעַד עוד .v		be warned
הוֹעִיד יעד .v		summon
הוֹעִיל יעל .v		a. help b. do good c. be profitable
הוּפַר פרר .v		be annulled; be voided
הוּצָא יצא .v		be removed
הוֹצִיא יצא .v		a. bring out; bring forth b. liberate
הוּצַק יצק .v		a. be poured b. be cast (metal)
הוּצַר יצר .v		be created
הוּקַד יקד .v		be burned
הוֹקִיעַ יקע .v		hang
הוֹקִיר יקר .v		value; have regard for
הוּקַם קום .v		a. be raised b. be fulfilled
הוּקַע יקע .v		be hanged

1) קַל (פָּעַל) 2) נִפְעַל 3) פִּעֵל 4) פֻּעַל 5) הִתְפַּעֵל 6) הִפְעִיל 7) הָפְעַל

הוּרַד ירד v. be lowered

הוֹרָה ירה v. a. shoot
b. teach; guide
c. refresh

הוֹרִיד ירד v. lower; bring down

הוֹרִישׁ ירש v. a. give as inheritance
b. expel
c. dispossess
d. make poor

הוּרַם רום v. a. be lifted
b. be offered

הוּשַׁב ישב v. be inhabited

הוּשַׁב שוב v. be returned

הוֹשִׁיב ישב v. settle; cause to reside

הוֹשִׁיעַ ישע v. deliver; defend; save

הוּשַׂם שים v. be placed

הוֹשֵׁעַ pr.n.m. a. Joshua
b. Hosea ("save") (root: ישע)

הוּשַׁר שיר v. be sung

הוּשַׁת שית v. be set; be made

הוֹתִיר יתר v. leave

הִזָּה נזה v. sprinkle

הִזְהִיר זהר v. a. warn
b. guide

הֵזִיד זוד v. act maliciously

הִזִּיל נזל v. cause to drip

הִזִּיר נזר v. set apart

הִזְעִיק זעק v. call up; gather; alert

הִזְקִין זקן v. grow old

הִזְרִיעַ זרע v. produce seed

הֶחְבִּיא חבא v. hide

הֵחַד חדד v. sharpen

הֶחֱזִיק חזק v. a. hold; grab
b. strengthen; support

הֶחֱטִיא חטא v. cause to sin; mislead

הֶחֱיָה חיה v. a. revive
b. let live

הֵחִיל חיל v. cause to tremble

הֵחִישׁ חוש v. speed up; rush

הֶחְכִּים חכם v. make wise

הֵחֵל חלל v. begin

הֶחֱלָה חלה v. sicken

הֶחֱלִיף חלף v. change

הֶחֱלִיק חלק v. make smooth

הֶחֱנִיף חנף v. a. defile
b. pollute

הֶחְסִיר חסר v. lessen

הֶחְפִּיר חפר v. a. be ashamed
b. cause shame

הֶחֱרִיב חרב v. a. destroy
b. dry

הֶחֱרִישׁ חרש v. a. think
b. be silent

הֶחֱשָׁה חשה v. a. be silent
b. silence

הֶחֱשִׁיךְ חשך v. darken

הֵחַת חתת v. a. break
b. scare

הַט, הַטֵּה, הַטָּה נטה see

הִטַּהֵר טהר v. cleanse oneself

הֵטִיב טוב v. a. do good
b. be generous

הֵטִיל טול v. throw; cast

הִטִּיף נטף v. preach

הִטַּמָּא טמא v. a. defile oneself
b. desecrate

הִטְמִין טמן v. hide; bury

הִיא (הוּא) pron.f.s. a. she
b. it
c. that
d. which

הֵידָד interj. hurrah!; cheer!

היה v.
1) הָיָה a. be; exist
b. happen; come
c. become
וְהָיָה d. (precedes a statement in the future tense)
וַיְהִי e. (precedes a statement in the past tense)
2) נִהְיָה a. become
b. happen

הַיּוֹם n.m. today

הֵיטֵב adv. a. well
b. plenty

הֵיטִיב יטב v. do well; do right

הֵיכָל, הֵיכַל-; הֵיכָלוֹת, הֵיכְלֵי- n.m.
a. palace
b. the Temple in Jerusalem

הֵילִיל ילל v. a. mourn
b. howl; cry

הִין, הִין- n.m. hin
(a measure of liquid)

הֵישִׁיר ישר v. straighten; level

הִכְבִּיד כבד v. make heavy

הִכָּה נכה v. a. smite
b. kill
c. conquer

הֻכָּה נכה v. a. be smitten
b. be killed
c. be conquered

הִכְזִיב כזב v. prove wrong

הִכְחִיד כחד v. a. destroy
b. hide

הֵכִיל כול v. a. contain; hold
b. endure

הֵכִין כון v. a. prepare
b. arrange

הִכִּיר נכר v. a. recognize
b. note
c. know

הַכֹּל n.m. all; everything (root: כֹּל)

הִכְלִים כלם v. shame

1) קַל (פָּעַל) 2) נִפְעַל 3) פִּעֵל 4) פֻּעַל 5) הִתְפַּעֵל 6) הִפְעִיל 7) הָפְעַל

הָכְלַם כלם v. — be ashamed

הִכְנִיעַ כנע v. — subdue; vanquish

הִכְעִיס כעס v. — anger

הִכְרִיעַ כרע v. — a. bring down
b. strike down

הִכְרִית כרת v. — destroy

הָכְרַת כרת v. — be cut off

הִכְשִׁיל כשל v. — cause to fall

הִכַּת כתת v. — smash; beat

הֻכַּת כתת v. — be smashed

הֲלֹא, הֲלוֹא conj. — see לֹא

הֶלְאָה לאה v. — tire; exhaust

הָלְאָה adv. — a. farther
b. further
c. from...on (time)

הִלְבִּין לבן v. — a. turn white
b. explain

הִלְבִּישׁ לבש v. — clothe;
dress (someone)

הִלְוָה לוה v. — lend

הַלָּז adj.m.f. — this

הֲלִיכָה ; הֲלִיכוֹת n.f. — a. walking
b. way
c. caravan (root: הלך)

הֵלִין (הִלִּין) לון v. — complain;
rail against

הֵלִיץ לוץ v. — scoff

הלך v.
1) הָלַךְ — a. walk; march
b. move
c. travel
d. behave
הָלַךְ בְּ- ; הָלַךְ אַחֲרֵי- ; הָלַךְ בְּדֶרֶךְ- ;
e. (continuing action) הָלוֹךְ וְ-
f. (continuing action) הוֹלֵךְ וְ-
3) הִלֵּךְ — move
5) הִתְהַלֵּךְ — a. walk; move
b. follow
6) הוֹלִיךְ — a. carry
b. lead

הלל v.
1) הָלַל — act foolishly
3) הִלֵּל — praise
3) הוֹלֵל — make a fool of
4) הֻלַּל — be praised
5) הִתְהַלֵּל — a. brag
b. be glorified
5) הִתְהוֹלֵל — dash madly about;
act crazily

הַלְלוּיָהּ interj. — hallelujah
("praise God") (roots: הלל, יָהּ)

הלם v.
1) הָלַם — strike; hit

הֲלֹם adv. — a. here
b. near

הִלְעִיג לעג v. — mock

הֵם pron.m.pl. — a. they
b. those הָהֵם

המה v.
1) הָמָה — a. roar
b. moan

הֵמָּה pron. m. pl. — they
(a variation of הֵם)

הָמוֹן, הֲמוֹן-; הֲמוֹנִים n.m. — a. noise
b. crowd

הִמְחָה מחה v. — erase

הֵמִיל מול v. — destroy; cut down

הֵמִית מות v. — kill; slay

הִמְלִיט מלט v. — a. rescue
b. give birth

הִמְלִיךְ מלך v. — crown as a king; enthrone

הָמְלַךְ מלך v. — be enthroned

הָמַם v.
1) הָמַם — a. confuse
b. cause panic

הֵמֵס מסס v. — a. melt
b. weaken

הִמְעִיד מעד v. — cause to stumble

הִמְעִיט מעט v. — reduce

הִמְצִיא מצא v. — bring; provide

הֵמֵק מקק v. — fester; rot

הֵמַר מרר v. — a. mourn
b. cause pain

הִמְרָה מרה v. — defy; disobey

הִמְשִׁיל משל v. — a. enthrone; cause to reign
b. compare

הִמְתִּיק מתק v. — sweeten

הֵן interj. — a. now that...
b. but
c. indeed ; surely

הֵן pr.f.pl. — they

הֵנָּה pr.f.pl. — they (see also הֵן)

הֵנָּה adv. — a. to here
b. till now

הִנֵּה adv., conj.
a. (word introducing a question or a statement)
b. now
c. here
d. behold
declension: הִנְנִי, הִנְּךָ, הִנּוֹ, ... הִנֵּה אֲנִי, הִנֵּה אַתָּה, הִנֵּה הוּא ...

הִנְחָה נחה v. — guide

הִנְחִיל נחל v. — give as inheritance

הֵנִיא נוא v. — prevent

הֵנִיד נדד v. — drive; move

הֵנִיד נוד v. — a. shake
b. move

הֵנִיחַ נוח v. — a. give rest
b. relieve
c. place
d. leave
e. tolerate
f. let

הֵנִיס נוס v. — chase

הֵנִיעַ נוע v. — a. shake
b. move

הֵנִיף נוף v. — wave; wield

הֵנִיק ינק v. — nurse a baby

1) קַל (פָּעַל) 2) נִפְעַל 3) פִּעֵל 4) פֻּעַל 5) הִתְפַּעֵל 6) הִפְעִיל 7) הָפְעַל

הִנְנִי, הִנְּךָ, הִנָּךְ, הִנּוֹ	here I am, you are (m.s.), you are (f.s.), he is ... (see הִנֵּה)
הַס interj.	hush!; silence!
הֵסֵב סבב v.	a. bring over b. turn
הִסְגִּיר סגר v.	a. isolate b. deliver
הִסִּיג נסג v.	move; shift
הִסִּיךְ נסך v.	a. pour b. annoint c. cast
הֵסִיךְ סוך v.	a. cover b. anoint
הִסִּיעַ נסע v.	a. cause to move b. move
הֵסִיף סוף v.	bring to an end
הֵסִיר סור v.	remove
הֵסִית סות v.	a. incite b. seduce
הֵסֵךְ סכך v.	screen; cover
הִסְכִּיל סכל v.	act foolishly
הִסְכִּין סכן v.	be in the habit of
הִסְתִּיר סתר v.	hide
הִסְתַּתֵּר סתר v.	hide oneself
הֶעֱבִיד עבד v.	make work; enslave
הֶעֱבִיר עבר v.	a. lead across b. send c. deliver
הֶעְדִּיף עדף v.	exceed
הֶעֱוָה עוה v.	a. sin b. twist
הֶעֱטִיר עטר v.	a. adorn b. crown
הֵעִיד עוד v.	a. testify b. call to witness c. warn
הֵעִיר עור v.	a. waken b. encourage c. stir up
הֶעֱלָה עלה v.	a. raise; lift b. present
הֶעְלִים עלם v.	hide
הָעֳמַד עמד v.	be placed
הֶעֱמִיד עמד v.	a. place b. put up c. erect d. establish
הֶעֱמִיס עמס v.	load
הֶעְמִיק עמק v.	a. be deep b. exceed
הֶעֱנָה ענה v.	a. answer b. oppress
הֶעֱצִיב עצב v.	cause sorrow
הֶעֱצִים עצם v.	strengthen
הֶעֱרָה ערה v.	expose
הֶעֱרִיךְ ערך v.	estimate

הֶעֱרִיץ ערץ v. a. scare
b. hold in awe

הֶעֱשִׁיר עשר v. a. become rich
b. make rich

הֶעֱשִׂיר עשׂר v. set a tithe

הֶעְתִּיק עתק v. a. move
b. copy

הֶעְתִּיר עתר v. plead

הִפְגִּיעַ פגע v. a. intervene
b. demand
c. bring about; visit upon

הִפְדָּה פדה v. redeem

הִפְחִיד פחד v. scare

הִפִּיחַ נפח v. blow

הֵפִיחַ פוח v. a. snort
b. blow
c. utter

הִפִּיל נפל v. a. cause to fall
b. lower
c. defeat; conquer
d. omit

הֵפִיץ פוץ v. scatter

הֵפִיק פוק v. a. totter; wobble
b. attain
c. succeed

הֵפִיר פרר v. a. annul
b. frustrate

הפך v.
1) הָפַךְ a. overturn; reverse
b. change
c. turn away
d. destroy
2) נֶהְפַּךְ a. be diverted, turned away
b. be changed
c. be destroyed

הִפְלָה פלה v. set apart

הִפְלִיא פלא v. a. cause to marvel
b. act marvelously
c. dedicate

הִפְלִיט פלט v. save

הִפְנָה פנה v. turn

הָפְנָה פנה v. be turned

הֻפְקַד (הָפְקַד) פקד v. be appointed

הִפְקִיד פקד v. a. appoint
b. deposit
c. entrust

הֵפֵר פרר v. a. annul
b. frustrate

הִפְרָה פרה v. make fruitful

הִפְרִיד פרד v. separate

הִפְרִיחַ פרח v. cause to bloom

הִפְרִיס פרס v. have hoofs (animal)

הִפְרִיעַ פרע v. a. distract
b. disturb

הִפְשִׁיט פשט v. a. undress someone
b. flay (hide)
c. remove

הִפְתָּה פתה v. enlarge

הִצְבִּיא צבא v. be in command

הִצְדִּיק צדק v. a. vindicate

1) קַל (פָּעַל) 2) נִפְעַל 3) פִּעֵל 4) פֻּעַל 5) הִתְפַּעֵל 6) הִפְעִיל 7) הָפְעַל

b. justify

הִצָּה נצה v. agitate

הִצְטַדֵּק צדק v. apologize

הִצִּיב יצב v. a. set up
b. erect

הִצִּיג יצג v. a. present
b. set up

הִצִּיל נצל v. save; rescue

הֵצִיץ צוץ v. a. sprout flowers
b. look

הֵצִיק צוק v. a. oppress
b. afflict

הִצִּית יצת v. set on fire

הִצְלִיחַ צלח v. a. prosper
b. succeed
c. make prosperous

הִצְמִיחַ צמח v. cause to grow

הִצְמִית צמת v. a. destroy
b. put an end to

הִצְעִיק צעק v. assemble; gather

הִצְפִּין צפן v. hide

הֵצֵר צרר v. oppress

הִקְבִּיל קבל v. correspond to; parallel

הִקְדִּים קדם v. a. be early
b. hasten

הִקְדִּיר קדר v. darken

הִקְדִּישׁ קדש v. a. consider holy
b. designate

הִקְהִיל קהל v. gather; assemble

הִקְטִיר קטר v. burn ritual incense

הֵקִיא קיא v. vomit; spew out

הֵקִים קום v. a. raise; erect
b. perform
c. fulfill

הִקִּיף נקף v. surround; encircle

הֵקִיץ קיץ v. a. awake
b. rouse to action

הֵקֵל קלל v. a. make light
b. ease
c. slight

הֻקַּם נקם v. be avenged

הִקְנִיא קנא v. anger

הִקְצִיף קצף v. irritate; vex

הִקְרָה קרה v. a. cause to happen
b. cause to meet

הִקְרִיב קרב v. a. bring near
b. offer a sacrifice
c. come near

הִקְרִיחַ קרח v. shave smooth

הִקְשָׁה קשה v. a. make difficult
b. make hard

הִקְשִׁיב קשב v. listen

הַר, הַר־; הָרִים, הָרֵי־ n.m. mountain

הֶרְאָה ראה v. show; cause to see

הָרְאָה ראה .v be shown

הִרְבָּה רבה .v a. increase
b. extend
c. do more

הַרְבֵּה .adv much

הִרְבִּיעַ רבע .v mate (an animal)

הִרְבִּיץ רבץ .v a. cause to lie down
b. set (precious stones)

הרג .v
1) הָרַג kill; slay
2) נֶהֱרַג be killed

הֶרֶג, הֶרֶג-; .n.m slaughter (root: הרג)

הֲרֵגָה .n.f slaughter (root: הרג)

הִרְגִּיז רגז .v a. make shudder
b. disturb

הִרְגִּיעַ רגע .v a. calm
b. give rest

הִרְדִּיף רדף .v a. push
b. chase

הרה .v
1) הָרָה a. become pregnant
b. think

הָרָה, הֲרַת-; הָרוֹת, הָרוֹת-; .n.f
pregnant woman (root: הרה)

הִרְוָה רוה .v a. water
b. make drink
c. rain

הִרְחִיב רחב .v a. make wide;
increase in size
b. relieve from distress

הֵרִים רום .v a. lift; raise
b. remove
c. offer (a gift)

הֵרִיעַ רוע .v a. shout
b. blow a trumpet or a shofar

הֵרִיץ רוץ .v a. cause to run
b. rush

הרס .v
1) הָרַס a. destroy; ruin
b. break through
2) נֶהֱרַס be destroyed
3) הֵרַס smash

הֵרַע רעע .v a. cause harm
b. do evil

הִרְעִישׁ רעש .v shake; cause to quake

הִרְפָּה רפה .v let go; slacken

הָרָפָה .pr.n.m chieftain of the tribe Rephaim (see רְפָאִים)

הֵרַץ רצץ .v crush

הִרְצָה רצה .v accept favorably

הִרְקִיד רקד .v cause to jump

הִרְקִיעַ רקע .v a. spread out
b. soar sky-high

הִרְשִׁיעַ רשע .v a. find guilty
b. do evil

הִשְׁאָה שאה .v destroy

הִשְׁאִיל שאל .v lend

הִשְׁאִיר שאר .v a. leave
b. spare

הָשֵׁב, הֵשִׁיב see שוב

הִשְׁבִּיחַ שבח v. calm; soothe

הִשְׂבִּיעַ שׂבע v. feed to fullness; satisfy

הִשְׁבִּיעַ שבע v. cause to take an oath; exact an oath

הִשְׁבִּיר שבר v. sell food

הִשְׁבִּית שבת v. a. cause to cease; put an end to
b. destroy

הִשְׁגָּה שגה v. mislead; lead astray

הִשָּׁה נשה v. a. make forget
b. lessen
c. exact a payment

הִשְׁוָה שוה v. make like; liken

הֵשַׁח שחח v. a. lay low
b. humble

הִשְׁחָה שחה v. cause to bow down

הִשְׂחִיק שׂחק v. mock

הִשְׁחִית שחת v. a. spoil; ruin
b. corrupt (morally)

הִשִּׁיא נשא v. dupe; mislead

הֵשִׁיב שוב v. a. return; give back
b. reply
c. cancel; revoke

הִשִּׂיג נשׂג v. a. overtake
b. be able; manage הִשִּׂיגָה יָדוֹ

הִשִּׁיךְ נשך v. lend with usury

הֵשִׂים שׂים v. make; cause

הֵשִׁיר (הֵשַׁר) שׁרר v. make king

הִשְׁכִּיב שכב v. cause to lie down

הִשְׁכִּיחַ שכח v. cause to forget

הִשְׂכִּיל שׂכל v. a. act wisely
b. observe
c. teach

הִשְׁכִּיל שכל v. bereave of children

הִשְׁכִּים שכם v. rise early

הִשְׁכִּין שכן v. a. cause to dwell
b. establish

הִשְׁכִּיר שכר v. cause to be drunk

הַשְׁכֵּם וְ... adv. (do) repeatedly

הִשְׁלָה שלה v. deceive

הִשְׁלִיחַ שלח v. a. send
b. bring about

הִשְׁלִיךְ שלך v. a. throw; cast
b. remove; drive away

הִשְׁלִים שלם v. a. finish; complete
b. make peace

הָשְׁלַךְ שלך v. be thrown

הָשְׁלַם שלם v. be made (peace)

הָשַּׁם שמם v. be horrified

הִשְׁמִיד שמד v. destroy; exterminate

הִשְׂמִיחַ שׂמח v. cause to rejoice

הִשְׁמִיט שמט v. cause to drop

הִשְׁמִים שמם v. a. destroy

	b. horrify
הִשְׁמִין שמן .v	a. fatten b. be fat
הִשְׁמִיעַ שמע .v	a. announce b. summon
הִשְׁעָה שעה .v	a. remove b. seal
הִשְׁפִּיל שפל .v	a. lower b. humiliate
הִשְׁקָה שקה .v	a. give a drink b. water
הִשְׁקִיט שקט .v	give rest; pacify; calm
הִשְׁקִיעַ שקע .v	cause to sink
הִשְׁקִיף שקף .v	look
הִשְׁרִישׁ שרש .v	a. grow roots b. thrive
הִשְׁתָּאָה שאה .v	wonder
הִשְׁתַּבֵּחַ שבח .v	boast
הִשְׁתַּגֵּעַ שגע .v	go mad
הִשְׁתַּוָּה שוה .v	be equal
הִשְׁתּוֹלֵל שלל .v	be despoiled
הִשְׁתּוֹמֵם שמם .v	a. be amazed b. be horrified
הִשְׁתַּחֲוָה שחה .v	bow down; prostrate oneself
הִשְׁתּוֹחֵחַ שחח .v	be downcast
הִשְׁתִּין שתן .v	urinate
הִשְׁתַּכֵּחַ שכח .v	be forgotten
הִשְׂתַּכֵּר שׂכר .v	earn wages
הִשְׁתַּכֵּר שכר .v	become drunk
הִשְׁתַּמֵּר שמר .v	a. be careful b. be guarded
הִשְׁתַּנָּה שנה .v	disguise oneself
הִשְׁתָּעָה שעה .v	look at each other
הִשְׂתָּעֵר שׂער .v	attack; storm
הִשְׁתַּעֲשַׁע שעשע .v	a. be delighted b. be amazed
הִשְׁתַּפֵּךְ שפך .v	a. be spilled b. run out
הִתְאַבֵּל אבל .v	mourn
הִתְאַדֵּם אדם .v	glow red
הִתְאַוָּה אוה .v	covet; desire
הִתְאַזֵּר אזר .v	strengthen oneself
הִתְאַנָּה אנה .v	seek a pretext; bait
הִתְאַמֵּץ אמץ .v	try; strive
הִתְאַפֵּק אפק .v	hold back; control oneself
הִתְבּוֹלֵל בלל .v	a. be mixed b. be assimilated
הִתְבּוֹנֵן בין .v	watch; pay attention
הִתְבּוֹסֵס בוס .v	wallow in; roll in

הִתְבָּרֵר ברר .v	a. be pure b. act purely
הִתְגָּאֵל גאל .v	defile oneself
הִתְגַּבֵּר גבר .v	prevail
הִתְגּוֹדֵד גדד .v	a. gash one's flesh b. assemble in groups
הִתְגּוֹרֵר גרר .v	whirl
הִתְגַּנֵּב גנב .v	sneak into
הִתְגָּעַשׁ געש .v	tremble; shake
הִתְגָּרָה גרה .v	a. harass b. wage war
הֵתָה (הֶאֱתָה) אתה .v	bring
הִתְהַלֵּךְ הלך .v	a. walk b. follow c. move
הִתְהַלֵּל הלל .v	a. brag b. be glorified
הִתְוַדַּע ידע .v	make oneself known
הִתְחַבֵּא חבא .v	hide
הִתְחַבֵּר חבר .v	become partners
הִתְחַזֵּק חזק .v	a. take courage b. become strong c. strive
הִתְחַטֵּא חטא .v	cleanse oneself
הִתְחַכֵּם חכם .v	a. pretend to be wise b. behave wisely
הִתְחַלָּה חלה .v	a. become ill b. feign illness
הִתְחַנֵּן חנן .v	appeal to; beseech
הִתְחַפֵּשׂ חפש .v	disguise oneself
הִתְחָרָה חרה .v	contend with
הִתְחַתֵּן חתן .v	a. marry b. intermarry
הִתִּיךְ נתך .v	melt down (metal)
הִתְיַפָּה יפה .v	beautify oneself
הִתְיַצֵּב יצב .v	a. present oneself b. stand ready
הִתִּיק נתק .v	draw away; distance
הִתִּיר נתר .v	a. untie b. set free
הֵתִיר תור .v	explore
הִתְכַּבֵּד כבד .v	a. put on airs b. be heavy
הִתְכּוֹנֵן כון .v	be established
הִתְכַּחֵשׁ כחש .v	cringe
הִתְכַּסָּה כסה .v	cover oneself
הִתְכַּפֵּר כפר .v	be forgiven
הֵתֵל תלל .v	a. mock b. deceive
הִתְלוֹנֵן לון .v	reside
הִתְלוֹצֵץ ליץ .v	mock
הִתְלַכֵּד לכד .v	a. be interlocked b. compact
הִתְלַקַּח לקח .v	flash

הִתְלַקֵּט לקט .v	gather together
הֵתֵם (הֵתֵּם) תמם .v	a. complete b. destroy
הִתַּמֵּהַּ תמה .v	be astonished
הִתְמַהְמֵהַּ מהמה .v	linger; tarry
הִתְמוֹדֵד מדד .v	stretch oneself
הִתְמַכֵּר מכר .v	commit oneself
הִתְמַלֵּט מלט .v	escape
הִתַּמֵּם תמם .v	behave honestly
הִתְנַדֵּב נדב .v	a. offer freely b. dedicate oneself
הִתְנַהֵל נהל .v	travel
הִתְנוֹדֵד נוד .v	sway
הִתְנַחֵל נחל .v	a. possess b. inherit
הִתְנַקֵּם נקם .v	avenge
הִתְנַשֵּׂא נשׂא .v	a. boast b. exalt
הִתְעַבֵּר עבר .v	be angry
הִתְעָה תעה .v	lead astray; mislead
הִתְעוֹפֵף עוף .v	fly away
הִתְעוֹרֵר עור .v	wake up
הִתְעַטֵּף עטף .v	a. be weak b. faint
הִתְעִיב תעב .v	behave abhorrently
הִתְעַלֵּל עלל .v	a. mock b. abuse
הִתְעַלֵּם עלם .v	ignore
הִתְעַנֵּג ענג .v	enjoy; delight in
הִתְעַנָּה ענה .v	a. suffer b. be oppressed
הִתְעַצֵּב עצב .v	a. be distressed b. be saddened
הִתְעָרֵב ערב .v	a. mingle with b. bet
הִתְעָרָה ערה .v	a. undress b. be rooted
הִתְפָּאַר פאר .v	boast
הִתְפּוֹרֵר פרר .v	collapse
הִתְפָּעֵם פעם .v	be agitated
הִתְפַּקֵּד (הָתְפַּקֵּד) פקד .v	be counted
הִתְפָּרֵד פרד .v	separate
הִתְפָּרֵץ פרץ .v	revolt
הִתְפָּרֵק פרק .v	a. break b. remove from oneself
הִתְפַּתֵּחַ פתח .v	untie oneself
הִתְקַבֵּץ קבץ .v	gather; be assembled
הִתְקַדֵּר קדר .v	become dark
הִתְקַדֵּשׁ קדש .v	be sanctified
הִתְקוֹטֵט קוט .v	a. be disgusted b. quarrel with

1) קַל (פָּעַל) 2) נִפְעַל 3) פִּעֵל 4) פֻּעַל 5) הִתְפַּעֵל 6) הִפְעִיל 7) הָפְעַל

הִתְקוֹמֵם קום .v a. rise up
b. stand against

הִתְקַשֵּׁר קשר .v conspire

הִתְרָאָה ראה .v see each other

הִתְרַגֵּז רגז .v a. be excited
b. be enraged

הִתְרוֹמֵם רום .v a. exalt oneself
b. raise oneself

הִתְרוֹעֵעַ רוע .v shout

הִתְרוֹצֵץ רוץ .v run back and forth

הִתְרוֹצֵץ רצץ .v struggle with each other

הִתְרַחֵץ רחץ .v wash oneself

הִתְרַפֵּא רפא .v recover; be healed

הִתְרַפָּה רפה .v be lax

הִתְרַצָּה רצה .v a. reconcile
b. appease

ו

וְ-, וּ-, וַ-, וָ-, וֶ-, וֵ- prefix
a. with
b. and
c. or
d. however
e. while
f. in order
g. even
h. that
i. (special tenses - see "Grammar", sections 7 and 15.7)

וָו ; וָוִים n.m. hook

וַיָּבֶז v. see בזה

וַיֵּבְךְּ v. see בכה

וַיִּבֶן v. see בנה

וַיַּגֵּד v. see נגד

וַיִּגַל v. see גלה

וַיָּגָר v. see גור

וַיָּהָם v. see המם

וַיּוּשַׂם v. see שׂים

וַיֵּז v. see נזה

וַיָּחַל v. see חלה

וַיִּחַן v. see חנה

וַיִּחַר v. see חרה

וַיֵּט, וַיֵּט v. see נטה

וַיִּטֹּשׁ v. see נטש

וַיִּירָא v. see ירא

וַיַּךְ v. see נכה

וַיְכַל v. see כלה

וַיָּלֶן v. see לון, לין

וַיָּמָד v. see מדד

וַיִּמַח v. see מחה

וַיָּמָל v. see מול

וַיָּנַח v. see נוח

וַיָּנַע v. see נוע

וַיֹּסֶף v. see יסף

וַיָּסַר v. see סור

וַיָּעָף v. see עוף

וַיֵּפֶן, וַיִּפֶן v. see פנה

וַיַּצֵּל v. see נצל

וַיָּצֹק v. see יצק

וַיִּקֶן v. see קנה

וַיִּקָּר v. see קרה

וַיִּקְרָא v. see קרא
"He called" - the Book of Leviticus

וַיַּרְא, וַיֵּרָא v. see ראה

וַיָּרֶב v. see ריב

וַיֹּרֶשׁ v. see ירש

וַיִּשָּׂא v. see נשׂא

וַיֵּשֶׁב v. see ישב

וַיָּשָׁב v. see שוב

וַיִּשְׁבְּ v. see שבה

וַיַּשַּׁח v. see שחח

וַיִּשַּׁק v. see נשק

וַיֵּשְׁתְּ v. see שתה

וַיִּשְׁתַּחוּ v. see שחה

וַיִּתְגַּל v. see גלה

וַנְּהִי v. see היה

וָעֶד v. see עַד

וַתִּדַּד v. see נדד

וַתַּהַר v. see הרה

וַתָּחֵל, וַתָּחֹל v. see חול

וַתִּקֹּד v. see קדד

וַתֵּרֶב v. see רבה

וַתָּשַׁר v. see שיר

זְאֵב, זְאֵב-; זְאֵבִים, זְאֵבֵי- ; n.m.
a. wolf
b. Zeeb ("Wolf") pr.n.m.

זֹאת pron., adj.f.
a. this
b. this (following a definite noun) הַזֹּאת

זְבוּל, זְבוּל- ; n.m.
abode; stately house

זבח v.
1) זָבַח a. sacrifice (religious)
b. slaughter; kill
3) זִבֵּחַ sacrifice

זֶבַח, זֶבַח-; זְבָחִים, זִבְחֵי- ; n.m.
a. sacrifice (religious)
b. slaughter (root: זבח)

זְבֻלוּן, זְבוּלוּן pr.n.m.
Zebulun ("he will dwell" ?) (root: זְבוּל ?)

זֵד; זֵדִים n., adj.m.
evil

זָדוֹן, זְדוֹן- ; n. m.
evil; insolence

זֶה pron., adj.m.
a. this
b. which
c. that
d. (to emphasize a length of time)
e. here בָּזֶה
f. this (a definite noun) הַזֶּה
g. from here; from this thing מִזֶּה

זָהָב, זְהַב- ; n.m.
a. gold
b. gold coin

זהר v.
2) נִזְהַר be careful
6) הִזְהִיר warn

זוֹ adj., pron.
which; that

זוב v.
1) זָב a. flow (menstrual blood)
b. emit semen (man)

זוֹב n.m.
a. woman's menstrual flow
b. man's semen discharge (root: זוב)

זוד v.
1) זָד act maliciously
6) הֵזִיד a. act maliciously
b. cook

זוּלַת prep.
except; other than

זוֹנָה; זוֹנוֹת n.f.
prostitute (root: זנה)

זור v.
1) זָר a. turn aside
b. squeeze
2) נָזוֹר a. retreat
b. turn back on
7) מוּזָר a. distant
b. strange

זַיִת, זֵית-; זֵיתִים, זֵיתֵי- ; n.m.
olive (tree and fruit)

זַךְ, זַכָּה adj.
pure; clean (root: זכה)

זכה v.
1) זָכָה be pure
3) זִכָּה purify; cleanse

זכר v.
1) זָכַר remember
2) נִזְכַּר be remembered
6) הִזְכִּיר remind; recall

זָכָר; זְכָרִים n.m.
male

זֵכֶר, זֵכֶר- ; n.m. a. memory; remembrance
b. fame; name (root: זכר)

זִכָּרוֹן, זִכְרוֹן- ; n.m. a. reminder; remembrance
b. memorial (root: זכר)

זְכַרְיָה(וּ) pr.n.m. Zechariah ("God remembers") (roots: זכר, יָהּ)

זלל v.
1) זָלַל a. be worthless; be abject
b. be a glutton

זִמָּה, זִמַּת- ; **זִמּוֹת** ; n.f. a. plan
b. wickedness
c. incest

זְמוֹרָה, זְמוֹרַת- ; **זְמוֹרוֹת** ; n.f.
branch (root: זמר)

זָמִיר, זְמִיר- ; **זְמִירוֹת, זְמִירוֹת-** ; n.m.
a. pruning
b. song (root: זמר)

זמם v.
1) זָמַם a. scheme
b. plot to do evil

זְמַן ; **זְמַנִּים** ; n.m. a. time
b. appointed time

זמר v.
1) זָמַר prune; trim
3) זִמֵּר a. sing
b. play an instrument

זִמְרָה, זִמְרַת- ; n.f. a. music (instrumental and /or vocal) (root: זמר)
b. choice fruit
c. strength

זָנָב ; **זְנָבוֹת, זַנְבוֹת-** ; n.m. tail

זנה v.
1) זָנָה a. commit adultery
b. betray
6) הִזְנָה a. fornicate
b. lead astray

זְנוּנִים, זְנוּנֵי- ; n.m.pl. harlotry (root: זנה)

זְנוּת n.f. harlotry (root: זנה)

זנח v.
1) זָנַח a. abandon
b. be abandoned
6) הִזְנִיחַ abandon; neglect

זַעֲוָה n.f. horror

זעם v.
1) זָעַם a. be angry
b. curse

זַעַם, זַעַם- ; n.m. anger

זַעַף, זַעַף- ; n.m. anger; rage

זעק v.
1) זָעַק shout; cry
2) נִזְעַק be assembled; rally
6) הִזְעִיק call up; alert; gather

זְעָקָה, זַעֲקַת- ; n.f. cry; outcry (root: זעק)

זקן v.
1) זָקֵן age; grow old
6) הִזְקִין grow old

זָקֵן, זְקַן- ; **זְקֵנִים, זִקְנֵי-** ; adj., n.m.
a. old man
b. elder; leader (root: זקן)

זָקָן, זְקַן- ; n.m. beard (root: זקן)

זִקְנָה, זִקְנַת- ; n.f. old age (root: זקן)

זקק v.
1) זָקַק refine; purify
3) זִקֵּק refine; purify
4) מְזֻקָּק refined; purified

זָר ; זָרָה ; זָרִים ; זָרוֹת n., adj.
a. strange; foreign
b. layman, laywoman

זֵר, זֵר- n.m. a. moulding
b. rim

זרה v.
1) זָרָה winnow; fan
3) זֵרָה scatter

זְרוֹעַ, זְרוֹעַ- ; זְרוֹעִים, זְרוֹעֵי- ;
זְרוֹעוֹת, זְרוֹעוֹת- n.f. a. arm
b. hand
c. strength; might

זרח v.
1) זָרַח shine; glow

זֶרֶם, זֶרֶם- n.m. a. flood
b. rainstorm

זרע v.
1) זָרַע a. sow; plant seed
b. spread
2) נִזְרַע be sowed; be planted
6) הִזְרִיעַ produce seed

זֶרַע, זֶרַע- n.m. a. seed
b. grain
c. offspring
d. semen (root: זרע)

זרק v.
1) זָרַק a. dash; spray
b. scatter
c. throw
4) זֹרַק be sprayed

זֶרֶת n.f. span (of a hand)

ח

חבא v.
2) נֶחְבָּא hide oneself
5) הִתְחַבֵּא hide oneself
6) הֶחְבִּיא hide; conceal

חַבּוּרָה ; חַבּוּרוֹת n.f. sore; wound

חבט v.
1) חָבַט thresh; beat (wheat, olives)
2) נֶחְבַּט be threshed

חבל v.
1) חָבַל a. take in pledge
b. damage
3) חִבֵּל a. ruin; harm
b. be pregnant
4) חֻבַּל be damaged

חֶבֶל, חֶבֶל- ; חֲבָלִים, חַבְלֵי- n.m.
a. rope; cord
b. snare; trap
c. share; portion
d. region
e. group

חֵבֶל ; חֲבָלִים, חֶבְלֵי- n.m. birth pain; labor

חבק v.
1) חָבַק embrace
3) חִבֵּק embrace

חֲבַקּוּק pr.n.m. Habakkuk
("the embraced one" ?) (root: חבק?)

חבר v.
1) חָבַר join; attach
3) חִבֵּר attach; tie
4) חֻבַּר be tied together
5) הִתְחַבֵּר become partners

חֶבֶר, חֶבֶר- ; חֲבָרִים n.m. a. group
(root: חבר)
b. magic; spell

חָבֵר ; חֲבֵרִים, חַבְרֵי- n.m. friend
(root: חבר)

חבש v.
1) חָבַשׁ a. tie; bind
b. saddle
3) חִבֵּשׁ bandage a wound

חַג, חַג- ; חַגִּים, חַגֵּי- n.m.
a. holiday; feast
b. the sacrifice of a feast
c. Festival of the Tabernacles הֶחָג

חָגָב ; חֲגָבִים n.m. grasshopper

חגג v.
1) חָגַג celebrate (a festival)

חֲגוֹרָה ; חֲגוֹרוֹת n.f. a. girdle
b. belt (root: חגר)

חַגַּי pr.n.m. Haggai ("festal")
(root: חגג)

חגר v.
1) חָגַר gird; tie on

חדד v.
1) חָדַד, חַד be sharp
6) הֵחַד sharpen
7) הוּחַד be sharpened

חדל v.
1) חָדַל cease; stop

חֶדֶר, חֲדַר- ; חֲדָרִים, חַדְרֵי- n.m.
room; chamber

חדש v.
3) חִדֵּשׁ renovate; restore

חָדָשׁ ; **חֲדָשָׁה** ; **חֲדָשִׁים, חֲדָשׁוֹת** ; adj.
new (root: חדש)

חֹדֶשׁ, חֹדֶשׁ- ; **חֳדָשִׁים, חָדְשֵׁי-** ;n.m.
a. month
b. new moon

חוֹבֵל ; **חוֹבְלִים, חוֹבְלֵי-** ; n.m. sailor
(root: חבל)

חוה v.
3) חִוָּה announce; say

חַוָּה ; **חַוּוֹת, חַוּוֹת-** ; n.f. a. village
b. encampment

חוֹזֶה, חוֹזֵה- ; **חוֹזִים** n.m. seer;
prophet (root: חזה)

חוֹחַ ; **חוֹחִים** ; n.m. thistle; thorn

חוּט, חוּט- ; n.m. thread

חִוִּי pr.n.m. Hivite
(ancient people of Canaan)

חול v.
1) חָל a. dance
b. turn
c. befall; descend upon
d. happen
e. tremble; shake
3) חוֹלֵל dance
5) הִתְחוֹלֵל spin

חוֹל, חוֹל- ; n.m. sand

חוֹלֶה v. see חלה

חוֹלֵל חיל v. cause birth

חוֹמָה, חוֹמַת- ; **חוֹמוֹת, חוֹמוֹת-** ; n.f.
wall

חוס v.
1) חָס care about; pity

חוֹף, חוֹף- ; n.m. seashore

חוּץ, חוּץ- ; **חוּצוֹת, חוּצוֹת-** ; n.m.
a. the outside
b. street

חוֹקֵק חקק v. legislate

חוֹר (חֹר), חוֹר- ; **חוֹרִים, חוֹרֵי-** ; n.m.
a. hole
b. noblemen (only in pl.)

חוֹרֵב (חֹרֵב) pr.n.m. Horeb; Mt. Sinai
("desert", "waste") (root: חרב)

חוש v.
1) חָשׁ hurry
6) הֵחִישׁ speed up; rush

חוֹשֵׁב n.m. artisan; designer
(root: חשב)

חוֹתָם n.m. seal; stamp (root: חתם)

חוֹתֵן n.m. father-in-law

חזה v.
1) חָזָה a. see; observe; behold
b. understand
c. prophesy

חָזֶה, חֲזֵה- ; **חָזוֹת** ; n.m. a. chest
b. breast

חָזוֹן, חֲזוֹן- ; n.m. vision; prophecy
(root: חזה)

חָזוּת n.f. a. vision; prophecy
b. contract (root: חזה)

חִזָּיוֹן, חֶזְיוֹן- ; **חֶזְיוֹנוֹת, חֶזְיוֹנוֹת-** ;
vision; prophecy (root: חזה) n.m.

1) קַל (פָּעַל) 2) נִפְעַל 3) פִּעֵל 4) פֻּעַל 5) הִתְפַּעֵל 6) הִפְעִיל 7) הָפְעַל

חֲזִיר n.m. pig

חזק v.
1) חָזַק a. be strong
b. gain the upper hand
c. become severe
3) חִזֵּק a. strengthen
b. tighten
c. fortify
d. harden
5) הִתְחַזֵּק a. take courage
b. become strong
c. strive
6) הֶחֱזִיק a. hold
b. grab
c. strengthen
d. support

חָזָק, חֲזָקָה, חֲזָקִים adj. a. strong
b. mighty
c. hard (root: חזק)

חֹזֶק n.m. a. might
b. strength (root: חזק)

חָזְקָה n.f. strength (root: חזק)

חִזְקִיָּה, חִזְקִיָּהוּ pr.n.m. Hezekiah
("might of God") (roots: חֹזֶק, יָהּ)

חָח ; חַחִים n.m. a. ring
b. hook

חטא v.
1) חָטָא a. sin; err; transgress
b. be guilty
3) חִטֵּא a. bring a sin offering
b. cleanse; purge
5) הִתְחַטֵּא cleanse oneself
6) הֶחֱטִיא cause to sin; mislead

חַטָּא, חַטָּאָה, חַטָּאִים n., adj.
a. sinner
b. sinful

חֵטְא, חֵטְא- ; חֲטָאִים, חֲטָאֵי- n.m.;
a. sin; transgression
b. guilt (root: חטא)

חֲטָאָה (חַטָּאָה) (חַטָּאת) ; חַטָּאוֹת, חַטֹּאת ; n.f. a. sin
b. sin offering (root: חטא)

חטב v.
1) חָטַב cut (wood)

חִטָּה ; חִטִּים, חִטֵּי- ; n.f. wheat

חַי, חַיָּה, חַיִּים, חַיּוֹת adj., n. a. live
b. raw
c. natural

חִידָה ; חִידוֹת ; n.f. a. riddle
b. lesson

חיה v.
1) חָיָה a. live
b. thrive
c. recover
3) חִיָּה a. survive
b. let live
c. revive
6) הֶחֱיָה a. let live
b. revive

חַיָּה, חַיַּת- (חַיְתוֹ-) ; חַיּוֹת ; n.f.
a. animal
b. beast
c. soul
d. group (root: חיה)

חַיִּים, חַיֵּי- ; n.m.pl. life (root: חיה)

חיל v.
1) חָל a. tremble
b. succeed
c. hope
d. wait
3) חוֹלֵל a. bring forth
b. hope
5) הִתְחוֹלֵל a. be made
b. hope
6) הֵחִיל cause to tremble

חַיִל, חֵיל-; חֲיָלִים n.m.
a. strength
b. might
c. courage
d. army
e. retinue
f. riches; property
g. success

חֵיל (חֵל), חֵיל- ; n.m. wall; rampart

חִיל n.m. agony

חִיצוֹן, חִיצוֹנָה adj. outer; external

חֵיק, חֵיק- ; n.m.
a. bosom
b. hollow
c. midst

חֵךְ n.m. palate

חכה v.
3) חִכָּה a. await
b. expect

חכם v.
1) חָכַם a. be wise
b. acquire wisdom
3) חִכֵּם enlighten; make wise
5) הִתְחַכֵּם a. pretend to be wise
b. behave wisely
6) הֶחְכִּים make wise

חָכָם, חֲכָמָה, חֲכָמִים, חֲכָמוֹת n., adj.
a. wise
b. clever
c. wily
d. expert
e. learned one
f. craftsman (root: חכם)

חָכְמָה, חָכְמַת-; חָכְמוֹת ; n.f.
a. wisdom
b. cleverness
c. expertise (root: חכם)

חֹל n.m. something profane or secular

חֶלְאָה, חֶלְאַת- ; n.f.
a. rust
b. scum

חָלָב, חֲלֵב- ;n.m. milk

חֵלֶב, חֵלֶב-; חֲלָבִים, חֶלְבֵי- ; n.m.
a. animal fat
b. the fat of, the best of (metaphor)

חלה v.
1) חָלָה a. ail
b. ache
c. become weak
2) נֶחֱלָה be ill
3) חִלָּה a. beseech; ask
b. cause illness
5) הִתְחַלָּה a. become ill
b. feign illness
6) הֶחֱלָה sicken

חַלָּה, חַלַּת-; חַלּוֹת, חַלּוֹת- ; n.f.
loaf of bread ("challah")

חֲלוֹם, חֲלוֹם-; חֲלוֹמוֹת, חֲלוֹמוֹת- ;
n.m. dream (root: חלם)

חַלּוֹן, חַלּוֹן-; חַלּוֹנִים, חַלּוֹנֵי- ;
חַלּוֹנוֹת, חַלּוֹנוֹת- ; n.m.f. window

חָלוּץ, חֲלוּץ-; חֲלוּצִים, חֲלוּצֵי- ; n.m.
a. armed soldier
b. shock-fighter
c. vanguard

חֳלִי; חֳלָיִים n.m. disease (root: חלה)

חָלִיל; חֲלִילִים n.m. flute

חָלִילָה interj. a. far be it!
b. heaven forbid!
c. never!

חֲלִיפָה; חֲלִיפוֹת, חֲלִיפוֹת- ; n.f.
a. set of clothing
b. change (root: חלף)

חלל v.
2) נִחַל be defiled; be desecrated
3) חִלֵּל desecrate
6) הֵחֵל a. begin
b. be first

חָלָל, חֲלַל-; חֲלָלִים, חַלְלֵי-; n.m.
slain person

חלם v.
1) חָלַם dream

חַלָּמִישׁ, חַלְמִישׁ-; n.m. flint

חלף v.
1) חָלַף a. pass
b. sprout
c. pierce
6) הֶחֱלִיף change

חלץ v.
1) חָלַץ remove
2) נֶחֱלַץ a. be rescued
b. hasten
3) חִלֵּץ a. rescue
b. remove

חֲלָצַיִם n.m.pl. loins

חלק v.
1) חָלַק a. be smooth
b. divide; distribute
c. share
2) נֶחֱלַק be divided
3) חִלֵּק divide
6) הֶחֱלִיק make smooth

חָלָק adj.m. smooth (root: חלק)

חֵלֶק, חֵלֶק-; חֲלָקִים; n.m.
a. share; part
b. lot; fate
c. field; area (root: חלק)

חֶלְקָה, חֶלְקַת-; n.f.
a. field; piece of land
b. smooth place (root: חלק)

חֹם, חֹם-; n.m. heat

חֶמְאָה n.f. a. butter
b. curd

חמד v.
1) חָמַד a. be eager
b. want
c. covet
2) נֶחְמָד pleasant; delightful

חֶמְדָּה, חֶמְדַּת-; n.f. a. glory
b. preciousness (root: חמד)

חַמָּה n.f. sun (root: חמם)

חֵמָה, חֲמַת-; חֵמוֹת n.f. a. fury; anger
b. poison

חָמוּד, חֲמוּד-; n., adj.m.
a. precious object
b. precious (root: חמד)

חֲמוֹר, חֲמוֹר-; חֲמוֹרִים; n.m.
a. donkey; ass
b. heap; mass

חָמוֹת n.f. mother-in-law

חֲמִישִׁי, חֲמִישִׁית adj. fifth
See also "Grammar", section 9

חֲמִישִׁית n.f. one fifth

חמל v.
1) חָמַל pity; have compassion

חמם v.
1) חָמַם, חַם become warm
2) נֵחַם become warm

חַמָּן; חַמָּנִים n.m.
altar for sun worshipping (root: חַמָּה)

חמס v.
1) חָמַס a. violate
b. rob

חָמָס, חֲמַס-; חֲמָסִים n.m.
a. lawlessness
b. violence (root: חמס)

חָמֵץ n.m. leavened (soured) bread

חֹמֶץ, חֹמֶץ-; n.m. vinegar

חֹמֶר, חֹמֶר-; חֳמָרִים n.m.
a. homer (a dry measure)
b. pile; heap
c. mortar; clay

חָמֵשׁ, חֲמֵשׁ-; adj., n.f. five
See also "Grammar", section 9

חֲמִשָּׁה, חֲמֵשֶׁת-; adj., n.m. five
See also "Grammar", section 9

חֲמִשִּׁים adj., n., m.f. fifty
See also "Grammar", section 9

חֵן n.m. a. grace
b. beauty

חנה v.
1) חָנָה pitch camp; encamp

חַנּוּן adj.m. merciful (root: חנן)

חֲנִית, חֲנִית-; חֲנִיתִים, חֲנִיתוֹת; n.f.
spear

חנך v.
1) חָנַךְ a. dedicate
b. teach

חֲנֻכָּה, חֲנֻכַּת-; n.f. dedication
(root: חנך)

חִנָּם adv. a. without reward; for free
b. in vain; for naught

חנן v.
1) חָנַן a. grant
b. pity
c. be gracious
5) הִתְחַנֵּן appeal to; beseech

חנף v.
1) חָנֵף be defiled
6) הֶחֱנִיף pollute; defile

חָנֵף; חֲנֵפִים, חַנְפֵי-; adj.m.
a. ungodly
b. hypocritical
c. sinful (root: חנף)

חֶסֶד, חֶסֶד-; חֲסָדִים, חַסְדֵי-; n.m.
a. charity
b. grace
c. steadfast love
d. kindness
e. shame

חסה v.
1) חָסָה find shelter

חָסִיד; חֲסִידִים adj., n.m. a. faithful
b. righteous (root: חסד)

חֲסִידָה n.f. stork

חָסִיל n.m. locust

חֹסֶן, חֹסֶן-; n.m. wealth; treasure

חסר v.
1) חָסֵר diminish; lack; want
3) חִסֵּר lessen
6) הֶחְסִיר lessen

חָסֵר, חֲסַר-; adj. m. lacking;
devoid of

חפה v.
1) חָפָה cover
3) חִפָּה overlay

חפז v.
1) חָפַז hurry; rush
2) נֶחְפַּז hurry; rush

חֹפֶן ; חָפְנַיִם n.m. handful

חפץ v.
1) חָפֵץ want; wish; desire

חֵפֶץ, חֵפֶץ- ; חֲפָצִים n.m. a. desire; need
b. purpose

חפר v.
1) חָפַר a. dig
b. spy
c. be ashamed
6) הֶחְפִּיר a. be ashamed
b. cause shame

חָפְשִׁי ; חָפְשִׁים adj.m. free; liberated

חפש v.
1) חָפַשׂ a. search
b. reveal
3) חִפֵּשׂ search
5) הִתְחַפֵּשׂ disguise oneself

חֵץ, חֵץ- ; חִצִּים, חִצֵּי- ; n.m. arrow

חצב v.
1) חָצַב hew; cut; carve

חצה v.
1) חָצָה split; divide
2) נֶחֱצָה be split

חֲצוֹצְרָה ; חֲצוֹצְרוֹת, חֲצוֹצְרוֹת- ; n.f.
trumpet

חֲצִי, חֲצִי n.m. a. half
b. middle
c. arrow (see חֵץ)

חָצִיר, חֲצִיר- ; n.m. grass; hay

חָצֵר, חֲצַר- ; חֲצֵרוֹת, חַצְרוֹת- ;
חֲצֵרִים, חַצְרֵי- ; n.f.m. a. courtyard
b. villages חֲצֵרִים

חֵק see חֵיק

חֹק, חָק- ; חֻקִּים, חֻקֵּי- ; n.m.
a. judgement; ruling
b. rule
c. allotment (root: חקק)

חֻקָּה, חֻקַּת- ; חֻקּוֹת, חֻקּוֹת- ; n.f.
law; rule (root: חקק)

חקק v.
1) חָקַק a. carve
b. legislate
3) חוֹקֵק legislate

חקר v.
1) חָקַר a. inquire; check; search
b. spy
2) נֶחְקַר be reckoned

חֵקֶר, חֵקֶר- ; חִקְרֵי- ; n.m. search;
examination (root: חקר)

חֹר see חוֹר

חרב v.
1) חָרַב a. be destroyed
b. dry up
2) נֶחֱרַב be destroyed
4) חֹרַב be dry
6) הֶחֱרִיב a. dry
b. destroy
7) הָחֳרַב be destroyed

חָרֵב ; חֲרֵבָה ; חֲרֵבוֹת adj.
destroyed; desolate

חֶרֶב, חֶרֶב- ; חֲרָבוֹת, חַרְבוֹת- ; n.f.
sword

חֹרֵב pr.n.m. Horeb; Mt. Sinai
("desert", "waste") (root: חרב)

חֹרֶב n.m. a. dryness
b. desolation (root: חרב)

חָרְבָּה ; חֳרָבוֹת, חָרְבוֹת- ; n.f.
destruction; ruin (root: חרב)

חָרָבָה ; חֲרָבוֹת ; n.f. dry land
(root: חרב)

חרד v.
1) חָרַד a. fear
b. tremble
c. hurry
6) הֶחֱרִיד a. scare
b. trouble

חֲרָדָה, חֶרְדַּת- ; חֲרָדוֹת ; n.f. a. fear
b. trembling

חרה v.
1) חָרָה ... אַף flare up (anger)
2) נֶחֱרָה contend with
5) הִתְחָרָה contend with

חָרוֹן, חֲרוֹן-אַף ; n.m.
anger; wrath

חָרוּץ n.m. a. gold
b. threshing board

חָרוּץ adj.m. a. diligent
b. maimed
c. total; decisive (root: חרץ)

חַרְטֹם ; חַרְטֻמִּים, חַרְטֻמֵּי- ; n.m.
magician

חֳרִי (-אַף) n.m. anger (root: חרה)

חרם v.
6) הֶחֱרִים a. destroy
b. devote to God
c. dry
7) הָחֳרַם be destroyed

חֵרֶם ; חֲרָמִים n.m.
a. thing devoted to God
b. proscribed thing
c. destruction
d. fishing net

חרף v.
1) חָרַף a. curse
b. spend winter
3) חֵרֵף a. curse
b. belittle

חֹרֶף n.m. winter

חֶרְפָּה, חֶרְפַּת- ; חֲרָפוֹת, חֶרְפּוֹת- ; n.f.
shame

חרץ v.
1) חָרַץ a. cut
b. whet
חָרוּץ decisive
2) נֶחֱרַץ be decreed

חרק v.
1) חָרַק gnash (teeth)

חרר v.
1) חָרַר (חַר) burn
2) נִחַר burn; dry

חרש v.
1) חָרַשׁ a. plow
b. forge (iron)
c. think; plan
d. be silent
2) נֶחֱרַשׁ be plowed
6) הֶחֱרִישׁ a. think
b. be silent

חֹרֶשׁ (חֹרְשָׁה) n.m.f. forest

חָרָשׁ, חָרַשׁ- ; חָרָשִׁים, חָרָשֵׁי- ; n.m.
artisan; craftsman

חֵרֵשׁ ; חֵרְשִׁים adj.m. deaf

חֶרֶשׂ n.m. a earthenware

b. clay

חשב v.
1) חָשַׁב a. think
b. plan
c. account
d. make designs (art)
2) נֶחֱשַׁב a. be considered
b. be accounted
3) חִשֵּׁב compute; count

חֵשֶׁב n.m. band

חֶשְׁבּוֹן ; חֶשְׁבּוֹנוֹת n.m. reckoning; account

חשה v.
1) חָשָׁה be silent
6) הֶחֱשָׁה a. be silent
b. silence

חָשׁוּק (חִשּׁוּק) ; חֲשׁוּקִים, חֲשׁוּקֵי- ; n.m. metal band (root: חשק)

חשך v.
1) חָשַׁךְ a. be dark
b. become blind
6) הֶחֱשִׁיךְ darken

חֹשֶׁךְ n.m. darkness (root: חשך)

חשך v.
1) חָשַׂךְ a. withhold
b. save
2) נֶחְשַׂךְ a. be prevented
b. be saved

חֲשֵׁכָה, חֶשְׁכַת- ; חֲשֵׁכִים ; n.f. darkness (root: חשך)

חֹשֶׁן, חֹשֶׁן- ; n.m. breastpiece (of the garments of the High Priest)

חשף v.
1) חָשַׂף a. uncover; bare; show
b. yield (water)

חשק v.
1) חָשַׁק desire
3) חִשֵּׁק fasten a metal band
4) חֻשַּׁק be fastened (a metal band)

חָתוּם adj., n.m. a. sealed; signed
b. sealed document

חִתִּי ; חִתִּים pr.n.m. Hittite (a Canaanite people)

חִתִּית n.f. fear (root: חתת)

חתם v.
1) חָתַם seal; sign
2) נֶחְתַּם be sealed

חתן v.
5) הִתְחַתֵּן a. marry someone's daughter
b. become related through marriage

חָתָן, חֲתַן- ; חֲתָנֵי- ; n.m.
a. bridegroom
b. son-in-law

חתר v.
1) חָתַר a. dig (under a wall)
b. row (a boat)

חתת v.
1) חתת (חת) a. break
b. be cowed; be scared
2) נחת fear
3) חִתַּת a. scare
b. break
6) החת a. break
b. scared

ט

טבח v.
1) טָבַח — slaughter

טֶבַח n.m. — slaughter (root: טבח)

טַבָּח ; טַבָּחִים n.m.
a. cook
b. stewart (root: טבח)

טבל v.
1) טָבַל — dip
2) נִטְבַּל — be dipped

טבע v.
1) טָבַע — sink; drown
4) טֻבַּע — be sunk; be drowned
7) הָטְבַּע — be sunk

טַבַּעַת, טַבַּעַת- ; טַבָּעוֹת, טַבְּעוֹת- ; n.f.
a. ring
b. signet ring

טָהוֹר ; טְהוֹרָה ; טְהוֹרִים ; טְהוֹרוֹת ; adj.
a. pure
b. ritually clean (root:טהר)

טהר v.
1) טָהַר — become clean; become pure
3) טִהֵר — cleanse; purify
5) הִטַּהֵר — cleanse oneself

טָהֳרָה, טָהֳרַת- ; n.f. — purification; cleansing (root: טהר)

טוב v.
1) טוֹב — a. be pleased; rejoice
b. be pleasant
6) הֵטִיב — a. do good
b. be generous

טוֹב n., adj., adv., interj.
a. good
b. good; nice; useful
c. preferably
d. very well

טוּב, טוּב- ; n.m.
a. wealth
b. good things
c. grace
d. pleasantness

טוֹבָה, טוֹבַת- ; טוֹבוֹת ; n.f.
a. good deed
b. happiness
c. prosperity
d. charity
e. mercy (root: טוב)

טוח v.
1) טָח — a. plaster (a wall)
2) נִטּוֹחַ — be plastered

טול v.
6) הֵטִיל — throw
7) הוּטַל — be thrown

טוּר ; טוּרִים, טוּרֵי- ; n.m. — row; line

טְחוֹרִים, טְחוֹרֵי- ; n.m.pl.
hemorrhoids

טחן v.
1) טָחַן — a. grind
b. oppress

טִיט n.m. — mud

טִירָה, טִירַת- ; טִירוֹת ; n.f.
a. encampment
b. wall

טַל, טַל- ; n.m. — dew

טלא v.

1) טָלוּא — a. speckled; spotted
b. tapestried

4) מְטֻלָּא — patched

טמא v.

1) טָמֵא — be unclean (ritually); be defiled

2) נִטְמָא — become unclean, defiled

3) טִמֵּא — a. defile; desecrate
b. pronounce as unclean

5) הִטַּמָּא — a. defile oneself
b. desecrate

טָמֵא ; טְמֵאָה, טְמֵאַת- ; טְמֵאִים ; adj.
unclean; defiled (root: טמא)

טֻמְאָה, טֻמְאַת- ; טֻמְאוֹת, טֻמְאוֹת- ;
a. defilement; uncleanliness n.f.
b. unclean matter (root: טמא)

טמן v.

1) טָמַן — a. bury
b. hide

2) נִטְמַן — a. be hidden
b. be buried

6) הִטְמִין — a. hide
b. bury

טעם v.

1) טָעַם — taste

טַעַם, טַעַם- ; n.m. — a. taste
b. sense (root: טעם)

טַף n.m.pl. — children

טֶפַח (טֹפַח) n.m. — handbreadth

טֶרֶם adv. — a. not yet
b. prior to; before בְּטֶרֶם

טרף v.

1) טָרַף — a. devour
b. tear to pieces

2) נִטְרַף — a. be devoured
b. be torn to pieces

טֶרֶף n.m. — a. prey
b. food (root: טרף)

טְרֵפָה n.f. — animal torn by beasts

י

יְאוֹר ; **יְאוֹרִים, יְאוֹרֵי-** ;.n.m
a. the river Nile (s.)
b. river

יאל .v
2) נוֹאַל — act foolishly
6) הוֹאִיל — venture; undertake

יאשׁ .v
2) נוֹאַשׁ — despair

יְבוּל, יְבוּל- ; .n.m — crop; produce

יְבוּסִי .adj.m — Jebusite
(a Canaanite people)

יבל .v
6) הוֹבִיל — a. lead
b. bring
7) הוּבַל — a. be lead
b. be brought

יָבָם ; **יְבָמָה** .n.m.f
a. brother-in-law (m.)
b. sister-in-law (f.)

יבשׁ .v
1) יָבֵשׁ — dry up
3) יִבֵּשׁ — cause to dry
5) הִתְיַבֵּשׁ — dry up
6) הוֹבִישׁ — cause to dry

יָבֵשׁ ; **יְבֵשָׁה** ; **יְבֵשִׁים** ; **יְבֵשׁוֹת** ; .adj
dry (root: יבש)

יַבָּשָׁה (יַבֶּשֶׁת) .n.f — dry land
(root: יבש)

יגה .v
2) נוּגֶה — sad
3) יִגָּה — a. make sad
b. oppress
6) הוֹגָה — a. oppress
b. afflict

יָגוֹן .n.m — grief (root: יגה)

יְגִיעַ, יְגִיעַ- ; .n.m — a. toil
b. effort
c. labor
d. gain
e. wealth (root: יגע)

יגע .v
1) יָגַע — a. toil; labor
b. be weary
3) יִגַּע — a. trouble
b. wear out
6) הוֹגִיעַ — weary

יגר .v
1) יָגֹר — fear

יִגַּשׁ נגשׁ .v — approach; come near
(future, imperative)

יָד, יַד- ; **יָדַיִם, יְדֵי-** ; **יָדוֹת, יְדוֹת-** ;
.n.f
a. hand
b. handle
c. portion; share
d. area
e. monument
f. through, by בְּיַד
g. as befits כְּיַד
h. near לְיַד
i. from מִיַּד
j. near אֶל-יַד
k. near; with עַל-יַד
l. by means of, by עַל-יְדֵי
m. from מִידֵי

ידה .v
1) יָדָה — throw
3) יִדָּה — throw; cast
5) הִתְוַדָּה — confess
6) הוֹדָה — a. praise
b. thank
c. confess

יְדִיד, יְדִיד- ; n.m. beloved one

יְדִידְיָה pr.n.m. Jedidiah
("beloved of God") (roots: יְדִיד, יָהּ)

ידע v.
1) יָדַע a. know
b. be aware
c. be concerned
d. experience
e. copulate
2) נוֹדַע a. be known
b. become known
5) הִתְוַדַּע make oneself known
6) הוֹדִיעַ a. inform
b. tell
7) הוּדַע be known

יִדְּעוֹנִי ; **יִדְּעוֹנִים** n.m. sorcerer
(root: ידע)

יָהּ pr.n.m. one of God's names

יהב v.
1) הַב (הָבָה), הָבִי, הָבוּ a. give!
(imperative)
b. let us...

יְהוּדָה pr.n.m. Judah
("praise God") (roots: יָהּ, ידה)

יְהוּדִי ; **יְהוּדִים** adj., n.
a. Judean; of Judah
b. Hebrew; Jew

יְהוּדִית n.f.
the Judean language, Hebrew

יְהֹוָה pr.n.m. God; Lord
(name unpronounced literally)
"Jehova", "YHWE" (transliterated).
Written as יְיָ, both pronounced אֲדֹנָי
See also "Grammar", section 16

יְהוֹנָתָן (יוֹנָתָן) pr.n.m. Jonathan
("God has given") (roots: יָהּ, נתן)

יְהוֹשֻׁעַ pr.n.m. Joshua
("God will save") (roots: יָהּ, ישע)

יְהוֹשָׁפָט pr.n.m. Jehoshaphat
("God has judged") (roots: יָהּ, שפט)

יוֹאֵל pr.n.m. Joel
("God is lord") (roots: יָהּ, אֵל)

יוֹבֵל ; **יוֹבְלִים** ; n.m.
a. 50th year ("jubilee")
b. ram's horn (for blowing)

יוֹדֵעַ see ידע

יוֹלֵדָה n.f. woman in labor; mother
(root: ילד)

יוֹם, יוֹם- ; **יָמִים, יְמֵי-** ; n.m. day
today הַיּוֹם
at this time, now כְּהַיּוֹם, כַּיּוֹם

יוֹמָם adv. by day; during the day
(root: יוֹם)

יָוָן pr.n.m. a. Noah's grandchild
b. Greece
c. Greek people

יוֹנָה, יוֹנַת- ; **יוֹנִים, יוֹנֵי-** ; n.f. dove

יוֹנָה pr.n.m. Jonah
("dove") (root: יוֹנָה)

יוֹנֵק n.m. suckling; baby (root: ינק)

יוֹנֶקֶת; יוֹנְקוֹת n.f. twig (root: ינק)

יוֹנָתָן pr.n.m. Jonathan
("God has given") (roots: יָהּ, נתן)

יוֹסֵף pr.n.m. Joseph
("God will add") (roots: יָהּ, יסף)

יוֹעֵץ, יוֹעֵץ- ; **יוֹעֲצִים, יוֹעֲצֵי-** ; n.m.
advisor; counselor (root: יעץ)

יוֹצֵר ; יוֹצְרִים, יוֹצְרֵי- ; n.m. potter
(root: יצר)

יוֹשֵׁב, יוֹשֵׁב- ; יוֹשְׁבִים, יוֹשְׁבֵי- ; n.m.
resident; inhabitant (root: ישב)

יוֹתֵר adv. a. more
b. over
c. even better

יוֹתֶרֶת n.f. lobe of the liver

יִז, יֵז, יַז see נזה

יִזְרְעֶאל pr.n. Jezreel
("God will seed") (roots: זרע, אֵל)

יַחַד, יַחְדָּו adv. together

יְחֶזְקֵאל pr.n.m. Ezekiel
("God will strengthen") (roots: חזק, אֵל)

יְחִי v. חיה (long) live!

יָחִיד ; יְחִידָה n., adj. a. single
b. alone

יחל v.
3) יִחֵל a. hope
b. expect
6) הוֹחִיל a. await
b. hope

יחם v.
1) יָחַם be sexually aroused
3) יִחֵם be sexually aroused

יחשׂ v.
5) הִתְיַחֵשׂ belong genealogically ;
be a member of a family

יטב v.
1) יָטַב a. do well
b. be well
(only in the future יִיטַב)
6) הֵיטִיב a. do well
b. do a favor
c. do right

יְיָ see יְהוָה

יַיִן, יֵין- ; n.m. wine

יכח v.
2) נוֹכַח be judged
5) הִתְוַכַּח have a dispute with
6) הוֹכִיחַ a. reprove
b. judge
c. decree
7) הוּכַח be punished

יכל v.
1) יָכֹל a. can ; be able
b. overpower; overcome

ילד v.
1) יָלַד a. beget; father; sire
b. give birth (f.)
c. cause
2) נוֹלַד be born
3) יִלֵּד deliver (a newborn)

יֶלֶד, יֶלֶד- ; יְלָדִים, יַלְדֵי- ; n.m.
a. boy
b. child
c. baby
d. young man

יִלּוֹד, יָלוּד adj., n.m. newborn
(root: ילד)

יָלִיד, יְלִיד- ; יְלִידֵי- ; n.m.
a. descendant
b. homeborn slave (root: ילד)

יֵלֵךְ see הלך

ילל v.
6) הֵילִיל a. mourn
b. cry
c. howl

יְלָלָה, יִלְלַת- ; n.f. outcry (root: ילל)

יֶלֶק n.m.
a. locust
b. grasshoppers

יָם, יַם-; יַמִּים n.m.
a. sea
b. west
c. large vessel; tank
d. the sea of reeds
("the Red Sea" today) יַם-סוּף

יָמוֹת, יָמִים see יוֹם

יָמִין, יְמִין- adj., n.m.f.
a. right side
b. right hand
c. south

יְמִינִי adj.m.
Benjaminite
(root: בִּנְיָמִין)

ימן v.
6) הֵימִין turn right

יְמָנִי, יְמָנִית adj.
right-hand

ינה v.
6) הוֹנָה
a. oppress
b. wrong

ינק v.
1) יָנַק suck
6) הֵינִיק nurse a baby

יסד v.
1) יָסַד
a. found
b. make firm
2) נוֹסַד
a. be founded
b. congregate
3) יִסֵּד
a. lay foundations
b. give orders
4) יֻסַּד be founded
7) הוּסַד be founded

יְסוֹד, יְסוֹד-; יְסוֹדוֹת n.m.
foundation (root: יסד)

יסף v.
1) יָסַף
a. continue
b. add
c. increase
2) נוֹסַף
a. be added to
b. join
6) הוֹסִיף
a. continue
b. increase

יסר v.
1) יָסַר
a. punish
b. discipline
2) נוֹסַר be punished
3) יִסֵּר punish

יעד v.
1) יָעַד designate
2) נוֹעַד meet
6) הוֹעִיד summon
7) הוּעַד be directed

יָעֶה; יָעִים n.m.
a. scraper
b. shovel

יעל v.
6) הוֹעִיל
a. help
b. be of use
c. be profitable

יַעַן conj.
a. because
b. due to (also: יַעַן אֲשֶׁר, יַעַן כִּי)

יָעֵן; יְעֵנִים n.m.
ostrich
(also: בַּת-יַעֲנָה)

יעף v.
1) יָעַף
a. tire
b. be weary

יעץ v.
1) יָעַץ advise
2) נוֹעַץ consult
see also יוֹעֵץ

יַעֲקֹב pr.n.m.
Jacob
("he will be on the heel of...")
(root: עָקֵב)

יַעַר, יַעַר-; יְעָרִים, יְעָרוֹת n.m.
forest

יפה v.
1) יָפָה be beautiful
3) יִפָּה adorn
5) הִתְיַפָּה beautify oneself

יָפֶה, יְפֵה-; יָפָה, יְפַת-; יָפוֹת, יְפוֹת-; adj. beautiful (root: יפה)

יָפֶה adv. well

יֳפִי, יׇפִי, יְפִי-; n.m. beauty (root: יפה)

יפע v.
6) הוֹפִיעַ a. appear
b. shine

יצא v.
1) יָצָא a. exit
b. leave
c. go away
d. come out
e. be redeemed
f. come to an end
6) הוֹצִיא a. bring out
b. bring forth
c. liberate
d. expel
e. remove
7) הוּצָא be removed

יצב v.
2) נִצַּב stand erect
5) הִתְיַצֵּב a. present oneself
b. stand ready
6) הִצִּיב a. set up
b. erect
7) הֻצַּב a. be set up
b. be erected

יצג v.
6) הִצִּיג a. present
b. set up

יִצְהָר n.m., pr.n.m. a. pure oil
b. Itzhar

יִצְחָק pr.n.m. Isaac ("he will laugh") (root: צחק)

יצק v.
1) יָצַק a. pour (liquid)
b. cast (metal)
6) הוֹצִיק present
7) הוּצַק a. be cast (metal)
b. be poured
solid; hard מוּצָק

יצר v.
1) יָצַר a. create
b. make
potter יוֹצֵר
2) נוֹצַר be created
4) יֻצַּר be created
7) הוּצַר be created

יֵצֶר, יֵצֶר-; n.m. a. thought
b. product of a potter (root: יצר)

יצת v.
1) יָצַת burn
2) נִצַּת be burned; be kindled
6) הִצִּית set on fire

יֶקֶב; יְקָבִים, יִקְבֵי-; n.m.
a. wine press
b. vat

יקד v.
1) יָקַד burn
7) הוּקַד be burned

יקע v.
1) יָקַע displace
6) הוֹקִיעַ hang
7) הוּקַע be hanged

יקץ v.
1) יִיקַץ wake up (only in the future)
(for past, present and imperative see קוץ)

1) קַל (פָּעַל) 2) נִפְעַל 3) פִּעֵל 4) פֻּעַל 5) הִתְפַּעֵל 6) הִפְעִיל 7) הָפְעַל

יקר v.
1) יָקַר be dear
6) הוֹקִיר value; have regard for

יָקָר, יְקַר-; יְקָרָה; יְקָרִים; יְקָרוֹת adj.
a. dear
b. heavy
c. rare (root: יקר)

יְקָר n.m
a. glory
b. honor
c. valuable

יקש v.
1) יָקַשׁ set a snare; entrap
2) נוֹקַשׁ be snared

ירא v.
1) יָרֵא a. fear
b. obey; worship
2) נוֹרָא see
3) יֵרֵא scare; intimidate

יָרֵא, יְרֵא-; יִרְאַת-; יְרֵאִים, יִרְאֵי-; adj.
God-fearing; pious

יִרְאָה, יִרְאַת-; n.f.
a. fear
b. awe (root: ירא)

יְרֻבַּעַל pr.n.m.
Jerubaal
(Gideon's epithet)
"(let) Baal contend (with him)"
(roots: ריב, בַּעַל)

ירד v.
1) יָרַד a. descend; go down
b. fall; sink
6) הוֹרִיד lower; bring down
7) הוּרַד be lowered; be brought down

יַרְדֵּן pr.n.m.
Jordan river
(root: ירד)

ירה v.
1) יָרָה a. shoot arrows
b. throw; cast
2) נוֹרָה be shot (by an arrow)
6) הוֹרָה a. shoot
b. teach; guide
c. water; refresh

יְרוּשָׁלַיִם pr.n.f.
Jerusalem

יָרֵחַ n.m.
moon

יֶרַח, יֶרַח-; יְרָחִים, יַרְחֵי-; n.m.
month (root: יָרֵחַ)

יְרֵחוֹ, יְרִיחוֹ pr.n.f.
Jericho

יְרַחְמְאֵל pr.n.m.
Jerahmeel
("God will have mercy")
(roots: רחם, אֵל)

יְרִיעָה; יְרִיעוֹת, יְרִיעוֹת-; n.f.
curtain

יָרֵךְ, יֶרֶךְ-; יְרֵכַיִם; n.f.
a. thigh
b. side of a vessel or of a building

יַרְכָה; יַרְכָתַיִם, יַרְכְּתֵי-; n.f.
a. edge
b. flank

יִרְמְיָה, יִרְמְיָהוּ pr.n.m.
Jeremiah
("God is lofty") (roots: רום, יָהּ)

יָרָק, יְרַק-; n.m.
vegetable

יֶרֶק, יֶרֶק-; n.m.
green vegetation

יֵרָקוֹן n.m.
mildew

ירש v.
1) יָרַשׁ inherit
2) נוֹרַשׁ be impoverished
3) יֵרֵשׁ take over
6) הוֹרִישׁ a. give as inheritance
b. dispossess
c. expel
d. make poor

יְרֵשָׁה (יְרֵשָׁה), יְרֻשַּׁת-; n.f.
inheritance

יֵשׁ adv., n.m. there is; there are
you are ready יֶשְׁךָ
he is; it is יֶשְׁנוֹ
you (m.pl.) are יֶשְׁכֶם

יֶשְׁךָ see יֵשׁ

יֶשְׁכֶם see יֵשׁ

יֶשְׁנוֹ see יֵשׁ

ישב v.
1) יָשַׁב a. sit
b. reside; dwell
2) נוֹשַׁב be inhabited
6) הוֹשִׁיב settle; make reside
7) הוּשַׁב be settled; be inhabited

יֵשׁוּעַ pr.n.m. Jeshua
("salvation") (root: ישע)

יְשׁוּעָה, יְשׁוּעַת-; יְשׁוּעוֹת, יְשׁוּעוֹת-;
a. salvation n.f.
b. triumph; success (root: ישע)

יִשַׁי pr.n.m. Jesse
("there is God" ?) (roots: ? יֵשׁ, יָהּ)

יְשִׁימוֹן n.m. wasteland; desert

יִשְׁמָעֵאל pr.n.m. Ishmael
("God will hear") (roots: שמע, אֵל)

ישן v.
1) יָשֵׁן sleep
2) נוֹשַׁן become old
3) יִשֵּׁן lull to sleep

יָשָׁן; יְשָׁנָה; יְשָׁנִים adj. old

ישע v.
2) נוֹשַׁע be saved
6) הוֹשִׁיעַ a. save
b. deliver
c. defend

יֶשַׁע n.m. salvation
(see also יְשׁוּעָה) (root: ישע)

יְשַׁעְיָהוּ pr.n.m. Isaiah
("God will save") (roots: ישע, יָהּ)

ישר v.
1) יָשַׁר seem good
3) יִשֵּׁר straighten; level
6) הֵישִׁיר straighten; level

יָשָׁר, יְשָׁרָה; יְשָׁרִים, יִשְׁרֵי-; יְשָׁרוֹת
a. right adj.
b. straight
c. honest (root: ישר)

יֹשֶׁר, יֹשֶׁר-; n.m. uprightness
(root: ישר)

יִשְׂרָאֵל pr.n.m. Israel
("will strive with God")
(roots: שׂרה, אֵל)

יִשָּׂשכָר pr.n.m. Issachar
("God's reward") (roots: יָהּ, שָׂכָר)

יָתֵד, יְתַד-; יְתֵדוֹת, יִתְדוֹת-; n.f.
peg; pin

יָתוֹם; יְתוֹמִים n.m. orphan

יִתֵּן see נתן

יתר v.
2) נוֹתַר remain
6) הוֹתִיר leave over

יֶתֶר, יֶתֶר-; n.m. a. excess; rest;
remainder (root: יתר)
b. rope; string

יִתְרוֹן, יִתְרוֹן-; n.m. advantage
(root: יתר)

כ

כְּ, כַּ, כָּ, כֶּ, כִּ, כֵּ prep.
a. as (prefix)
b. like
c. approximately
d. when
e. after
Declension : כָּמוֹנִי, כָּמוֹךָ, כָּמוֹךְ, כָּמוֹהוּ, כָּמוֹהָ כָּמוֹנוּ, כָּכֶם, כָּכֶן, כָּהֵם, כָּהֵן (כָּהֵנָּה)
like me, like you (m.s.), like you (f.s.), like him, like her, like us, like you (m.pl.), like you (f.pl.), like them (m.) like them (f.)
See also "Grammar", section 6.2

כאב v.
1) כָּאַב a. ache
b. be in pain
6) הִכְאִיב hurt; cause pain

כְּאֵב, כְּאֵב- ; n.m. pain
(root: כאב)

כַּאֲשֶׁר conj. as (roots: כְּ, אֲשֶׁר)

כבד v.
1) כָּבַד a. weigh
b. be haughty
2) נִכְבַּד be important
3) כִּבֵּד a. honor
b. reward
c. strengthen
4) כֻּבַּד be honored
5) הִתְכַּבֵּד a. put on airs
b. be heavy
6) הִכְבִּיד make heavy

כָּבֵד n.m. liver

כָּבֵד ; כְּבֵדִים, כִּבְדֵי- ;.adj.m a. hard
b. heavy
c. mighty (root: כבד)

כבה v.
1) כָּבָה be extinguished
3) כִּבָּה extinguish; quench; douse

כָּבוֹד, כְּבוֹד- ; n.m. a. honor
b. glory
c. treasure (root: כבד)

כַּבִּיר ; כַּבִּירִים adj.m. mighty; strong

כבס v.
3) כִּבֵּס launder; wash
4) כֻּבַּס be washed

כְּבָר adv. a. already
b. previously

כֶּבֶשׂ ; כְּבָשִׂים n.m. sheep

כבש v.
1) כָּבַשׁ conquer
2) נִכְבַּשׁ be conquered
3) כִּבֵּשׁ conquer

כִּבְשָׂה (כַּבְשָׂה), כִּבְשַׂת- ; כְּבָשׂוֹת, כִּבְשׂוֹת- ; n.f. ewe; female lamb

כַּד ; כַּדִּים n.m.f. pitcher; jar

כְּדֵי adv. enough

כֹּה adv. a. so; thus
b. here
c. now

כהה v.
1) כָּהָה a. dim
b. become weak
3) כִּהָה a. rebuke
b. become weak

כֵּהֶה ; כֵּהָה ; כֵּהוֹת ; adj. a. dim
b. weak

כְּהַיּוֹם adv. at this time; now
(roots: כְּ, יוֹם)

כָּהֶם (כָּהֵם) ; כָּהֵן (כָּהֵנָּה) prep.
like them (m.), like them (f.) (root: כְּ)

כהן v.
3) כִּהֵן — serve as a priest; minister

כֹּהֵן, כֹּהֵן- ; כֹּהֲנִים, כֹּהֲנֵי- ; n.m.
priest (root: כהן)

כְּהֻנָּה, כְּהֻנַּת- ; כְּהֻנּוֹת ; n.f.
priesthood (root: כהן)

כּוֹבַע, כּוֹבַע- ; כּוֹבָעִים ; n.m. — hat

כּוֹכָב ; כּוֹכָבִים, כּוֹכְבֵי- ; n.m. — star

כול v.
1) כָּל — measure
6) הֵכִיל — a. contain
b. hold
c. endure

כון v.
2) נָכוֹן — a. be secured
b. be established
c. be true
d. be ready
3) כּוֹנֵן — establish
4) כּוֹנַן — be established
5) הִתְכּוֹנֵן — be established
6) הֵכִין — a. prepare
b. arrange
7) הוּכַן — be established

כּוֹס, כּוֹס- ; כּוֹסוֹת ; n.f. — a. cup
b. portion
c. owl (m.)

כּוּר, כּוּר- ; n.m. — crucible; furnace

כּוֹרֵם ; כּוֹרְמִים n.m. — vineyard farmer
(root: כֶּרֶם)

כּוֹרֶשׁ (כֹּרֶשׁ) pr.n.m. — Cyrus

כּוֹתֶרֶת ; כּוֹתָרוֹת n.f. — capital;
upper part of a column (root: כתר)

כזב v.
1) כָּזַב — lie
2) נִכְזַב — be proved a liar
3) כִּזֵּב — lie; deceive
6) הִכְזִיב — prove wrong

כָּזָב ; כְּזָבִים n.m. — lie (root: כזב)

כֹּחַ, כֹּחַ- ; n.m. — strength

כחד v.
2) נִכְחַד — a. be hidden; escape notice
b. be destroyed
3) כִּחֵד — withhold; hide
6) הִכְחִיד — a. destroy
b. hide

כחש v.
1) כָּחַשׁ — be lean
2) נִכְחַשׁ — cringe
3) כִּחֵשׁ — a. lie; deceive
b. deny
5) הִתְכַּחֵשׁ — cringe

כִּי conj. — a. that
b. because; since
c. when; as
d. if
e. like
f. but
g. even though
h. only; just
i. whether הֲכִי
j. not so לֹא-כִי

כִּידוֹן n.m. — spear

כִּיּוֹר, כִּיּוֹר- ; כִּיּוֹרִים ; כִּיּוֹרוֹת ; n.m.
laver; wash basin

כִּיס n.m. — a. purse
b. pouch

כִּי עַל-כֵּן adv. — seeing that...;
since; for

כָּכָה adv. — so; thus

כָּכֶם conj. — as you (m.pl.) (root: כְּ)

כִּכָּר, כִּכַּר- ; n.f. plain; valley

כִּכָּר, כִּכַּר- ; כִּכָּרִים, כִּכְּרֵי-, כִּכְּרוֹת- ;
a. talent (gold coin; weight) n.f.
b. loaf (of bread)

כֹּל, כָּל- ; adj., pron., n.m. a. all
b. none (in the negative sense)
Declension: כֻּלִּי, כֻּלְּךָ, כֻּלֵּךְ, כֻּלּוֹ, כֻּלָּהּ ...
all of me, all of you (m.s.), all of you (f.s.), all of him, all of her …
all; everything הַכֹּל

כלא v.
1) כָּלָא a. prevent; stop
b. jail
2) נִכְלָא be stopped

כֶּלֶא ; כְּלָאִים n.m. prison (root: כלא)

כֶּלֶב ; כְּלָבִים, כַּלְבֵי- ; n.m. a. dog
b. male prostitute

כָּלֵב pr.n.m. Caleb ("dog") (root: כֶּלֶב)

כלה v.
1) כָּלָה a. end; cease
b. be consumed
3) כִּלָּה a. complete; finish
b. destroy

כָּלָה adv., n.f. a. altogether (adv.)
b. decision (n.)
c. destruction (n.)

כַּלָּה ; כַּלּוֹת ; n.f. a. bride
b. beloved woman
c. daughter-in-law

כְּלִי, כְּלִי- ; כֵּלִים, כְּלֵי- ; n.m.
a. object
b. instrument
c. apparel

כִּלְיָה ; כְּלָיוֹת, כִּלְיוֹת- ; n.f.
a. kidney
b. mind
c. conscience

כָּלִיל adj., adv., n.m. a. pure (adj.)
b. totally; entirely (adv.)
c. burnt offering (n.) (root: כלה)

כלכל v.
3) כִּלְכֵּל a. feed
b. suffer

כלם v.
2) נִכְלַם be ashamed
6) הִכְלִים shame
7) הָכְלַם be shamed

כְּלִמָּה, כְּלִמַּת- ; כְּלִמּוֹת ; n.f. shame
(root: כלם)

כַּמָּה (כַּמֶּה) adv., adj. a. how many?
b. how much?
c. till when?
d. several

כְּמוֹ adv. a. as; like
b. when
Declension: כָּמוֹנִי, כָּמוֹךָ, ...
like me, like you (m.s.), ...

כֵּן adv. a. so; thus
b. truly; right
c. now

כֵּן ; כֵּנִים adj.m. true; honest

כֵּן, כֵּן- ; n.m. a. stand; basis
b. post
c. lice (pl.כִּנִּים)

כִּנּוֹר ; כִּנּוֹרוֹת ; n.m. lyre; harp

כנס v.
1) כָּנַס gather
3) כִּנֵּס gather

כנע v.
2) נִכְנַע humble oneself

6) הִכְנִיעַ subdue; vanquish

כָּנָף, כְּנַף-; כְּנָפַיִם, כַּנְפֵי-; כַּנְפוֹת-; n.f.
a. wing (of a bird)
b. corner (of a garment; of the earth)

כִּנֶּרֶת pr.n.f. Kineret
(ancient Canaanite city)
Sea of Galilee יָם-כִּנֶּרֶת

כִּסֵּא, כִּסֵּא-; כִּסְאוֹת; n.m. a. chair
b. throne
c. authority

כסה v.
1) כָּסָה cover; hide
2) נִכְסָה be covered
3) כִּסָּה cover up
4) כֻּסָּה be covered; be coated
5) הִתְכַּסָּה cover oneself

כִּסֶּה, כֶּסֶה see כִּסֵּא

כְּסוּת n.f. clothing; cover (root: כסה)

כְּסִיל, כְּסִיל-; כְּסִילִים adj., n.m.
a. foolish
b. fool
c. Orion (constellation)

כֶּסֶל; כְּסָלִים n.m. a. stupidity
b. trust; security
c. loins (pl.)

כסף v.
1) כָּסַף desire
2) נִכְסַף a. yearn
b. be shamed

כֶּסֶף, כֶּסֶף-; n.m. a. silver
b. silver coin
c. price

כעס v.
1) כָּעַס be angry
3) כִּעֵס anger; vex
6) הִכְעִיס anger

כַּעַס (כַּעַשׂ), כַּעַס-; כְּעָסִים n.m.
anger; vexation (root: כעס)

כַּף, כַּף-; כַּפּוֹת, כַּפּוֹת-; כַּפַּיִם, כַּפֵּי-; n.f.
a. hand
b. sole (of the foot)
c. socket (of a limb)
d. authority
e. ladle
f. palm tree
branches (pl.כַּפּוֹת)

כְּפוֹר n.m. a. frost
b. cup
c. bowl

כִּפּוּרִים n.m.pl. atonement (root: כפר)

כְּפִי prep. a. per; in accordance with
b. because of

כְּפִיר, כְּפִיר-; כְּפִירִים; n.m. lion cub

כפר v.
1) כָּפַר coat; cover
3) כִּפֵּר expiate; make atonement
4) כֻּפַּר be forgiven
5) הִתְכַּפֵּר be forgiven

כֹּפֶר, כֹּפֶר-; כְּפָרִים; n.m. a. tar; pitch
b. ransom
c. henna tree
d. village

כַּפֹּרֶת, כַּפֹּרֶת-; n.f. cover
(of the Holy Ark)

כַּפְתּוֹר; כַּפְתּוֹרִים n.m. a. calyx
b. capital (at the top of a post)
c. isle of Crete (pr.n.m.s.)

כַּר; כָּרִים n.m. a. lamb
b. battering ram
c. cushion
d. pasture

כֹּר; כֹּרִים n.m. unit of dry measure
(equal to ten אֵיפוֹת)

כרה v.
1) כָּרָה a. dig
b. open

c. buy
d. prepare a meal
2) נִכְרָה be dug

כְּרוּב ; כְּרוּבִים n.m. a. angel
b. "cherub", a celestial being

כֶּרֶם, כֶּרֶם- ; כְּרָמִים, כַּרְמֵי- ; n.m.
vineyard

כַּרְמֶל n.m., pr.n. a. farmland
b. grain on the stalk
c. city in Judea (pr.n.f.)
d. Carmel, mountain range near the valley of Zebulun (pr.n.m.)

כרע v.
1) כָּרַע a. kneel
b. lie down
6) הִכְרִיעַ bring down; strike down

כְּרָעַיִם n.f.pl. animal's legs
(root: כרע)

כרת v.
1) כָּרַת a. cut
b. hew
כָּרַת בְּרִית make a covenant
2) נִכְרַת a. be destroyed
b. be cut off
4) כֹּרַת be cut off
6) הִכְרִית destroy
7) הָכְרַת be cut off

כֶּשֶׂב ; כְּשָׂבִים n.m. sheep

כַּשְׂדִּים pr.n.pl. Chaldeans
(south Babylonians)

כשל v.
1) כָּשַׁל a. stumble
b. fall
c. fail
d. weaken
2) נִכְשַׁל stumble
6) הִכְשִׁיל cause (someone) to fall
7) הֻכְשַׁל be made to fall

כשף v.
3) כִּשֵּׁף practice witchcraft

כְּשָׁפִים n.m.pl. witchcraft; sorcery
(root: כשף)

כתב v.
1) כָּתַב a. write
b. inscribe
2) נִכְתַּב a. be written
b. be inscribed
3) כִּתֵּב write

כְּתָב, כְּתָב- ; n.m. a. letter
b. edict
c. script

כָּתוּב adj.m.s. written (root: כתב)

כְּתוּבִים adj.m.pl. Writings,
Hagiographa (third division of the Bible) (root: כתב)
See also "Grammar", section 17

כֶּתֶם, כֶּתֶם- ; n.m. fine gold

כֻּתֹּנֶת (כְּתֹנֶת), כְּתֹנֶת- ; כֻּתֳּנוֹת
(כָּתְנוֹת), כָּתְנוֹת- ; n.f. a. tunic
b. shirt

כָּתֵף, כֶּתֶף- ; כְּתֵפוֹת, כִּתְפוֹת- ; n.f.
a. shoulder
b. side; flank
c. shoulder pieces (pl.)

כתר v.
3) כִּתֵּר surround

כֶּתֶר, כֶּתֶר- ; n.m. crown (root: כתר)

כתת v.
1) כָּתַת break; smash
3) כִּתֵּת a. beat
b. demolish
4) כֻּתַּת be demolished
6) הִכַּת smash; beat
7) הֻכַּת be smashed

ל

לְ, לַ, לָ, לֶ, לִ, לֵ prep.
a. to
b. near (time)
c. of (nouns)
d. about
e. (before a direct object, like אֶת)
f. according to
Declension: לִי, לְךָ, לָךְ, לוֹ, לָהּ, לָנוּ, לָכֶם, לָכֶן, לָהֶם (לָמוֹ), לָהֶן
to me, to you (m.s.), to you (f.s.), to him, to her, to us, to you (m.pl.), to you (f.pl.), to them (m.), to them (f.)
See also "Grammar", section 6.3

לֹא (לוֹא) adv., adj.
a. no
b. do not...
c. not so
d. or not אִם לֹא
e. without בְּלֹא
f. is it not...? הֲלֹא

לאה v.
1) לָאָה — a. be tired
b. be unable
2) נִלְאָה — a. be tired
b. be unable
6) הֶלְאָה — tire; exhaust

לְאֹם ; לְאֻמִּים n.m. — nation; people

לֵאמֹר v. אמר
a. to say; to command
b. that is; to wit; as follows

לֵב, לֵב- ; לִבּוֹת ; n.m.
a. heart
b. center

לֵבָב, לְבַב- ; לְבָבוֹת n.m.
a. heart
b. center

לְבַד adv.
a. alone
b. separately
in addition to ... לְבַד מִ-

לְבוֹנָה n.f. — frankincense

לְבוּשׁ ; לְבוּשִׁים n.m. — garment
(root: לבש)

לָבֶטַח adv. — safely; securely
(root: בטח)

לָבִיא ; לְבָאִים n.m. — lion
(see also אַרְיֵה)

לבן v.
1) לָבַן — make bricks
6) הִלְבִּין — a. turn white
b. explain

לָבָן, לְבֶן- ; לְבָנָה ; לְבָנִים ; לְבָנוֹת adj.
white (root: לבן)

לְבֵנָה, לִבְנַת- ; לְבֵנִים n.f. — brick
(root: לבן)

לבש v.
1) לָבַשׁ — a. wear (clothing)
b. cover
c. wrap
6) הִלְבִּישׁ — dress (someone)

לֹג, לֹג- ; n.m. — liquid measure
(1/12 of a הִין)

לַהַב, לַהַב- ; לְהָבִים, לַהֲבֵי- ; n.m.
a. flame
b. glitter
c. blade (of a knife or of a sword)

לֶהָבָה ; לֶהָבוֹת, לַהֲבוֹת- ; n.f.
flame of fire

להט v.
1) לָהַט — burn

1) קַל (פָּעַל) 2) נִפְעַל 3) פִּעֵל 4) פֻּעַל 5) הִתְפַּעֵל 6) הִפְעִיל 7) הָפְעַל

3) לְהֵט burn

לָהֶם, לָהֶן see לְ

לוּ (לוּא) conj. a. if
b. what if
c. oh that... (wish)

לוה v.
1) לָוָה borrow
2) נִלְוָה join
6) הִלְוָה lend

לוּחַ, לוּחַ-; לוּחוֹת, לוּחוֹת- n.m.
tablet

לֵוִי; לְוִיִּם pr.n.m. a. Levy
("join") (root: לוה)
b. Levite

לִוְיָתָן n.m. leviathan; sea monster

לוּלֵא (לוּלֵי) conj. a. if not
b. were it not
c. except (roots: לוּ, לֹא)

לוּלָאָה; לוּלָאוֹת, לוּלְאוֹת- n.f. loop

לון (לין) v.
1) לָן a. sleep; spend the night
b. stay; remain
2) נָלוֹן complain
5) הִתְלוֹנֵן reside
6) הִלִּין, הֵלִין complain; rail against

לוֹצֵץ v. ליץ mock

לוש v.
1) לָשׁ knead

לַח; לַחִים adj.m. moist

לְחִי, לְחִי-; לְחָיַיִם n.f. cheek

לחך v.
1) לָחַךְ a. lick
b. eat
3) לִחֵךְ lick

לחם v.
1) לָחַם a. eat
b. fight
2) נִלְחַם fight

לֶחֶם, לֶחֶם-; n.m. a. bread
b. food

לחץ v.
1) לָחַץ a. press
b. oppress
2) נִלְחַץ be pressed

לַחַץ, לַחַץ-; n.m. oppression
(root: לחץ)

לטש v.
1) לָטַשׁ sharpen

לִי see לְ

לַיִל, לֵיל see לַיְלָה

לַיְלָה; לֵילוֹת, לֵילוֹת-; n.m. night
tonight הַלַּיְלָה

לין see לון

ליץ v.
1) לָץ scoff; scorn
3) לוֹצֵץ mock
5) הִתְלוֹצֵץ mock
6) הֵלִיץ scoff
see also מֵלִיץ

לֵךְ, לְכִי, לְכוּ (m.s., f.s., pl.) go!
imperative tense of הלך

לְךָ, לָךְ, לָכֶם, לָכֶן see לְ

לכד v.
1) לָכַד capture
2) נִלְכַּד be captured
5) הִתְלַכֵּד be interlocked; compact

לְכָה variation of לֵךְ see above

לָכֵן conj. therefore

לֶכֶת הלך v.
a. go
b. walk
c. travel (infinitive construct)

למד v.
1) לָמַד learn
3) לִמֵּד teach; train
4) לֻמַּד be trained

לָמָּה conj.
a. why?
b. for what? (roots: לְ, מָה)

לָמוֹ, לְמוֹ see לְ

לִמּוּד ; לִמּוּדִים, לִמּוּדֵי- ; n., adj.m.
a. pupil
b. trained (root: למד)

לְמַעַן prep.
a. for; to; so that (before a verb)
b. for; on account of (before a noun)
c. so that לְמַעַן אֲשֶׁר

לעג v.
1) לָעַג mock
6) הִלְעִיג mock

לַעַג ; לַעֲגֵי- ; n.m. mockery; scorn
(root: לעג)

לָעַד see עַד

לְעֻמַּת prep.
a. opposite
b. next to

לַעֲנָה n.f. wormwood

לְפִי prep. according to; per

לַפִּיד, לַפִּיד- ; לַפִּידִים, לַפִּידֵי- ; n.m.
torch

לִפְנוֹת adv. toward; close to (root: פנה)

לִפְנֵי prep.
a. before
b. in the presence of
c. prior to
d. ahead (root: פָּנִים)

לְפָנִים adv. formerly

לֵץ ; לֵצִים n.m. scoffer; scorner
(root: ליץ)

לקח v.
1) לָקַח
a. take
b. hold
c. possess
d. marry a woman
2) נִלְקַח
a. be caught
b. be taken
c. be removed
4) לֻקַּח be taken
5) הִתְלַקַּח flash (fire)

לֶקַח n.m.
a. lesson
b. discourse
c. doctrine

לקט v.
1) לָקַט collect; gather
3) לִקֵּט gather; amass
4) לֻקַּט be gathered
5) הִתְלַקֵּט gather together

לקק v.
1) לָקַק lap; lick
3) לִקֵּק lap; lick

לִקְרַאת see קְרַאת

לָשׁוֹן, לְשׁוֹן- ; לְשׁוֹנוֹת, לְשׁוֹנוֹת- ; n.f.
a. tongue
b. language
c. speech

לִשְׁכָּה, לִשְׁכַּת- ; לְשָׁכוֹת, לִשְׁכוֹת- ;
chamber; room n.f.

מִ, מֵ prep. a. from
b. of
c. more than
d. because of
See also "Grammar", section 6.4

מְאֹד adv., n.m. a. very; very much
b. might; strength

מְאָדָּם ; מְאָדָּמִים adj., v. painted red
(root: אדם)

מֵאָה, מְאַת- ; מֵאוֹת ; n. hundred

מְאוּמָה (מְאוּם) n.m. a. nothing
b. anything

מָאוֹר, מְאוֹר- ; מְאוֹרוֹת, מְאוֹרֵי- ;
n.m. a. light
b. lighting
c. glow (root: אור)

מֹאזְנַיִם, מֹאזְנֵי- ; n.m.pl. scales;
balance (root: אזן)

מַאֲכָל, מַאֲכַל- ; n.m. food (root: אכל)

מאן v.
3) מֵאֵן refuse

מאס v.
1) מָאַס a. reject
b. refuse
2) נִמְאַס be rejected

מַאֲרָב, מַאְרַב- ; n.m. ambush
(root: ארב)

מְאֵרָה, מְאֵרַת- ; מְאֵרוֹת ; n.f. curse
(root: ארר)

מֵאֵת conj. from

מָאתַיִם n.pl. two hundred
(dual plural of מֵאָה)

מָבוֹא, מְבוֹא- ; מְבוֹאוֹת, מְבוֹאֵי- ;
n.m. entrance (root: בוא)
מְבוֹא שֶׁמֶשׁ sunset

מַבּוּל n.m. flood

מִבְחָר, מִבְחַר- ; n.m. choice
(root: בחר)

מִבְטָח, מִבְטַח- ; מִבְטָחִים n.m.
trust; confidence (root: בטח)

מִבְצָר, מִבְצַר- ; מִבְצָרִים, מִבְצְרֵי- ;
n.m. fortress (root: בצר)

מֶגֶד, מֶגֶד- ; מְגָדִים n.m. a. bounty
b. sweetness

מִגְדָּל, מִגְדַּל- ; מִגְדָּלִים (מִגְדָּלוֹת) ;
מִגְדְּלוֹת- ; n.m. tower (root: גדל)

מָגוֹר n.m. fear (root: יגר)

מָגוֹר ; מְגוּרִים n.m. a. residence
b. sojourn (root: גור)

מַגִּיד see נגד

מְגִלָּה, מְגִלַּת- ; n.f. scroll (root: גלל)

מָגֵן, מָגֵן- ; מָגִנִּים, מָגִנֵּי- ; n.m.
shield; cover; protection (root: גנן)

מַגֵּפָה, מַגֵּפַת- ; מַגֵּפוֹת n.f. a. plague
b. slaughter (root: נגף)

מִגְרָשׁ, מִגְרַשׁ- ; מִגְרְשֵׁי- ; n.m.
plot of land

מַד ; מִדִּין n.m.
a. garment
b. rug
c. measure (root: מדד)

מִדְבָּר, מִדְבַּר- ; n.m.
a. desert
b. speech (root: דבר)

מדד v.
1) מָדַד measure
2) נָמַד be measured
3) מִדֵּד measure
5) הִתְמוֹדֵד stretch oneself

מִדָּה, מִדַּת- ; **מִדּוֹת, מִדּוֹת-** ; n.f.
a. measure
b. size (root: מדד)

מָדוֹן n.m. fight; strife

מַדּוּעַ adv. why?

מִדְיָן pr.n.m Midian

מְדִינָה ; **מְדִינוֹת, מְדִינוֹת-** ; n.f.
a. country
b. province

מִדְיָנִים (מְדָנִים) n.m.pl. quarrel; discord

מַדָּע n.m.
a. knowledge
b. thought (root: ידע)

מַה, מָה, מֶה pron., adv., conj.
a. which?
b. what?
c. how?
d. why?

מְהוּמָה, מְהוּמַת- ; **מְהוּמוֹת** n.f.
panic; turmoil (root: המה)

מַהֲלָךְ, מַהֲלַךְ- ; **מַהֲלְכִים** n.m.
a. walking
b. distance (root: הלך)

מהמה v.
5) הִתְמַהְמֵהַּ linger; tarry

מַהְפֵּכָה, מַהְפֵּכַת- ; n.f. destruction
(root: הפך)

מהר v.
1) מָהַר a. pay a bride's price
b. change
2) נִמְהַר be hasty
3) מִהֵר hurry; rush

מַהֵר, מְהֵרָה adv. quickly (root: מהר)

מוג v.
1) מָג melt
2) נָמוֹג a. melt
b. be weakened
3) מוֹגֵג melt
5) הִתְמוֹגֵג a. melt
b. be weakened

מוּזָר v.
a. strange
b. distant

מוט v.
1) מָט a. stumble
b. fall
c. crumble
2) נָמוֹט a. stumble
b. fall
c. crumble
5) הִתְמוֹטֵט a. stumble
b. fall
c. crumble

מוֹט n.m.
a. stick; rod
b. collapse (root: מוט)

מוֹטָה; מוֹטוֹת, מוֹטוֹת- ; n.f.
a. rod; stick
b. yoke ; burden

מוך v.
1) מָךְ a. be low
b. become poor

מול v.
1) מָל circumcise
2) נָמוֹל be circumcised
6) הֵמִיל a. destroy
b. cut down

מוּל (מוֹל) prep. opposite

מוֹלֶדֶת, מוֹלֶדֶת- ; **מוֹלְדוֹת-** ; n.f.
a. born (person)
b. birth
c. family (root: ילד)

מוּם n.m. defect; blemish

מוּסָד ; **מוּסָדוֹת, מוּסְדוֹת-, מוּסְדֵי-** ;
n.m. basis; foundation (root: יסד)

מוּסָר, מוּסַר- ; n.m. a. correction
b. warning
c. discipline; punishment (root: יסר)

מוֹסֵרָה ; **מוֹסֵרוֹת, מוֹסְרוֹת-** ; n.f.
bond; tie

מוֹעֵד, מוֹעֵד- ; **מוֹעֲדִים (מוֹעֲדוֹת), מוֹעֲדֵי-** ; n.m.
a. appointed time
b. festival; holy day
c. festival sacrifice
d. meeting; convention (root: יעד)

מוֹעֵצָה ; **מוֹעֵצוֹת** n.f. a. counsel
b. device
c. plan (root: יעץ)

מוֹפֵת ; **מוֹפְתִים** n.m. a. miracle
b. portent; sign

מוֹץ (מֹץ), מוֹץ- ; n.m. chaff

מוֹצָא, מוֹצָא- ; **מוֹצָאֵי-** ; n.m.
a. source; starting point
b. exit (root: יצא)

מוּצָק יצק .v solid; hard

מוֹקֵשׁ ; **מוֹקְשִׁים, מוֹקְשֵׁי-** ; n.m.
trap; snare (root: יקש)

מוֹר (מֹר), מָר- ; n.m. myrrh

מור v.
2) נָמַר change
6) הֵמִיר exchange

מוֹרָא ; **מוֹרָאִים** n.m. fear (root: ירא)

מוֹרָד, מוֹרַד- ; n.m. descent; slope
(root: ירד)

מוֹרֶה n.m. a. teacher
b. early rain
c. archer
d. rebellious (adj.m.) See also v. ירה

מוֹרָשָׁה n.f. a. heritage
b. possession (root: ירש)

מוש v.
1) מָשׁ a. move
b. remove
c. feel; touch
6) הֵמִישׁ let touch

מוֹשָׁב, מוֹשַׁב- ; **מוֹשְׁבוֹת-, מוֹשְׁבֵי-** ;
n.m. a. seat
b. abode
c. company (root: ישב)

מוֹשִׁיעַ n.m. savior (root: ישע)

מוֹשֵׁל n.m. ruler (root: משל)

מות v.
1) מֵת die
3) מוֹתֵת kill; slay
6) הֵמִית kill; slay
7) הוּמַת be slain

מָוֶת ; **מוֹתֵי-** ; n.m. death (root: מות)

מִזְבֵּחַ, מִזְבַּח- ; **מִזְבְּחוֹת, מִזְבְּחוֹת-** ;
n.m. altar (root: זבח)

מְזוּזָה, מְזוּזַת- ; **מְזוּזוֹת, מְזוּזוֹת-** ;
n.f. doorpost

מַזְלֵג ; מִזְלָגוֹת n.m. a. fork
b. meat hook

מְזִמָּה ; מְזִמּוֹת, מְזִמּוֹת- ; n.f. plan; scheme (root: זמם)

מִזְמוֹר n.m. psalm; song (root: זמר)

מִזְרָח, מִזְרַח- ; n.m. east (root: זרח)

מִזְרָק ; מִזְרָקִים (מִזְרָקוֹת), מִזְרְקֵי- ;
n.m. bowl

מַחְבֶּרֶת ; מַחְבְּרוֹת n.f. a. loop
b. coupling
c. clasp (root: חבר)

מַחֲבַת, מַחֲבַת- ; n.f. frying pan

מחה v.
1) מָחָה a. erase; eradicate
b. destroy
c. wipe
d. touch; abut
2) נִמְחָה be destroyed; be eradicated
6) הִמְחָה erase

מָחוֹל, מְחוֹל- ; **מְחוֹלוֹת** n.m. dance
(root: חול)

מִחְיָה, מִחְיַת- ; n.f. a. sustenance
b. raw flesh in a wound (root: חיה)

מְחִיר, מְחִיר- ; n.m. price; cost

מַחֲלָה n.f. illness (root: חלה)

מַחֲלֶה n.m. illness (root: חלה)

מַחְלְקָה (מַחֲלֹקֶת), מַחְלֹקֶת- ;
מַחְלְקוֹת, מַחְלְקוֹת- ; n.f. a. division
b. group (root: חלק)

מַחְמָד (מַחֲמוּד), מַחְמַד- ; **מַחֲמַדִּים,**
מַחֲמַדֵּי- ; n.m. prized item
(root: חמד)

מַחֲנֶה, מַחֲנֵה- ; **מַחֲנִים, מַחֲנוֹת,**
מַחֲנוֹת- ; n.m.f. a. camp
b. troop (root: חנה)

מַחְסֶה, מַחְסֵה- ; n.m. shelter; refuge
(root: חסה)

מַחְסוֹר n.m. need; want (root: חסר)

מחץ v.
1) מָחַץ a. crush
b. wound

מַחֲצִית, מַחֲצִית- ; n.f. half
(root: חצה)

מָחָר adv. a. tomorrow
b. in the future

מָחֳרָת, מָחֳרַת- ; n.f.
day after tomorrow

מַחֲשָׁבָה, מַחֲשֶׁבֶת- ; **מַחֲשָׁבוֹת,**
מַחְשְׁבוֹת- ; n.f. a. thought
b. evil plot (root: חשב)

מַחֲשֶׁבֶת ; מַחֲשָׁבוֹת n.f.
designer's craft

מַחְשָׁךְ ; מַחֲשַׁכִּים, מַחֲשַׁכֵּי- ; n.m.
dark place (root: חשך)

מַחְתָּה ; מַחְתּוֹת, מַחְתּוֹת- ; n.f.
a. fire pan
b. censer (root: חתה)

מְחִתָּה, מְחִתַּת- ; n.f. a. destruction
b. shock

מַטֶּה, מַטֵּה- ; **מַטּוֹת, מַטּוֹת-** ; n.m.
a. rod; staff
b. branch
c. tribe (of the twelve tribes of Israel)
(root: נטה)

מִטָּה, מִטַּת- ; **מִטּוֹת, מִטּוֹת-** ; n.f.
bed

מַטָּה adv. below; down

מְטֻלָּא טלא v. patched

מַטָּע, מַטַּע- ; **מַטָּעֵי-** ; n.m.
plantation (root: נטע)

מַטְעַמִּים n.m.pl. tasty food
(root: טעם)

מטר v.
2) נִמְטַר be rained on
6) הִמְטִיר cause to rain

מָטָר, מְטַר- ; **מִטְרוֹת-** ; n.m. rain
(root: מטר)

מַטָּרָה n.f. a. target
b. prison

מֵי- see מַיִם

מִי pron. a. who?
b. whose
c. whom
d. whoever
e. oh that...; if only...

מֵיטָב, מֵיטַב- ; n.m. choice;
the best of (root: טוב)

מִיכָאֵל pr.n.m. Michael
("who is like God!")
(roots: מִי, כְּ, אֵל)

מִיכָה pr.n.m. Micah
("who is like God!")
(roots: מִי, כְּ, יָהּ)

מַיִם, מֵי- ; **מֵימֵי-** ; n.m.pl. water

מִין ; **מִינִים** n.m. kind; type

מִישׁוֹר n.m. a. plain; tableland
b. justice; equity (root: ישר)

מֵישָׁרִים n.m.pl. justice; equity
(root: ישר)

מֵיתָר ; **מֵיתָרִים, מֵיתָרֵי-** ; n.m.
string; cord

מַכְאוֹב ; **מַכְאוֹבִים** n.m. pain
(root: כאב)

מִכְבָּר, מִכְבַּר- ; n.m. net; grating

מַכָּה, מַכַּת- ; **מַכּוֹת, מַכּוֹת-** ; n.f.
a. blow; strike
b. plague (root: נכה)

מָכוֹן, מְכוֹן- ; **מְכוֹנִים** n.m. a. place
b. habitation

מְכוֹנָה ; **מְכוֹנוֹת** n.f. basis; foundation
(root: כון)

מִכְנָסַיִם, מִכְנְסֵי- ; n.m.pl. pants;
breeches (root: כנס)

מֶכֶס n.m. a. levy; tax
b. worth

מִכְסָה n.f. number; amount

מִכְסֶה (מְכַסֶּה), מִכְסֵה- ; n.m.
cover; lid (root: כסה)

מכר v.
1) מָכַר sell
2) נִמְכַּר be sold
5) הִתְמַכֵּר commit oneself

מִכְשׁוֹל, מִכְשׁוֹל- ; **מִכְשׁוֹלִים** n.m.
stumbling block (root: כשל)

מִכְתָּב, מִכְתַּב- ; n.m. letter; writing
(root: כתב)

מִכְתָּם n.m. type of poem (in Psalms)

מלא v.
1) מָלֵא a. fill
b. complete (time)
2) נִמְלָא be filled
3) מִלֵּא a. fill
b. fulfill
4) מֻלָּא be filled

מָלֵא ; מְלֵאָה ; מְלֵאִים ; מְלֵאוֹת adj.
full (root: מלא)

מְלֹא see מְלוֹא

מַלְאָךְ, מַלְאַךְ- ; מַלְאָכִים, מַלְאֲכֵי- ;
n.m. a. messenger
b. God's messenger

מְלָאכָה, מְלֶאכֶת- ; מַלְאֲכוֹת- ; n.f.
a. work; labor
b. task
c. property; wealth

מַלְאָכִי pr.n.m. Malachi
("my messenger") (root: מלאך)

מִלְּבַד prep. in addition to...

מַלְבּוּשׁ n.m. clothing; garment
(root: לבש)

מִלָּה ; מִלִּים (מִלִּין) n.f. word;
utterance (root: מלל)

מְלוֹא n.m. entirety; fullness
(root: מלא)

מִלּוֹא n.m. dirt rampart

מִלּוּאִים n.m.pl.
a. setting (of precious stones)
(root: מלא)
b. ordination (of priests)

מְלוּכָה n.f. kingdom; monarchy
(root: מלך)

מָלוֹן, מְלוֹן- ; n.m. inn;
night encampment (root: לון)

מֶלַח n.m. salt

מִלְחָמָה (מִלְחֶמֶת) ; מִלְחָמוֹת,
מִלְחֲמוֹת- ; n.f. war (root: לחם)

מלט v.
2) נִמְלַט a. escape
b. run
3) מִלֵּט rescue; save
5) הִתְמַלֵּט escape
6) הִמְלִיט a. rescue
b. give birth (animals)

מֵלִיץ ; מְלִיצֵי- ; n.m. a. advocate
b. interpreter (root: ליץ)

מלך v.
1) מָלַךְ rule; be king
6) הִמְלִיךְ crown as a king
7) הָמְלַךְ be crowned as a king

מֶלֶךְ, מֶלֶךְ- ; מְלָכִים, מַלְכֵי- ; n.m.
king (root: מלך)
the Book of Kings מְלָכִים

מֹלֶךְ n.m. Moloch
(fire god of ancient origin)

מַלְכָּה, מַלְכַּת- ; מְלָכוֹת n.f. queen
(root: מלך)

מַלְכוּת, מַלְכוּת- ; מַלְכֻיּוֹת n.f.
a. kingdom
b. reign (root: מלך)

מַלְכִּיָּה(וּ) pr.n.m. Malkiah
("my king is God ") (roots: מֶלֶךְ, יָהּ)

מלל v.
1) מָלַל rub
2) נָמַל wither
3) מִלֵּל speak
3) מוֹלֵל wither
5) הִתְמוֹלֵל be rubbed

מַלְקוֹחַ n.m. booty; spoil (root: לקח)

מַלְקוֹשׁ n.m. latc rain

מֶלְקָחַיִם n.m.pl. pair of tongs (root: לקח)

מִמְכָּר, מִמְכַּר- ; n.m.
a. sale
b. wares (root: מכר)

מַמְלָכָה, מַמְלֶכֶת- ; **מַמְלָכוֹת, מַמְלְכוֹת-** ; n.f.
reign; kingdom (root: מלך)

מַמְלְכוּת n.f. reign; kingdom

מִמֶּנִּי, מִמְּךָ, מִמֵּךְ, מִמֶּנּוּ, מִמֶּנָּה, מִמֶּנּוּ, מִכֶּם, מֵהֶם (מֵהֵמָּה), מֵהֶן (מֵהֵנָּה)
declension of מִן or of מֵ-:
from me, from you (m.s.), from you (f.s.), from him, from her, from us, from you (m.pl.), from you (f.pl.), from them (m.), from them (f.)
See also "Grammar", section 6.4

מֶמְשָׁלָה, מֶמְשֶׁלֶת- ; **מֶמְשְׁלוֹת-** ; n.f.
a. government
b. dominion (root: משל)

מָן n.m. manna

מִן prep.
a. from
b. of
c. than
d. because of
e. lest
See the declension above, under מִמֶּנִּי
See also מֵ, מִ

מנה v.
1) מָנָה a. count
b. destine
2) נִמְנָה be counted
3) מִנָּה appoint
4) מֻנָּה be appointed

מָנָה ; **מָנוֹת** n.f. portion (root: מנה)

מָנֶה ; **מָנִים** n.m. mina
(a coin and a weight)

מָנוֹחַ, מְנוֹחַ- ; n.m. rest (root: נוח)

מְנוּחָה ; **מְנוּחוֹת** n.f.
a. rest
b. resting place (root: נוח)

מָנוֹס n.m.
מְנוּסָה n.f.
a. escape
b. shelter (root: נוס)

מְנוֹרָה, מְנוֹרַת- ; **מְנוֹרוֹת, מְנוֹרוֹת-** ; n.f.
a. lampstand
b. candlestick

מִנְחָה, מִנְחַת- ; **מִנְחוֹת-** ; n.f.
a. gift
b. meal-offering to God

מְנַחֵם pr.n.m. Menahem
("one who comforts") (root: נחם)

מִנִּי, מִנֵּי see מִן

מנע v.
1) מָנַע prevent
2) נִמְנַע be prevented

מַנְעוּל n.m. lock; padlock (root: נעל)

מְנַצֵּחַ n.m.
a. musical conductor (?)
b. musical symbol (?) (root: נצח)

מְנַשֶּׁה pr.n.m. Manasseh
("causes to forget") (root: נשה)

מְנָת, מְנַת- ; **מְנָאוֹת (מְנָיוֹת)** n.f.
share; portion (root: מנה)

מַס, מַס- ; **מִסִּים** n.m. tax; levy

מַסְגֵּר n.m.
a. prison
b. blacksmith (root: סגר)

מִסְגֶּרֶת ; **מִסְגְּרוֹת** n.f.
a. frame
b. stronghold (root: סגר)

מסך v.
1) מָסַךְ pour; mix (a drink)

מָסָךְ, מָסַךְ- ; n.m. curtain; screen (root: סכך)

מַסֵּכָה, מַסֶּכֶת- ; **מַסֵּכוֹת** n.f.
a. metal-cast idol
b. scheme
c. cover (root: נסך)

מִסְכְּנוֹת n.f.pl. store-cities

מְסִלָּה, מְסִלַּת- ; **מְסִלּוֹת** n.f.
a. highway
b. path (root: סלל)

מַסְמֵר ; **מַסְמְרִים, מַשְׂמְרוֹת** n.m.
nail; peg

מסס v.
2) נָמֵס melt
6) הֵמֵס a. melt
b. weaken

מַסָּע ; **מַסְעֵי-** ; n.m. journey (root: נסע)

מִסְפֵּד, מִסְפַּד- ; n.m. mourning (root: ספד)

מִסְפּוֹא n.m. feed (for animals)

מִסְפָּר, מִסְפַּר- ; **מִסְפְּרֵי-** ; n.m.
a. number
b. count
c. a few
d. story (root: ספר)

מִסְתָּר ; **מִסְתָּרִים** n.m. hiding place (root: סתר)

מַעְבָּרָה ; **מַעְבָּרוֹת, מַעַבְּרוֹת-** ; n.f.
a. crossing
b. bridge (root: עבר)

מַעְגָּל, מַעְגַּל- ; **מַעְגְּלֵי-** ; n.m. a. circle
b. path (root: עגל)

מעד v.
1) מָעַד stumble
6) הִמְעִיד cause to stumble

מָעוֹז, מָעוֹז- ; n.m. a. stronghold
b. refuge; shelter (root: עוז/עזז)

מָעוֹן, מְעוֹן- ; n.m.
מְעוֹנָה ; **מְעוֹנוֹת, מְעוֹנוֹת-** ; n.f. abode

מְעוֹנֵן n.m. soothsayer (root: ענן)

מעט v.
1) מָעַט decrease
3) מִעֵט decrease
6) הִמְעִיט reduce

מְעַט adj., adv. a. little
b. few
c. small
d. a little
e. almost
f. nearly
g. is it not enough that...? הַמְעַט

מֵעַיִם, מְעֵי- ; n.m.pl. intestines; bowels

מְעִיל, מְעִיל- ; n.m. coat; mantle

מַעְיָן, מַעְיַן- ; **מַעְיָנִים, מַעְיְנֵי-** ;
מַעְיָנוֹת, מַעְיְנוֹת- ; n.m. a. fountain
b. spring

מעל v.
1) מָעַל betray confidence

מַעַל, מַעַל- ; n.m. betrayal (root: מעל)

מַעַל adv. a. above מִמַּעַל
b. on top מִמַּעַל לְ-
c. ... and over מִן ... וָמַעְלָה
d. from the top מִלְמַעְלָה (root: עלה)

מַעֲלֶה, מַעֲלֵה- ; n.m. a. ascent
b. uphill

c. raised platform (root: עלה)

מַעֲלָה ; מַעֲלוֹת, מַעֲלוֹת- ; n.f. a. rise
b. step (root: עלה)

מַעֲלָלִים, מַעַלְלֵי- ; n.m.pl. actions;
deeds (root: עלל)

מַעֲמָד n.m. a. station
b. position (root: עמד)

מַעֲמַקִּים, מַעֲמַקֵּי- ; n.m.pl. depths
(root: עמק)

מַעֲנֶה, מַעֲנֵה- ; n.m. reply (root: ענה)

מַעֲרָב n.m. a. west
b. merchandise (root: ערב)

מְעָרָה, מְעָרַת- ; **מְעָרוֹת, מְעָרוֹת-** ; n.f.
cave

מַעֲרָכָה ; מַעַרְכוֹת- ; n.f.
a. battleground
b. arrangement; order (root: ערך)

מַעֲרֶכֶת, מַעֲרֶכֶת- ; **מַעֲרָכוֹת** n.f.
row (of bread offering at the Temple)

מַעֲשֶׂה, מַעֲשֵׂה- ; **מַעֲשִׂים, מַעֲשֵׂי-** ;
a. action n.m.
b. work
c. deed
d. creation (root: עשׂה)

מַעֲשֵׂיָהוּ pr.n.m. Maaseiah
("creation of God") (roots: מַעֲשֶׂה, יָהּ)

מַעֲשֵׂר, מַעֲשַׂר- ; **מַעַשְׂרוֹת** n.m.
a. one tenth
b. tithe (root: עשׂר)
מַפָּלָה, מַפֶּלֶת- ; n.f. destruction; fall
(root: נפל)

מִפְּנֵי prep. a. from
("from the face of...")
b. because
c. on account of (root: פָּנִים)

מִפְקָד, מִפְקַד- ; n.m. census
(root: פקד)

מִפְתָּן, מִפְתַּן- ; n.m. threshold;
doorstep

מצא v.
1) מָצָא a. find
b. discover c. meet
d. be enough; make do
2) נִמְצָא a. be found
b. exist
c. be enough
d. respond
6) הִמְצִיא a. bring
b. provide

מַצָּב, מַצַּב- ; n.m. a. stand; position
b. outpost; garrison (root: נצב)

מַצֵּבָה, מַצֶּבֶת- (מַצְּבַת-) ; **מַצֵּבוֹת,**
מַצְּבוֹת- ; n.f. cult or memorial post
(root: נצב)

מְצָד ; **מְצָדוֹת, מְצָדוֹת-** ; n.m. fort

מצה v.
1) מָצָה a. drain
b. squeeze
2) נִמְצָה be drained

מַצָּה ; **מַצּוֹת** n.f. a. unleavened bread
("matzo")
b. quarrel

מְצוּדָה, מְצוּדַת- ; **מְצוּדוֹת** n.f.
a. fortress
b. shelter
c. net; trap (root: צוד)

מִצְוָה, מִצְוַת ; **מִצְוֹת, מִצְוֹת-** ; n.f.
commandment; precept (root: צוה)

מְצוּלָה ; **מְצוּלוֹת, מְצוּלוֹת-** ; n.f.
depth (of the sea) (root: צלל)

מְצוּקָה ; **מְצוּקוֹת** n.f. trouble;
distress (root: צוק)

מָצוֹר, מְצוֹר- ; n.m. a. distress
b. siege (root: צור)
c. Egypt (pr.n.m.)

מְצוּרָה ; **מְצוּרוֹת** n.f. fortress
(root: צור)

מֵצַח, מֵצַח- ; **מִצְחוֹת** n.m. forehead

מְצִלְתַּיִם n.m.f.pl. cymbals (root: צלל)

מִצְנֶפֶת, מִצְנֶפֶת- ; n.f. headdress
(a priest's)

מִצְרִי ; **מִצְרִית** ; **מִצְרִים** ; **מִצְרִיּוֹת** adj.
Egyptian (root: מִצְרַיִם)

מִצְרַיִם pr.n.m. a. Egypt
b. Egyptian nation

מְצֹרָע adj.m. leprous (root: צרע)

מַקֶּבֶת ; **מַקָּבוֹת** n.f. hammer
(root: נקב)

מִקְדָּשׁ, מִקְדַּשׁ- ; **מִקְדָּשִׁים,**
מִקְדְּשֵׁי- ; n.m. a. temple
b. the Temple in Jerusalem (root: קדש)

מִקְוֶה, מִקְוֵה- ; n.m. a. hope
b. body of water (root: קוה)

מָקוֹם, מְקוֹם- ; **מְקוֹמוֹת, מְקוֹמוֹת-** ;
place; location (root: קום) n.m.

מָקוֹר, מְקוֹר- ; n.m. a. source
b. flow

מַקֵּל, מַקֵּל- ; **מַקְלוֹת** n.m. rod; stick

מִקְלָט, מִקְלַט- ; n.m. a. refuge
b. shelter (root: קלט)

מִקְנֶה, מִקְנֵה- ; n.m. a. livestock
b. purchase (root: קנה)

מִקְנָה, מִקְנַת- ; n.f.
a. purchase; acquisition
b. price (root: קנה)

מִקְצוֹעַ, מִקְצוֹעַ- ; **מִקְצוֹעוֹת,**
מִקְצוֹעֵי- ; n.m. corner

מִקְצָת, מִקְצַת- ; n.f. part; some

מקק v.
2) נָמַק fester; rot
6) הֻמַק fester; rot

מִקְרָא, מִקְרָא- ; **מִקְרָאֵי-** ; n.m.
convocation (root: קרא)

מִקְרֶה, מִקְרֵה- ; n.m. happening
(root: קרה)

מִקְשָׁה n.f. a. hammered metal work
b. field of gourds, watermelons, cucumbers, etc.

מַר ; **מָרָה** ; **מָרִים** adj. a. bitter
b. embittered

מַרְאֶה, מַרְאֵה- ; n.m. a. vision; sight
b. shape (root: ראה)

מַרְאָה ; **מַרְאוֹת-** ; n.f. a. vision
b. mirror (root: ראה)

מְרַאֲשׁוֹת n.f.pl. head of the bed
(root: רֹאשׁ)

מַרְבִּית, מַרְבִּית- ; n.f. a. greater part;
most of
b. usury (root: רבה)

מַרְגְּלוֹת n.f.pl. feet

1) קַל (פָּעַל) 2) נִפְעַל 3) פִּעֵל 4) פֻּעַל 5) הִתְפַּעֵל 6) הִפְעִיל 7) הָפְעַל

מרד v.
1) מָרַד — rebel

מרה v.
1) מָרָה — disobey
6) הִמְרָה — a. disobey
b. defy

מָרוֹם n.m., adv. — a. high place
b. upwards (root: רום)

מֶרְחָב ; **מֶרְחֲבֵי-** ; n.m. — wide place
(root: רחב)

מֶרְחָק ; **מֶרְחַקִּים** n.m. — a. distance
b. distant place (root: רחק)

מרט v.
1) מָרַט — a. pluck
b. polish
2) נִמְרַט — be plucked
4) מֹרַט — a. be plucked
b. be polished

מְרִי n.m. — a. disobedience; rebellion
b. bitterness
(root: מרה)

מְרִיא ; **מְרִיאִים, מְרִיאֵי-** ; n.m.
fatling

מְרִיבָה n.f., pr.n.f. — a. quarrel
b. Meribah ("quarrel") (root: ריב)

מֶרְכָּבָה, מִרְכֶּבֶת- ; **מַרְכָּבוֹת, מַרְכְּבוֹת-** ; n.f.
a. chariot
b. coach (root: רכב)

מִרְמָה ; **מִרְמוֹת** n.f. — falsehood
(root: רמה)

מִרְמָס, מִרְמַס- ; n.m.
trampled place or thing (root: רמס)

מֵרֵעַ ; **מֵרֵעִים** n.m. — friend

מִרְעֶה, מִרְעֵה- ; n.m. — pasture
(root: רעה)

מַרְעִית n.f. — a. pasture
b. flock (root: רעה)

מַרְפֵּא n.m. — cure; healing (root: רפא)

מרר v.
1) מָרַר, מַר — a. be bitter
b. be disconsolate
3) מֵרַר — embitter
6) הֵמַר — a. mourn
b. cause pain

מַשָּׂא, מַשָּׂא- ; **מַשְּׂאוֹת-** ; n.m.
a. burden
b. trouble
c. vision
d. prophecy (root: נשא)

מַשְׂאֵת, מַשְׂאַת- ; **מַשְׂאוֹת, מַשְּׂאוֹת-** ;
n.f.
a. signal
b. column
c. gift (root: נשא)

מִשְׁבֶּצֶת ; **מִשְׁבְּצוֹת** n.f. — setting
(for jewelry)

מִשְׁבָּר ; **מִשְׁבְּרֵי-** ; n.m.
breaker; large wave (root: שבר)

מִשְׂגָּב, מִשְׂגַּב- ; n.m. — a. haven
b. secure height (root: שגב)

מְשֻׁגָּע שגע v. — mad; madman

משה v.
1) מָשָׁה — draw out; pull

מֹשֶׁה pr.n.m. — Moses
"draws out of the water"? (root: משה)

מְשׁוּבָה, מְשׁוּבַת- ; **מְשׁוּבוֹת** ; n.f.
a. tranquility
b. deviation
c. apostasy (root: שוב)

מָשׁוּחַ adj.m. — anointed (root: משח)

singer (m.s.) **מְשׁוֹרֵר** v. שיר

joy (root: שׂישׂ) n.m. ; **מָשׂוֹשׂ, מְשׂוֹשׂ-**
interwoven **מָשְׁזָר** v. שזר

משח v.
a. anoint 1) מָשַׁח
b. smear

a. ointment n.f. ; **מִשְׁחָה, מִשְׁחַת-**
b. portion (root: משח)

a. destroyer n.m. **מַשְׁחִית**
b. raider
c. destruction (root: שחת)
anointed one n.m. ; **מָשִׁיחַ, מְשִׁיחַ-**
(king or priest) (root: משח)

ruined; spoiled adj.m. **מָשְׁחָת**
(root: שחת)

משך v.
a. drag; pull 1) מָשַׁךְ
b. gather
last; be long 2) נִמְשַׁךְ

a. bed n.m. ; **מִשְׁכָּב, מִשְׁכַּב-** ; **מִשְׁכְּבֵי-**
b. laying (root: שכב)

מַשְׂכִּיל ; **מַשְׂכִּילִים** adj.m.
a. style of a Psalm (?)
b. successful
c. wise

מִשְׁכָּן, מִשְׁכַּן- ; **מִשְׁכָּנוֹת, מִשְׁכְּנוֹת-** ;
a. abode; home n.m.
b. the Tent of the Covenant
c. the Temple in Jerusalem (root: שכן)

משל v.
a. rule; reign 1) מָשַׁל
b. speak in parables
resemble 2) נִמְשַׁל
speak in parables 3) מִשֵּׁל
resemble 5) הִתְמַשֵּׁל
a. cause to reign 6) הִמְשִׁיל
b. compare

מָשָׁל, מְשַׁל- ; **מְשָׁלִים, מִשְׁלֵי-** ; n.m.
a. proverb
b. fable; parable
c. byword
d. the Book of Proverbs ("the proverbs of...") מִשְׁלֵי

undertaking n.m. ; **מִשְׁלָח, מִשְׁלַח-**
(with יָד) (root: שלח)

a. three years old adj.m. **מְשֻׁלָּשׁ**
b. woven of three threads
c. of three floors (root: שָׁלֹשׁ)

desert; desolation n.f. **מְשַׁמָּה** ; **מְשַׁמּוֹת**

fat n.m. ; **מִשְׁמָן, מִשְׁמַן-** ; **מִשְׁמַנֵּי-** ;
(root: שמן)

a. guardhouse n.m. ; **מִשְׁמָר, מִשְׁמַר-**
b. guard
c. watch (root: שמר)

מִשְׁמֶרֶת, מִשְׁמֶרֶת- ; **מִשְׁמָרוֹת, מִשְׁמְרוֹת-** ;
a. guard n.f.
b. duty; charge
c. guard post

מִשְׁנֶה, מִשְׁנֵה- ; **מִשְׁנִים** n.m.
a. deputy; second in rank
b. double
c. copy (root: שנה)

loot n.f. **מְשִׁסָּה** ; **מְשִׁסּוֹת**

a. support n.f. ; **מִשְׁעֶנֶת, מִשְׁעֶנֶת-** ;
b. rod; staff (root: שען)

מִשְׁפָּחָה, מִשְׁפַּחַת- ; **מִשְׁפָּחוֹת, מִשְׁפְּחוֹת-** ;
a. family; household n.f.
b. clan

מִשְׁפָּט, מִשְׁפַּט- ; **מִשְׁפָּטִים, מִשְׁפְּטֵי-** ;
a. judgment n.m.

b. justice
c. verdict
d. legal suit
e. law; commandment
f. custom
g. norms; rules;
charges (pl.) (root: שפט)

מַשְׁקֶה, מַשְׁקֵה- ; **מַשְׁקִים** n.m.
a. cupbearer; butler
b. drink
c. watered area (root: שקה)

מִשְׁקָל, מִשְׁקַל- ; n.m. a. weight
b. weighing (root: שקל)

מְשָׁרֵת ; **מְשָׁרְתִים, מְשָׁרְתֵי-** ; n.m.
a. servant; attendant
b. minister in the Temple (root: שרת)

משש v.
1) מָשַׁש feel; touch
3) מִשֵּׁשׁ feel; grope

מִשְׁתֶּה, מִשְׁתֵּה- ; n.m. a. feast
b. drink (root: שתה)

מֵת ; **מֵתִים, מֵתֵי-** ; n.m. dead
(root: מות)

מָתוֹק ; **מְתוּקָה** ; **מְתוּקִים** adj. sweet
(root: מתק)

מָתַי adv. when?

מְתִים, מְתֵי- ; n.m.pl. men; people

מַתְכֹּנֶת, מַתְכֹּנֶת- ; n.f. a. quota
b. count
c. measurement (root: תכן)

מַתָּן n.m. gift (root: נתן)

מַתָּנָה, מַתְּנַת- ; **מַתָּנוֹת, מַתְּנוֹת-** ; n.f.
a. gift
b. donation (root: נתן)

מַתַּנְיָה pr.n.m. Mattaniah
("God's gift") (roots: מַתָּן, יָהּ)

מָתְנַיִם n.m.pl. a. hips
b. loins

מתק v.
1) מָתַק be sweet
6) הִמְתִּיק sweeten

מַתָּת, מַתַּת- ; n.f. gift (root: נתן)

נ

נָא interj.
a. please (after a verb)
b. (for emphasis) See also אָנָּא

נֹאד, נֹאד־ ; נֹאדוֹת, נֹאדוֹת־ ; n.m.
skin (bottle)

נָאָה ; נְאוֹת־ ; n.f. — pasture

נָאוֶה ; נָאוָה (נָוָה) adj.
a. fair; comely
b. suitable

נָאוֹר adj.m.
a. shining
b. enlightened

נֶאֱכַל אכל v. — be eaten

נֶאֱלַם אלם v. — be silenced

נְאֻם, נְאֻם־ ; n.m. — speech; saying

נֶאֱמָן adj.n.m. — steady (root: אמן)

נֶאֱמַר אמר v. — be said; be spoken

נֶאֱנַח אנח v. — moan; groan

נֶאֱסַף אסף v.
a. be gathered
b. be destroyed

נֶאֱסַר אסר v. — be tied

נאף v.
1) נָאַף — commit adultery
3) נִאֵף — commit adultery

נאץ v.
1) נָאַץ — a. spurn
b. detest
3) נִאֵץ — a. spurn
b. detest

נבא v.
2) נִבָּא — prophesy
5) הִתְנַבֵּא — prophesy

נִבְדַּל בדל v. — be separated

נִבְהַל בהל v. — panic; be scared

נָבוֹן adj.m. — wise (root: בין)

נִבְזֶה adj.m. — despised (root: בזה)

נִבְחַן בחן v. — be tested

נִבְחָר adj.m.
a. chosen
b. elected (root: בחר)

נבט v.
2) נִבַּט — look; gaze
6) הִבִּיט — look; gaze

נָבִיא ; נְבִיאָה ; נְבִיאִים, נְבִיאֵי־ ; n.
a. prophet (root: נבא)
b. נְבִיאִים "Prophets" (the second division in the Bible).
See "Grammar", section 17

נבל v.
1) נָבֵל — wither; dry up
3) נִבֵּל — a. spurn
b. dishonor

נָבָל ; נְבָלִים ; נְבָלוֹת adj., n. — villain; scoundrel

נֵבֶל, נֵבֶל־ ; נְבָלִים, נִבְלֵי־ ; n.m.
a. leather bottle
b. clay jar
c. lyre
d. psaltery

נְבָלָה n.f. — shameful act (root: נבל)

1) קַל (פָּעַל) 2) נִפְעַל 3) פִּעֵל 4) פֻּעַל 5) הִתְפַּעֵל 6) הִפְעִיל 7) הָפְעַל

נְבֵלָה, נִבְלַת- ; n.f. a. carcass
b. corpse

נִבְנָה בנה .v a. be built
b. be established

נבע .v
1) נָבַע burst forth; flow
6) הִבִּיעַ say; utter

נִבְעָר .adj.m foolish (root: בער)

נָבַק בקק .v be destroyed

נִבְקַע בקע .v burst open

נָבַר ברר .v be purified

נִבְרָא ברא .v be created

נִגְאַל גאל .v be saved

נֶגֶב, נֶגֶב- ; n.m. a. south
b. dryness
c. southern part of Israel הַנֶּגֶב
d. southward נֶגְבָּה

נגד .v
6) הִגִּיד tell
7) הֻגַּד be told

נֶגֶד .prep a. against
b. in front of
c. at a distance מִנֶּגֶד

נִגְדַּע גדע .v be smashed; be cut off

נֹגַהּ, נֹגַהּ- ; n.m. light; glow

נָגוּעַ .adj.m infected (root: נגע)

נִגְזַר גזר .v a. be cut
b. be decreed

נגח .v
1) נָגַח gore
3) נִגַּח a. smash
b. gore

נָגִיד, נְגִיד- ; נְגִידִים, נְגִידֵי- ; n.m.
ruler; leader

נְגִינָה, נְגִינַת- ; נְגִינוֹת- ; n.f. song;
singing (root: נגן)

נִגְלָה גלה .v a. be shown
b. be exiled

נִגְמַל גמל .v be weaned

נגן .v
3) נִגֵּן play music

נגע .v
1) נָגַע a. touch
b. harm
2) נִגַּע be harmed
4) נֻגַּע be afflicted
6) הִגִּיעַ a. make contact

נֶגַע, נֶגַע- ; נְגָעִים, נִגְעֵי- ; n.m.
a. affliction
b. disease
c. pain
d. assault (root: נגע)

נִגְעַל געל .v be defiled

נגף .v
1) נָגַף afflict; smite
2) נִגַּף be smited; be defeated
5) הִתְנַגֵּף stumble

נֶגֶף .n.m plague; affliction

נגר .v
2) נִגַּר flow; spill
6) הִגִּיר pour

נִגְרַע גרע .v be reduced

נִגְרַשׁ גרש .v be expelled

נגש .v

1) נָגַשׂ — oppress
2) נִגַּשׂ — be oppressed

נגשׁ v.
1) גֶּשֶׁת — approach; come near (infinitive)
(future, imperative) יִגַּשׁ
2) נִגַּשׁ — approach; come near
6) הִגִּישׁ — a. bring near
b. offer

נָד adj.m. — moving (root: נוד)

נדב v.
1) נָדַב — offer freely
5) הִתְנַדֵּב — a. offer freely
b. dedicate oneself

נְדָבָה, נִדְבַת-; נְדָבוֹת, נִדְבוֹת-; n.f.
a. offering
b. freewill offering
c. generosity (root: נדב)

נִדְבַּר דבר v. — talk with...

נדד v.
1) נָדַד — a. wander
b. pass
c. move
6) הֵנִיד — drive; cause to move

נִדָּה, נִדַּת-; n.f. — a. menstruation
b. uncleanliness

נָדוֹשׁ דוש v. — be crushed

נדח v.
1) נָדַח — wield
2) נִדַּח — a. be exiled
b. be lured
c. be lost
6) הִדִּיחַ — a. exile
b. push away

נָדִיב, נְדִיב-; נְדִיבִים, נְדִיבֵי-; n., adj.m.
a. noble
b. generous (root: נדב)

נִדְכָּה דכה v. — be oppressed

נָדַם דמם v. — be destroyed

נִדְמָה דמה v. — be lost; perish

נדף v.
1) נָדַף — disperse; drive
2) נִדַּף — be dispersed

נִדְקַר דקר v. — be stabbed

נדר v.
1) נָדַר — vow

נֶדֶר, נֶדֶר-; נְדָרִים n.m. — vow

נִדְרַשׁ דרש v. — a. respond to inquiry
b. be sought out

נהג v.
1) נָהַג — a. lead
b. herd
3) נִהֵג — a. lead
b. herd

נֵהוֹם הום v. — buzz with excitement

נְהִי n.m. — wailing

נהל v.
3) נִהֵל — lead
5) הִתְנַהֵל — travel

נהם v.
1) נָהַם — roar

נֶהְפַּךְ הפך v. — be diverted; be turned away

נהר v.
1) נָהַר — a. flow
b. gaze
c. glow

נָהָר, נְהַר-; נְהָרִים, נַהֲרֵי-; נְהָרוֹת, נַהֲרוֹת-; n.m. — river

נֶהֱרַג הרג v. — be killed

1) קַל (פָּעַל) 2) נִפְעַל 3) פִּעֵל 4) פֻּעַל 5) הִתְפַּעֵל 6) הִפְעִיל 7) הֻפְעַל

נֶהֱרַס הרס .v — be destroyed

נוא .v
6) הֵנִיא — prevent

נוֹאֵף.n.m — adulterer (root: נאף)

נוֹאַשׁ יאש .v — despair

נוּגֶה יגה .v — sad

נוד .v
1) נָד — a. wander; roam
b. pity
c. move
5) הִתְנוֹדֵד — sway
6) הֵנִיד — a. shake
b. move

נוֹדַע ידע .v — be known

נָוֶה, נְוֵה- ; .n.m — a. homestead; habitation
b. pasture

נוח .v
1) נָח — rest
6) הֵנִיחַ — a. give rest; relieve
b. place
c. leave
d. tolerate
e. let
7) הוּנַח (הֻנַּח) — a. be placed
b. be calmed

נוֹכַח יכח .v — be judged

נוֹלַד ילד .v — be born

נום .v
1) נָם — slumber

נוס .v
1) נָס — escape; flee
6) הֵנִיס — chase; cause to flee

נוֹסַד יסד .v — a. be founded
b. congregate

נוֹסַף יסף .v — a. join
b. be added

נוֹסַר יסר .v — be punished

נוע .v
1) נָע — a. move
b. shake
c. wander
6) הֵנִיעַ — a. move
b. shake

נוֹעַד יעד .v — meet

נוֹעַץ יעץ .v — consult

נוף .v
6) הֵנִיף — wave; wield

נוֹצַר יצר .v — be created

נוֹקַשׁ יקש .v — be trapped

נוֹרָא ; **נוֹרָאָה** ; **נוֹרָאוֹת** .adj
a. awesome
b. fearful (root: ירא)

נוֹרָה ירה .v — be shot

נוֹרַשׁ ירש .v — be impoverished

נוֹשַׁב ישב .v — be inhabited

נוֹתַר יתר .v — remain

נזה .v
1) נָזָה — be spattered
6) הִזָּה — sprinkle

נִזְהַר זהר .v — be careful

נָזִיד, נְזִיד- ; .n.m — stew; pottage

נָזִיר, נְזִיר- ; **נְזִירִים** .n.m — Nazarite; a consecrated man (root: נזר)

נזל v.
1) נָזַל a. drip
b. flow
6) הִזִּיל cause to flow

נֶזֶם, נֶזֶם-; נְזָמִים, נִזְמֵי- n.m.
nose-ring

נִזְעַק זעק v. be assembled;
be gathered

נזר v.
2) נִזַּר abstain
6) הִזִּיר set apart

נֵזֶר, נֵזֶר- n.m. a. crown
b. Nazarite's long hair
c. state of a Nazarite

נֶחְבָּא חבא v. hide

נֶחְבַּט חבט v. be beaten
(olives, wheat)

נחה v.
1) נָחָה lead
6) הִנְחָה guide

נַחוּם pr.n.m. Nahum
("the comforted one") (root: נחם)

נְחוּשָׁה n.f. copper

נחל v.
1) נָחַל a. inherit
b. accept
3) נִחֵל allot
5) הִתְנַחֵל a. possess
b. inherit
6) הִנְחִיל give as possession

נַחַל, נַחַל-; נְחָלִים, נַחֲלֵי- n.m.
a. wadi; valley
b. torrent; flow

נֶחֱלָה חלה v. be ill

נַחֲלָה, נַחֲלַת-; נְחָלוֹת n.f.
a. inheritance
b. property (root: נחל)

נֶחֱלַץ חלץ v. be rescued

נֶחֱלַק חלק v. be divided

נחם v.
2) נִחַם a. regret
b. be comforted
3) נִחַם comfort
5) הִתְנַחֵם receive comfort

נֵחַם חמם v. become warm

נֶחְמָד adj.m. a. pleasant
b. delightful
c. desirable (root: חמד)

נְחֶמְיָה pr.n.m. Nehemiah
("God comforts") (roots: נחם, יָהּ)

נַחְנוּ pron. we (see אֲנַחְנוּ)

נֶחְפַּז חפז v. hurry; rush

נֶחֱצָה חצה v. be split

נִחַר חרר v. be scorched

נֶחֱרַב חרב v. be destroyed

נֶחֱרַץ חרץ v. be decreed

נֶחֱרַשׁ חרש v. be plowed

נחש v.
3) נִחֵשׁ divine

נָחָשׁ, נְחַשׁ-; נְחָשִׁים n.m. snake

נֶחֱשַׁב חשב v. a. be considered
b. be accounted

נֶחְשַׂךְ חשך v. be prevented; be saved

נְחֹשֶׁת n.f. copper

נְחֻשְׁתַּיִם n.m.pl.
copper or brass fetters (root: נְחֹשֶׁת)

נִחַת חתת v. fear

נחת v.
1) נָחַת land; come down
3) נִחֵת a. bend
b. press down
6) הִנְחִית bring down

נַחַת n.f. a. gratification
b. rest (root: נוח)

נֶחְתַּם חתם v. be sealed

נִטְבַּל טבל v. be dipped; be immersed

נטה v.
1) נָטָה a. swerve
b. side with
c. stretch
d. send
e. pitch (a tent)
2) נִטָּה a. be pitched
b. be stretched
6) הִטָּה a. incline
b. turn back
c. twist
d. subvert
e. stretch

נָטוּי ; נְטוּיָה ; נְטוּיוֹת adj. stretched
(root: נטה)

נָטוּעַ adj.m. planted (root: נטע)

נְטוּשָׁה adj.f. a. whetted
b. neglected (root: נטש)

נִטְמָא טמא v. become defiled

נִטְמַן טמן v. be hidden

נטע v.
1) נָטַע a. plant
b. establish

נטף v.
1) נָטַף a. drip
b. preach
6) הִטִּיף a. drip
b. preach

נטר v.
1) נָטַר a. guard
b. bear a grudge

נִטְרַף טרף v. be torn to pieces;
be devoured

נטש v.
1) נָטַשׁ a. neglect; desert
b. spread
2) נִטַּשׁ spread

נִיחוֹחַ n.m. pleasure
רֵיחַ נִיחוֹחַ a pleasant smell

נִיר, נִיר- n.m. ; a. plowed field
b. lamp

נִכְבַּד כבד v. be important

נִכְבַּשׁ כבש v. be conquered

נכה v.
6) הִכָּה a. smite
b. kill
c. conquer
7) הֻכָּה a. be smitten
b. be killed
c. be conquered

נָכוֹן כון v. a. be established
b. be true
c. be ready

נִכְזַב כזב v.	be proved false
נֹכַח prep.	against; facing
נִכְחַד כחד v.	a. be hidden; escape notice b. be destroyed
נִכְחַשׁ כחש v.	cringe
נִכְלָא כלא v.	be stopped
נִכְלַם כלם v.	be ashamed
נִכְנַע כנע v.	humble oneself
נֶכֶס ; **נְכָסִים** n.m.	property; wealth
נִכְסָה כסה v.	be covered
נִכְסַף כסף v.	a. yearn b. be shamed
נכר v.	
2) נִכַּר	be known
6) הִכִּיר	a. recognize; note b. know
נֵכָר, נֵכַר- ; n.m.	a. alien b. foreign entity
נִכְרָה כרה v.	be dug
נָכְרִי ; **נָכְרִיָּה** ; **נָכְרִים** ; **נָכְרִיּוֹת** n., adj.	foreign(er); stranger
נִכְרַת כרת v.	a. be destroyed b. be cut off
נִכְשַׁל כשל v.	stumble; fall
נִכְתַּב כתב v.	be written; be inscribed
נִלְאָה לאה v.	a. be tired b. be unable
נִלְוָה לוה v.	join
נָלוֹן לון v.	complain
נִלְחַם לחם v.	fight
נִלְחַץ לחץ v.	be pressed
נִלְכַּד לכד v.	be captured
נִמְאַס מאס v.	be rejected
נִמְהַר מהר v.	be hasty
נִמּוֹל מול v.	be circumcised
נִמְחָה מחה v.	be destroyed; be eradicated
נִמְכַּר מכר v.	be sold
נִמְלָא מלא v.	be filled
נִמְלַט מלט v.	a. escape b. run
נָמֵס מסס v.	melt
נִמְצָא מצא v.	a. be found; exist b. be enough c. respond
נָמַק מקק v.	fester; rot
נָמַר מור v.	be changed
נָמֵר ; **נְמֵרִים** n.m.	leopard
נִמְשַׁל משל v.	resemble
נֵס n.m.	a. pole b. standard c. example
נָסַב סבב v.	a. turn b. surround

נסה v.
3) נִסָּה — try; test

נָסוֹג סוג v. — turn away from

נָסִיךְ ; **נְסִיכֵי-** ; n.m. — prince (root: נסך)

נסך v.
1) נָסַךְ — a. pour
b. anoint
c. cast
6) הִסִּיךְ — a. pour
b. anoint
c. cast

נֶסֶךְ, נֵסֶךְ- ; **נְסָכִים, נִסְכֵּי-** ; n.m.
libation (root: נסך)

נִסְכַּן סכן v. — be hurt

נִסְלַח סלח v. — be forgiven

נִסְמַךְ סמך v. — lean

נסע v.
1) נָסַע — a. travel
b. move
6) הִסִּיעַ — a. cause to move
b. move

נִסְעַר סער v. — be agitated

נִסְפַּד ספד v. — be mourned

נִסְפַּר ספר v. — be counted

נִסְקַל סקל v. — be stoned

נִסְתַּם סתם v. — be stopped up

נָע — v. see נוע

נֶעֱבַד עבד v. — be worked

נֶעְדַּר עדר v. — a. be tilled
b. be absent

נַעֲוָה עוה v. — twist

נְעוּרִים n.m.pl. — youth (root: נער)

נֶעֱזַב עזב v. — be forsaken

נֶעֱזַר עזר v. — a. be helped
b. be supported

נֶעֱטַף עטף v. — be weak

נָעִים, נְעִים- ; **נְעִימִים** adj.m. — pleasant
(root: נעם)

נעל v.
1) נָעַל — a. lock
b. shoe
6) הִנְעִיל — shoe

נַעַל ; **נַעֲלַיִם, נְעָלִים** n.f. — shoe
(root: נעל)

נַעֲלָה עלה v. — a. rise
b. be raised
c. move away

נֶעְלַם עלם v. — be hidden

נעם v.
1) נָעַם — be pleasing

נֹעַם, נֹעַם- ; n.m. — a. favor
b. beauty (root: נעם)

נַעֲנָה ענה v. — a. be answered
b. reply favorably
c. be oppressed

נֶעֱנַשׁ ענש v. — be punished

נֶעֱצַב עצב v. — a. be grieved
b. be pained

נֶעֱצַר עצר v. — be stopped

נער v.
1) נָעַר — a. roar
b. shake out
3) נִעֵר — shake

נַעַר, נַעַר-; נְעָרִים, נַעֲרֵי- ; n.m.
a. boy; lad
b. young man
c. servant; aide

נַעֲרָה (נַעֲרָ); נְעָרוֹת, נַעֲרוֹת- ; n.f.
a. young girl; maiden
b. maidservant

נַעֲרָה ערה .v be poured

נֶעֱרַץ ערץ .v be dreaded

נַעֲשָׂה עשה .v be done; be made

נֶעְתַּר עתר .v respond to a plea

נִפְגַּשׁ פגש .v meet

נִפְדָּה פדה .v be redeemed

נָפוֹץ פוץ .v be scattered

נִפְזַר פזר .v be scattered

נפח .v
1) נָפַח blow
6) הִפִּיחַ blow

נפל .v
1) נָפַל a. fall
b. drop
c. surrender; be defeated
d. fail; stumble
e. bend
f. bow down
5) הִתְנַפֵּל a. attack
b. prostrate oneself
6) הִפִּיל a. cause to fall; drop
b. lower
c. defeat; conquer
d. omit

נִפְלָא פלא .v a. be extraordinary
b. be wonderful

נִפְלָאוֹת, נִפְלְאוֹת- ; n.f.pl. wonders; miracles (root: פלא)

נִפְלָה פלה .v be separate; be distinguished

נִפְעַם פעם .v a. be moved
b. be troubled

נפץ .v
1) נָפַץ a. break; crush
b. scatter
3) נִפֵּץ smash

נִפְקַד פקד .v be absent

נִפְקַח פקח .v be opened (eyes)

נִפְרַד פרד .v be divided; be separate

נִפְרַע פרע .v be disorderly

נִפְרַשׂ פרשׂ .v be scattered; be spread out

נֶפֶשׁ, נֶפֶשׁ-; נְפָשׁוֹת, נַפְשׁוֹת- ; n.f.
a. soul
b. person
c. self
d. mind

נֹפֶת, נֹפֶת- ; n.f. honey

נַפְתָּלִי pr.n.m. Naphtali ("wrestled with God") (roots: פתל, יָהּ)

נִצַּב יצב .v stand erect

נְצַב ; נְצָבִים n.m. prefect; officer

נִצְדַּק צדק .v be justified

נצה .v
2) נִצָּה a. quarrel
b. be desolate
6) הִצָּה agitate

1) קַל (פָּעַל) 2) נִפְעַל 3) פִּעֵל 4) פֻּעַל 5) הִתְפַּעֵל 6) הִפְעִיל 7) הָפְעַל

נצח v.
3) נִצַּח a. conduct; be in charge
b. musical leader (?) מְנַצֵּחַ
c. musical sign (?)
d. supervisor

נֶצַח n.m., adv. a. triumph
b. glory
c. blood
d. forever

נְצִיב, נְצִיב-; נְצִיבִים, נְצִיבֵי-; n.m.
a. prefect; officer
b. pillar (root: יצב)

נצל v.
2) נִצַּל a. be saved
b. escape
3) נִצֵּל a. save
b. exploit; strip
6) הִצִּיל save; rescue

נִצְעַק צעק v. gather; be assembled

נִצְפַּן צפן v. be hidden

נצר v.
1) נָצַר guard

נִצַּת v. be kindled

נקב v.
1) נָקַב a. drill
b. fix
c. bestow
d. curse
2) נִקַּב be cited

נְקֵבָה n.f. female

נִקְבַּץ קבץ v. be gathered

נִקְבַּר קבר v. be buried

נָקֹד; נְקֻדִּים; נְקֻדּוֹת adj. spotted
(root: נקד)

נקה v.
2) נִקָּה a. be free of
b. be held innocent
3) נִקָּה clear; make blameless

נִקְוָה קוה v. be collected (water)

נָקוֹט קוט v. be disgusted

נָקִי, נְקִי-; נְקִיִּים adj.m. a. clean
b. innocent
c. free (root: נקה)

נִקָּיוֹן, נִקְיוֹן-; n.m. purity (root: נקה)

נָקֵל קלל v. a. be easy
b. be swift

נִקְלָה קלה v. be disgraced

נקם v.
1) נָקַם avenge
2) נִקַּם avenge
3) נִקֵּם avenge
5) הִתְנַקֵּם avenge oneself
7) הֻקַּם be avenged

נָקָם, נְקַם-; n.m. vengeance
(root: נקם)

נְקָמָה, נִקְמַת-; נְקָמוֹת n.f.
vengeance; revenge (root: נקם)

נקף v.
6) הִקִּיף surround; encircle

נִקְפַּץ קפץ v. be shut

נקר v.
1) נָקַר pierce
3) נִקֵּר a. pierce
b. gouge

נִקְרָא קרא v. a. be invited
b. be named
c. be read

d. happen to be

נִקְרַב קרב .v — be brought near

נִקְרָה קרה .v — a. happen to be
b. meet

נִקְרַע קרע .v — a. be cut
b. be destroyed

נקש .v
1) נָקַשׁ — trap; ensnare
2) נִקַּשׁ — fall in a snare
3) נִקֵּשׁ — snare
5) הִתְנַקֵּשׁ — lay a snare

נִקְשַׁר קשר .v — be tied

נֵר, נֵר-; **נֵרוֹת, נֵרוֹת-**; .n.m — a. candle
b. light
c. salvation

נִרְאָה ראה .v — a. be visible
b. appear

נִרְגַּע רגע .v — be calmed

נִרְדַּם רדם .v — fall asleep

נִרְדַּף רדף .v — be pursued

נָרוֹם רום .v — elevate oneself

נִרְפָּא רפא .v — a. be cured
b. be repaired

נִרְפָּה רפה .v — be lax

נָרֹץ רצץ .v — be broken

נִרְצָה רצה .v — be accepted

נִרְצַח רצח .v — be slain

נשא .v
1) נָשָׂא — a. carry
b. move
c. lift
d. take
e. forgive
f. suffer
g. count
h. prefer (with פָּנִים)
2) נִשָּׂא — a. be lifted
b. be moved
3) נִשֵּׂא — elevate
5) הִתְנַשֵּׂא — a. boast
b. exalt

נשא .v
1) נָשָׁא — a. forget
b. exact
2) נִשָּׁא — be deceived
6) הִשִּׁיא — dupe; deceive

נִשְׁאָה שאה .v — a. be desolate
b. rage; make noise

נִשְׁאַל שאל .v — ask permission

נִשְׁאַר שאר .v — remain; be left behind

נִשְׁבָּה שבה .v — be taken prisoner

נִשְׁבַּע שבע .v — take an oath

נִשְׁבַּר שבר .v — be broken; be destroyed

נִשְׁבַּת שבת .v — stop; cease

נשג .v
6) הִשִּׂיג — overtake
הִשִּׂיגָה יָדוֹ — be able; manage

נִשְׂגַּב שׂגב .v — be high; be exalted

נשה .v
1) נָשָׁה — a. forget
b. be a creditor
2) נִשָּׁה — be forgotten
3) נִשָּׁה — make forget
6) הִשָּׁה — a. make forget
b. lessen

c. exact a payment

נָשַׁח שחח .v a. be bowed down
b. be humiliated

נִשְׁחַט שחט .v be slaughtered

נִשְׁחַת שחת .v be destroyed; be spoiled

נִשְׁטַף שטף .v a. be rinsed
b. be swept away

נָשִׂיא, נְשִׂיא-; נְשִׂיאִים, נְשִׂיאֵי-; n.m.
a. chieftain; ruler
b. rain clouds (pl.)

נָשִׁים, נְשֵׁי-; n.f. a. women
b. wives (singular: אִשָּׁה)

נשך .v
1) נָשַׁךְ a. bite
b. take usury
3) נִשֵּׁךְ bite
6) הִשִּׁיךְ lend with usury

נֶשֶׁךְ, נֶשֶׁךְ-; n.m. interest; usury
(root: נשך)

נִשְׁכַּח שכח .v be forgotten

נשל .v
1) נָשַׁל dislodge; remove
3) נִשֵּׁל displace

נִשְׁלָה שלה .v be at ease

נִשְׁלַח שלח .v be sent

נשם .v
1) נָשַׁם breathe

נָשַׁם שמם .v a. be destroyed
b. be appalled

נִשְׁמַד שמד .v a. be destroyed
b. be exterminated

נְשָׁמָה, נִשְׁמַת-; נְשָׁמוֹת n.f. a. soul
b. living creature
c. breath (root: נשם)

נִשְׁמַט שמט .v a. be moved
b. be dropped

נִשְׁמַע שמע .v a. be heard
b. be accepted
c. obey

נִשְׁמַר שמר .v a. be careful
b. heed

נִשְׂנָא שׂנא .v be hated

נִשְׁנָה שנה .v be repeated

נָשַׁס שסס .v be plundered

נִשְׁעַן שען .v a. lean
b. trust
c. be near

נִשְׂעַר שׂער .v be stormy

נֶשֶׁף, נֶשֶׁף-; n.m. a. evening
b. darkness

נִשְׁפַּט שפט .v a. be judged
b. plead
c. punish

נִשְׁפַּךְ שפך .v a. be poured
b. be thrown

נשק .v
1) נָשַׁק kiss
3) נִשֵּׁק kiss
6) הִשִּׁיק touch

נֶשֶׁק, נֶשֶׁק-; n.m. weapons

נִשְׁקַל שקל .v a. be weighted
b. be paid

נִשְׁקַע שקע .v sink

נִשְׁקַף שקף .v — a. be seen
b. look

נֶשֶׁר ; נְשָׁרִים, נִשְׁרֵי- ; .n.m — eagle

נִשְׂרַף שׂרף .v — be burned

נִשְׁתָּה שתה .v — be drunk

נָתוּן .adj., n.m — see: v. נתן

נתח .v
3) נִתַּח — cut

נֵתַח ; נְתָחִים .n.m — piece; slice
(root: נתח)

נָתִיב, נְתִיב- ; .n.m — path

נְתִיבָה ; נְתִיבוֹת, נְתִיבוֹת- ; .n.f — path

נָתִין ; נְתִינִים .n.m — Temple servant
(root: נתן)

נתך .v
1) נָתַךְ — pour (only in the future: יִתַּךְ)
2) נִתַּךְ — pour
6) הִתִּיךְ — melt down (metal)

נִתְכַּן תכן .v — be measured;
be examined

נִתַּם תמם .v — a. be destroyed
b. be finished

נִתְמַךְ תמך .v — a. be supported
b. be held up

נתן .v
1) נָתַן — a. give
b. put
c. set
d. appoint
e. marry off (a daughter)
f. let; allow

g. consider
2) נִתַּן — be given
7) הֻתַּן — be given
(only in the future: יֻתַּן)

נְתַנְאֵל .pr.n.m — Nethanel
("God given") (roots: נָתַן, אֵל)

נִתְעַב תעב .v — be abhorred

נִתְעָה תעה .v — be led astray

נִתְפַּשׂ תפשׂ .v — be captured

נתץ .v
1) נָתַץ — smash; destroy
2) נִתַּץ — be destroyed
3) נִתֵּץ — smash; destroy

נתק .v
2) נִתַּק — be cut; be broken
3) נִתֵּק — a. tear
b. cut
6) הִתִּיק — a. draw away
b. distance

נֶתֶק .n.m — scall; scurf

נִתְקַע תקע .v — be blown
(ram's horn or trumpet)

נתר .v
3) נִתֵּר — jump
6) הִתִּיר — a. untie
b. set free

נתש .v
1) נָתַשׁ — destroy; smash
2) נִתַּשׁ — be destroyed

נָתַתִּי, נָתַתָּ (נָתַתָּה), נָתַתְּ, נָתַן, נָתְנָה, נָתַנּוּ, נְתַתֶּם, נָתְנוּ .v
I gave, you gave (m.s.), you gave (f.s.) ... (past tense of v. נתן)

סְאָה ; סְאִים n.f. unit of dry measure (one-third of אֵיפָה)

סבא v.
1) סָבָא guzzle

סבב v.
1) סָבַב a. encircle; surround
b. march around
c. turn
d. cause
2) נָסַב a. turn
b. surround
3) סִבֵּב change
3) סוֹבֵב encircle; surround
6) הֵסֵב a. bring about
b. cause to turn
7) הוּסַב be surrounded

סָבִיב ; סְבִיבִים, סְבִיבוֹת
a. all around prep., adv., n.m.
b. surroundings (root: סבב)

סְבַךְ (סְבֹךְ) ; סִבְכֵי- n.m. thicket

סבל v.
1) סָבַל bear a load

סֵבֶל, סֵבֶל- ; סִבְלוֹת- n.m. burden (root: סבל)

סַבָּל ; סַבָּלִים n.m. porter (root: סבל)

סְגֻלָּה, סְגֻלַּת- ; n.f. treasured possession

סָגָן ; סְגָנִים n.m. official

סגר v.
1) סָגַר close; shut
2) נִסְגַּר a. be closed
b. be imprisoned
3) סִגַּר deliver
4) סֻגַּר a. be closed
b. be imprisoned
6) הִסְגִּיר a. isolate
b. deliver

סֹהַר n.m. prison (usually בֵּית-הַסֹּהַר)

סוג v.
2) נָסוֹג turn away from
6) הִסִּיג move; shift

סוֹד, סוֹד- ; n.m. a. secret
b. counsel

סוֹחֵר, סוֹחֵר- ; סוֹחֲרִים, סוֹחֲרֵי- ; n.m. merchant (root: סחר)

סוך v.
1) סָךְ anoint
6) הֵסִיךְ anoint

סוֹלְלָה ; סוֹלְלוֹת n.f. siege mount (root: סלל)

סוּס, סוּס- ; סוּסִים, סוּסֵי- ; n.m. horse

סוף v.
1) סָף end
6) הֵסִיף bring to an end

סוֹף, סוֹף- ; n.m. end (root: סוף)

סוּף n.m. reeds
יַם-סוּף sea of reeds ("Red Sea" today)

סוּפָה ; סוּפוֹת n.f. storm

סוֹפֵר, סוֹפֵר- ; סוֹפְרִים, סוֹפְרֵי- ; n.m. scribe (root: ספר)

סור v.
1) סָר a. deviate
b. stop; cease

6) הֵסִיר remove
7) הוּסַר be removed

סוֹרֵר ; סוֹרֶרָה ; סוֹרְרִים adj.
rebellious (root: סרר)

סות v.
6) הֵסִית a. incite
b. seduce

סחב v.
1) סָחַב drag; pull

סחר v.
1) סָחַר trade

סַחַר, סְחַר- ; n.m. a. trade
b. merchandise (root: סחר)

סִיג ; סִיגִים n.m. dross

סִיר ; סִירִים (סִירוֹת) n.m. a. pot
b. pail
c. thorn

סֻכָּה, סֻכַּת- ; סֻכּוֹת n.f. booth
(root: סכך)

סכך v.
1) סָכַךְ cover
6) הֵסֵךְ a. screen
b. cover

סכל v.
2) נִסְכַּל act foolishly
3) סִכֵּל annul
6) הִסְכִּיל act foolishly

סָכָל ; סְכָלִים adj.m. foolish
(root: סכל)

סִכְלוּת n.f. folly (root: סכל)

סכן v.
1) סָכַן be of use
2) נִסְכַּן be hurt
6) הִסְכִּין be in the habit of

סַל, סַל- ; סַלִּים, סַלֵּי- ; n.m. basket

סֶלָה interj. "Selah"
a liturgical-musical sign

סלח v.
1) סָלַח forgive
2) נִסְלַח be forgiven

סלל v.
1) סָלַל pave

סֶלַע ; סְלָעִים n.m., pr.n.f. a. rock
b. capital of Edom, today's Petra(?)

סלף v.
3) סִלֵּף distort

סֹלֶת, סֹלֶת- ; n.f. fine flour

סַמִּים n.m.pl. aromatic incense

סמך v.
1) סָמַךְ a. lay
b. support
c. approach
2) נִסְמַךְ lean
3) סִמֵּךְ support

סֶמֶל, סֵמֶל- ; n.m. image

סְנֶה n.m. bush (Moses' burning bush)

סְנַפִּיר n.m. fin

סעד v.
1) סָעַד sustain
eat סָעַד לֵב

סְעִיף, סְעִיף- ; סְעִיפִים, סְעִיפֵי- ;
n.m. a. cleft of a rock
b. branch

סער v.
1) סָעַר grow stormy
2) נִסְעַר be agitated
3) סֵעֵר scatter
4) סֹעַר be scattered

סַעַר n.m. storm (root: סער)

1) קַל (פָּעַל) 2) נִפְעַל 3) פִּעֵל 4) פֻּעַל 5) הִתְפַּעֵל 6) הִפְעִיל 7) הָפְעַל

סְעָרָה, סַעֲרַת-; סְעָרוֹת, סַעֲרוֹת-;
storm (root: סער) n.f.

סַף, סַף-; סִפִּים, סִפּוֹת n.m.
a. threshold
b. goblet

ספד v.
1) סָפַד mourn
2) נִסְפַּד be mourned

ספה v.
1) סָפָה a. add
b. destroy
2) נִסְפָּה be destroyed; perish
6) הִסְפָּה add

ספח v.
1) סָפַח join
2) נִסְפַּח be joined
3) סִפֵּח add
4) סֻפַּח be added
5) הִסְתַּפֵּחַ join

סָפִיחַ, סְפִיחַ-; n.m. aftergrowth
(root: ספח)

סַפִּיר; סַפִּירִים n.m. sapphire

ספן v.
1) סָפַן a. cover
b. hide
a. hidden
b. covered (adj.m.) סָפוּן; סְפוּנִים

ספק v.
1) סָפַק clap

ספר v.
1) סָפַר count; number
2) נִסְפַּר be counted
3) סִפֵּר a. tell
b. count
4) סֻפַּר be told

סֵפֶר, סֵפֶר, סְפָרִים n.m. a. scroll
b. letter; message
c. literacy
d. record; history

סקל v.
1) סָקַל stone
2) נִסְקַל be stoned
3) סִקֵּל a. stone
b. clear (a field) of rocks
4) סֻקַּל be stoned

סָרָה n.f. a. rebellion
b. falsehood (root: סור)

סרח v.
1) סָרַח a. hang down
b. spread
2) נִסְרַח go stale

סָרִיס, סְרִיס-; סָרִיסִים, סָרִיסֵי-;
n.m. a. eunuch
b. officer
c. functionary

סֶרֶן; סְרָנִים, סַרְנֵי-; n.m.
a. Philistine officer
b. axle

סרר v.
1) סָרַר rebel

סתם v.
1) סָתַם a. plug; stop up
b. hide
סָתוּם a. covered
b. hidden (adj.m.s.)
2) נִסְתַּם be stopped up
3) סִתֵּם a. plug
b. stop up

סתר v.
2) נִסְתַּר be hidden
3) סִתֵּר hide
5) הִסְתַּתֵּר hide oneself
6) הִסְתִּיר hide; conceal

סֵתֶר, סֵתֶר-; n.m. a. hiding place
b. shelter
c. secret (root: סתר)
d. secretly בַּסֵּתֶר

עָב, עַב- ; **עָבִים, עָבֵי-** ; **עָבוֹת** n.m.f.
cloud

עבד v.
1) עָבַד work; labor
עָבַד אֶת ... serve (someone)
עָבַד בְּ... impose work (on someone)
2) נֶעֱבַד be worked
4) עֻבַּד be worked
6) הֶעֱבִיד make work; enslave

עֶבֶד, עֶבֶד- ; **עֲבָדִים, עַבְדֵי-** ; n.m.
a. slave; servant
b. (God's) worshipper (root: עבד)

עֹבַדְיָה pr.n.m. Obadiah
("servant of God") (roots: עבד, יָהּ)

עֲבוֹדָה, עֲבוֹדַת- ; n.f. a. work
b. religious service (root: עבד)

עֲבוֹת, עֲבוֹת- ; **עֲבוֹתִים, עֲבוֹתוֹת**
a. corded rope n.m.f.
b. thicket

עבט v.
1) עָבַט pawn
6) הֶעֱבִיט lend against a pawn

עבר v.
1) עָבַר a. pass through
b. end; be gone
c. transgress
d. forgive
3) עִבֵּר a. breed
b. connect
5) הִתְעַבֵּר be angry
6) הֶעֱבִיר a. lead across
b. send
c. deliver
הֶעֱבִיר מִן cancel

עֵבֶר, עֵבֶר- ; **עֲבָרִים, עֶבְרֵי-** ; n.m. side

עֶבְרָה, עֶבְרַת- ; **עֲבָרוֹת, עַבְרוֹת-** ; n.f.
anger (root: עבר)

עִבְרִי ; **עִבְרִיָּה** ; **עִבְרִים** ; **עִבְרִיּוֹת** adj.
Hebrew, a descendant of עֵבֶר ("Eber"); Jew; Israelite

עגב v.
1) עָגַב lust after

עָגֹל ; **עֲגֻלּוֹת** adj. round

עֵגֶל, עֵגֶל- ; **עֲגָלִים, עֶגְלֵי-** ; n.m. calf

עֶגְלָה, עֶגְלַת- ; **עֶגְלוֹת-** ; n.f. heifer

עֲגָלָה ; **עֲגָלוֹת, עֶגְלוֹת-** ; n.f. cart

עַד n.m. a. eternity
b. booty
c. forever לְעוֹלָם וָעֶד

עַד, עֲדֵי- ; prep. a. until; to; up to
b. while

עֵד, עֵד- ; **עֵדִים, עֵדֵי-** ; n.m. witness
(root: עוד)

עֵדָה ; **עֵדוֹת** n.f. a. witness
b. God's commandments (pl.)

עֵדָה, עֲדַת- ; n.f. a. community
b. assembly (root: יעד)

עדה v.
1) עָדָה deck; wear ornaments
6) הֶעֱדָה dress

עֵדוּת, עֵדוּת- ; n.f. a. testimony

1) קַל (פָּעַל) 2) נִפְעַל 3) פִּעֵל 4) פֻּעַל 5) הִתְפַּעֵל 6) הִפְעִיל 7) הָפְעַל

b. covenant (root: עוד)

ornament; jewelry — **עֲדִי, עֲדִי- ; עֲדָיִים** n.m.

a. pleasure
b. Eden — **עֵדֶן** n.m., pr.n.m.

עדף v.
remain; be left over — 1) עָדַף
exceed — 6) הֶעֱדִיף

עדר v.
arrange; set — 1) עָדַר
a. be tilled — 2) נֶעְדַּר
b. be absent

עֵדֶר, עֵדֶר- ; עֲדָרִים, עֶדְרֵי- n.m.
a. herd
b. drove

Obadiah — **עוֹבַדְיָה** pr.n.m.
("the servant of God") (roots: עבד, יָהּ)

cake — **עוּגָה, עוּגַת- ; עוּגוֹת** n.f.

עוד v.
a. strengthen — 3) עוֹדֵד
b. encourage
a. testify — 6) הֵעִיד
b. call to witness
c. warn
be warned — 7) הוּעַד

a. again — **עוֹד** adv., prep.
b. still
c. yet
d. in
e. while בְּעוֹד

עוה v.
sin — 1) עָוָה
twist — 2) נַעֲוָה
twist — 3) עִוָּה
a. sin — 6) הֶעֱוָה
b. twist

עוז v.
seek refuge — 1) עָז
shelter — 6) הֵעִיז

sinner; wrongdoer — **עַוָּל** adj., n.m.

iniquity — **עָוֶל, עֶוֶל- ;** n.m.

wrong; iniquity — **עַוְלָה** n.f.

עוֹלָה, עוֹלַת- ; עוֹלוֹת, עוֹלוֹת- n.f. ;
a. burnt offering
b. iniquity
c. step

עוֹלֵל (עוֹלָל) ; עוֹלָלִים, עוֹלְלֵי- n.m. ;
baby

עוֹלָם ; עוֹלָמִים, עוֹלְמֵי- n.m. ;
a. eternity
b. world
c. forever לְעוֹלָם, לְעוֹלָם וָעֶד
d. ever since מֵעוֹלָם

עָוֹן (עָווֹן), עֲוֹן- ; עֲוֹנוֹת, עֲוֹנוֹת- n.m. ;
sin; transgression (root: עוה)

עוף v.
fly — 1) עָף
a. fly — 3) עוֹפֵף
b. brandish
fly away — 5) הִתְעוֹפֵף

bird (root: עוף) — **עוֹף, עוֹף-** n.m. ;

lead (metal) — **עוֹפֶרֶת** n.f.

עור v.
be awake — 1) עֵר
waken — 3) עוֹרֵר
blind — 3) עִוֵּר
wake up — 5) הִתְעוֹרֵר
a. waken — 6) הֵעִיר
b. encourage
c. stir up

עִוֵּר ; עִוְרִים ; עִוְרוֹת adj. blind
(root: עור)

עוֹר, עוֹר- ; עוֹרוֹת n.m. a. skin
b. hide

עוֹרֵב ; עוֹרְבִים, עוֹרְבֵי- ; n.m. raven

עות v.
3) עִוֵּת distort; wrong
4) עֻוַּת be wronged

עֵז ; עִזִּים n.f. goat

עַז ; עַזָּה ; עַזִּים ; עַזּוֹת adj. strong;
mighty (root: עזז)

עֹז (עוֹז), עָז- (עֹז-) ; n.m.
strength; might (root: עזז)

עזב v.
1) עָזַב a. leave
b. forsake
c. help
d. repair
עָזוּב a. free
b. forsaken
2) נֶעֱזַב be forsaken

עִזְבוֹנִים n.m.pl. merchandise; wares

עזז v.
1) עָזַז be strong
6) הֵעֵז פָּנִים be brazen

עֻזִּיאֵל pr.n.m. Uziel
("God is my strength") (roots: עֹז, אֵל)

עֻזִּיָּהוּ pr.n.m. Uziah
("God is my strength") (roots: עֹז, יָהּ)

עזר v.
1) עָזַר a. help
b. support
c. save
2) נֶעֱזַר a. be helped
b. be supported

עֵזֶר n.m. a. support
b. help (root: עזר)

עֶזְרָא pr.n.m. Ezra ("helper")
(root: עזר)

עֶזְרָה, עֶזְרַת- ; n.f. a. help
b. salvation (root: עזר)

עֲזָרָה n.f. a. court in the Temple
b. enclosure

עטה v.
1) עָטָה a. wear
b. cover

עטף v.
1) עָטַף a. cover
b. be weak
2) נֶעֱטַף be weak
5) הִתְעַטֵּף be weak

עטר v.
1) עָטַר a. surround
b. crown
3) עִטֵּר a. crown
b. adorn
6) הֶעֱטִיר a. crown
b. adorn

עֲטָרָה, עֲטֶרֶת- ; עֲטָרוֹת ; n.f. crown
(root: עטר)

עִי, עִי- ; עִיִּים n.m. pile of ruins

עַיִט, עֵיט- ; n.m. bird of prey

עַיִן, עֵין- ; עֵינַיִם, עֵינֵי- ; n.f. a. eye
b. sight; view
c. water spring
d. in the presence of... ... לְעֵינֵי

עיף v.
1) עָיֵף be tired

עָיֵף ; עֲיֵפָה ; עֲיֵפִים adj. tired
(root: עיף)

עִיר, עִיר- ; עָרִים, עָרֵי- n.f. city

עַיִר ; עֲיָרִים n.m. jackass

עֵירֹם ; עֵירֻמִּים adj.m. naked

עַכְבָּר ; עַכְבְּרֵי- n.m. mouse

עכר v.
1) עָכַר a. cause trouble
b. muddy

עַל n.m. height (root: עלה)

עַל (עֲלֵי) prep. a. on
b. above
c. near; at
d. with
e. about
f. on account of
g. also; in addition
Declension: עָלַי, עָלֶיךָ, עָלַיִךְ, עָלָיו, עָלֶיהָ,
עָלֵינוּ, עֲלֵיכֶם, עֲלֵיכֶן, עֲלֵיהֶם (עָלֵימוֹ), עֲלֵיהֶן
on me, on you (m.s.), on you (f.s.), on him, on her, on us, on you (m.pl.), on you (f.pl.), on them (m.), on them (f.)

עַל-אוֹדוֹת prep. on account of

עַל-אַף conj. a. though
b. despite

עַל אֲשֶׁר conj. because of; on account of

עַל-יַד adv. "at hand"; near; by
(root: יָד)

עַל-כִּי conj. because

עַל-כֵּן adv. therefore

עַל-פִּי conj. in accordance with
(root: פֶּה)

עַל-פְּנֵי conj. "on the face of"; on
(root: פָּנִים)

עֹל, עֹל- ; n.m. a. yoke
b. burden
c. suffering

עלה v.
1) עָלָה a. rise
b. go up
c. grow
2) נַעֲלָה a. rise
b. be raised
c. move away
5) הִתְעַלָּה pride oneself; boast
6) הֶעֱלָה a. raise; lift
b. present
7) הֹעֲלָה a. be raised
b. be presented

עָלֶה, עֲלֵה- ; עֲלֵי- n.m. leaf

עָלָה ; עָלוֹת n.f. nursing animal

עֲלוּמִים n.m.pl. youth (root: עֶלֶם)

עלז v.
1) עָלַז rejoice

עֲלִיָּה, עֲלִיַּת- ; עֲלִיּוֹת n.f. a. attic
b. stair
c. sky (root: עלה)

עֶלְיוֹן ; עֶלְיוֹנָה ; עֶלְיוֹנוֹת adj.
a. highest
b. supreme
c. Most High (God) (root: עלה)

עַלִּיז ; עַלִּיזָה ; עַלִּיזִים adj. joyful
(root: עלז)

עֲלִילָה ; עֲלִילוֹת- ; n.f. a. action; deed
b. slander עֲלִילֹת דְּבָרִים

עלל v.
3) עוֹלֵל a. deal with

b. do harm
c. pick bare (a vine, a field)
5) הִתְעַלֵּל a. mock
b. abuse

עלם v.
2) נֶעֱלַם be hidden
5) הִתְעַלֵּם ignore
6) הֶעֱלִים hide

עֶלֶם ; עַלְמָה ; עֲלָמוֹת n.
a. young man (m.)
b. young woman (f.)

עלף v.
4) עֻלַּף a. become weak
b. be covered
5) הִתְעַלֵּף a. be weak
b. cover oneself

עלץ v.
1) עָלַץ rejoice

עַם (עָם), עַם- ; עַמִּים, עַמֵּי- ; n.m.
a. people; nation
b. crowd; group
c. population
d. people of Israel הָעָם
e. family; relatives (in pl.)

עִם prep.
a. with
b. near; at
c. and
d. from מֵעִם
Declension: עִמִּי (עִמָּדִי), עִמְּךָ, עִמָּךְ, עִמּוֹ, עִמָּהּ, עִמָּנוּ, עִמָּכֶם, עִמָּהֶם (עִמָּם)
with me, with you (m.s.), with you (f.s.), with him, with her, with us, with you (m.pl.), with them (m.)

עמד v.
1) עָמַד a. stand
b. remain
c. stop moving
d. persist
6) הֶעֱמִיד a. place
b. put up
c. erect
7) הָעֳמַד be placed

עִמָּדִי prep. see עִם

עַמּוּד, עַמּוּד- ; עַמּוּדִים, עַמּוּדֵי- ; n.m.
pillar (root: עמד)

עָמוֹס pr.n.m. Amos ("burdened" ?) (root: עמס)

עָמוּס adj.m.s. loaded (root: עמס)

עָמִית n.m. friend

עמל v.
1) עָמַל toil; labor

עָמָל, עֲמַל- ; n.m.
a. labor
b. woe
c. mischief (root: עמל)

עמס v.
1) עָמַס load
6) הֶעֱמִיס load

עמק v.
1) עָמַק be deep
6) הֶעְמִיק a. be deep
b. exceed

עָמֹק ; עֲמֻקָּה ; עֲמֻקִּים ; עֲמֻקּוֹת adj.
a. deep
b. profound
c. unclear; dim (root: עמק)

עֵמֶק, עֵמֶק- ; עֲמָקִים, עִמְקֵי- ; n.m.
valley (root: עמק)

עֹמֶר, עֹמֶר- ; עֳמָרִים n.m.
a. unit of dry measure (1/10 of אֵיפָה)
b. sheaf

עֲמֹרָה pr.n.f. Gomorrah

עֵנָב ; עֲנָבִים, עִנְבֵי- ; n.m. grape

ענג v.

5) הִתְעַנֵּג enjoy; find delight in

ענה v.

1) עָנָה a. answer
b. cry out
c. be humble
d. testify עָנָה בְּ-
2) נַעֲנָה a. be answered
b. reply favorably
c. be oppressed
3) עִנָּה a. oppress
b. sing
4) עֻנָּה be oppressed
5) הִתְעַנָּה suffer; be afflicted
6) הֶעֱנָה a. answer
b. oppress

עָנָו ; עֲנָוִים, עַנְוֵי- ; adj.m. a. humble
b. afflicted
c. poor (root: ענה)

עֲנָוָה n.f. modesty; humility
(root: ענה)

עָנִי ; עֲנִיָּה ; עֲנִיִּים, עֲנִיֵּי- ; n., adj.
a. poor
b. afflicted (root: ענה)

עֳנִי (עֹנִי), עֳנִי- ; n.m.
a. oppression; affliction
b. poverty (root: ענה)

עִנְיָן, עִנְיַן- ; n.m. a. business
b. action
c. task
d. matter (root: ענה)

ענן v.

3) עִנֵּן cover with clouds
3) עוֹנֵן practice soothsaying

עָנָן, עֲנַן- ; עֲנָנִים n.m. cloud (root: ענן)

עָנָף ; עֲנָפִים n.m. branch (of a tree)

עֲנָק ; עֲנָקִים n.m., pr.n.m. a. pendant
b. Anak (family of giant warriors)

ענש v.

1) עָנַשׁ punish
2) נֶעֱנַשׁ be punished

עָסִיס, עֲסִיס- ; n.m. fruit juice

עֹפֶל, עֹפֶל- ; n.m., pr.n.m.
a. fortified hill
b. a fort in Jerusalem

עַפְעַפַּיִם, עַפְעַפֵּי- ; n.m.pl. eyelids

עָפָר, עֲפַר- ; עַפְרוֹת- ; n.m.
a. dirt of the earth
b. dust
c. ashes

עֹפֶר, עֹפֶר- ; עֳפָרִים n.m. young hart

עֵץ, עֵץ- ; עֵצִים, עֲצֵי- ; n.m. a. tree
b. wood; timber

עצב v.

1) עָצַב scold
עָצוּב sad
2) נֶעֱצַב a. regret
b. be concerned
3) עִצֵּב a. mould
b. grieve
5) הִתְעַצֵּב a. be grieved
b. regret
6) הֶעֱצִיב cause sorrow

עֶצֶב ; עֲצָבִים, עַצְּבֵי- ; n.m. a. statue
b. sorrow
c. pain (root: עצב)

עַצֶּבֶת, עַצְּבַת- ; n.f. a. sorrow
b. pain (root: עצב)

עֵצָה, עֲצַת- ; עֵצוֹת n.f. a. advice

עֵצָה (continued)
b. counsel (root: יעץ)
c. trees

עָצוּב v. עצב — sad

עָצוּם ; עֲצוּמִים adj.m.
a. huge
b. strong (root: עצם)

עָצֵל n., adj.m. — lazy

עצם v.
1) עָצַם — a. increase (in number or strength)
b. shut (eyes)
3) עִצֵּם — crack; break
6) הֶעֱצִים — strengthen

עֶצֶם, עֶצֶם- ; עֲצָמוֹת, עַצְמוֹת- ; n.f.
a. bone
b. essence; core (root: עצם)

עצר v.
1) עָצַר — stop; prevent
עָצוּר — imprisoned
2) נֶעֱצַר — be stopped

עֲצֶרֶת, עֲצֶרֶת- ; n.f.
solemn gathering (root: עצר)

עָקֵב, עֲקֵב- ; עִקְבֵי-, עֲקֵבֵי-, עִקְבוֹת- ; n.m.
a. heel
b. track
c. footstep

עֵקֶב, עֵקֶב- ; n.m., conj., adv.
a. result; effect
b. because; since
c. to the utmost

עָקֹד ; עֲקֻדִּים adj.m. — striped (cattle)

עקר v.
1) עָקַר — a. move
b. uproot
2) נֶעֱקַר — be uprooted
3) עִקֵּר — hamstring; maim

עָקָר ; עֲקָרָה, עֲקֶרֶת- ; adj.
a. sterile (m.)
b. barren (f.) (root: עקר)

עַקְרָב ; עַקְרַבִּים n.m. — scorpion

עקש v.
1) עָקַשׁ — a. twist
b. pervert
2) נֶעְקַשׁ — be twisted
3) עִקֵּשׁ — twist

עִקֵּשׁ, עִקֵּשׁ- ; עִקְּשִׁים, עִקְּשֵׁי- ; adj.m.
a. stubborn
b. perverted (root: עקש)

ערב v.
1) עָרַב — a. trade
b. pawn
c. be a surety
d. dare
e. be pleasant
f. set (sun)
g. be banished
5) הִתְעָרֵב — a. mingle with
b. bet
6) הֶעֱרִיב — (do something) in the evening

עֶרֶב, עֶרֶב- ; עַרְבַּיִם n.m. — evening (root: ערב)

עֶרֶב (עֲרָב) pr.n.f. — Arabia

עֵרֶב n.m.
a. mixed multitude (root: ערב)
b. woof (as in "warp and woof")

עָרֹב n.m. — swarm of insects (the fourth plague in Egypt)

עֲרָבָה ; עֲרָבוֹת, עַרְבוֹת- ; n.f.
a. wilderness
b. willow
c. the Jordan valley הָעֲרָבָה

עֲרָבִי ; עַרְבִים adj.m.
Arab, resident of עֶרֶב

ערה v.
1) עָרָה undress; strip naked
2) נֶעֱרָה be shown
3) עֵרָה expose
5) הִתְעָרָה a. undress
b. be rooted
6) הֶעֱרָה expose

עֶרְוָה n.f. a. nakedness
b. shame (root: ערה)

עָרוּם ; עֲרוּמִים adj.m. a. clever
b. shrewd (root: ערם)

עָרוֹם see עֵרֹם

עֶרְיָה n.f. nakedness (see עֶרְוָה)

עָרִיץ ; עָרִיצִים, עָרִיצֵי- ; n., adj.m.
a. ruthless man
b. cruel

ערך v.
1) עָרַךְ a. arrange; set up
b. compare
עָרוּךְ ready; arranged
6) הֶעֱרִיךְ estimate

עֵרֶךְ n.m. a. set; arrangement
b. value; importance
c. equivalence (root: ערך)

עָרֵל, עֲרַל- ; עֲרֵלָה ; עֲרֵלִים, עַרְלֵי- ;
adj. a. uncircumcised
b. unreceptive (heart, etc.)

עָרְלָה, עָרְלַת- ; עֲרָלוֹת, עָרְלוֹת- ; n.f.
a. foreskin
b. fruit of a tree in its first three years

ערם v.
1) עָרַם be cunning
2) נֶעֱרַם pile up
6) הֶעֱרִים be cunning; plot

עֵרֹם ; עֲרֻמָּה ; עֲרוּמִּים adj. naked

עָרְמָה n.f. shrewdness; cunning
(root: ערם)

עֲרֵמָה, עֲרֵמַת- ; עֲרֵמוֹת, עֲרֵמוֹת- ; n.f.
pile (root: ערם)

ערף v.
1) עָרַף a. drip
b. break the neck
c. destroy

עֹרֶף, עָרְף- ; n.m. nape; neck

עֲרָפֶל n.m. fog; mist (root: ערף?)

ערץ v.
1) עָרַץ a. scare; make tremble
b. fear
2) נֶעֱרַץ be dreaded
6) הֶעֱרִיץ a. scare
b. hold in awe

עֶרֶשׂ, עֶרֶשׂ- ; n.f. bed

עָשׁ n.m. moth

עֵשֶׂב, עֵשֶׂב- ; עִשְׂבוֹת- ; n.m. grass

עשה v.
1) עָשָׂה a. do; make; create
b. set
c. yield; provide
d. cause
e. appoint
2) נַעֲשָׂה be done; be made
3) עִשָּׂה squeeze

עָשׂוֹר n.m. a. ten
b. ten-stringed harp (root: עשׂר)

עָשִׁיר ; עֲשִׁירִים, עֲשִׁירֵי- ; n., adj.m.
rich (root: עשׁר)

עֲשִׂירִי ; עֲשִׂירִית adj. tenth
(root: עשׂר)

עֲשִׂירִיָּה (עֲשִׂירִית) n.f. one-tenth
(root: עשׂר)

עשן v.
1) עָשַׁן a. smoke
b. be angry

עָשָׁן, עֲשַׁן- ; n.m. smoke
(root: עשן)

עשק v.
1) עָשַׁק a. oppress
b. rob

עֹשֶׁק n.m. a. oppression
b. robbery (root: עשק)

עשר v.
1) עָשַׁר become rich
5) הִתְעַשֵּׁר pretend to be rich
6) הֶעֱשִׁיר a. become rich
b. make rich

עֹשֶׁר n.m. riches (root: עשר)

עשׂר v.
1) עָשַׂר take a tenth part
3) עִשֵּׂר tithe
6) הֶעֱשִׂיר tithe

עֶשֶׂר adj., n.f. ten
See "Grammar", section 14

עָשָׂר adj., n.m. suffix "ten"
in the numbers eleven to nineteen, similar to "-teen" in 'thirteen, ..., nineteen'.
See "Grammar", section 14

עֲשָׂרָה, עֲשֶׂרֶת- ; עֲשָׂרוֹת adj., n.m. ten

עֶשְׂרֵה adj., n.f. suffix "ten"
in the numbers eleven to nineteen, similar to "-teen" in 'thirteen, ..., nineteen'.
See "Grammar", section 14

עִשָּׂרוֹן ; עֶשְׂרוֹנִים n.m.
unit of dry measure (1/10 of אֵיפָה)
(root עשׂר)

עֶשְׂרִים adj., n.m.f. twenty

עַשְׁתֵּי עָשָׂר adj., n.m. eleven

עַשְׁתֵּי עֶשְׂרֵה adj., n.f. eleven

עֵת, עֵת- ; עִתִּים (עִתּוֹת) n.f. a. time
b. period
c. season
d. now כָּעֵת

עַתָּה adv. now
now that וְעַתָּה

עַתּוּד ; עַתּוּדִים, עַתּוּדֵי- ; n.m.
a. he-goat
b. leader

עָתִיד ; עֲתִידִים ; עֲתִידוֹת adj. ready

עתק v.
1) עָתַק a. move
b. grow
6) הֶעְתִּיק a. move
b. copy

עתר v.
1) עָתַר plead; pray
2) נֶעְתַּר respond to a plea
6) הֶעְתִּיר plead

פ

פֵּאָה, פְּאַת-; **פֵּאוֹת, פַּאֲתֵי-** n.f.
a. corner
b. side
c. sidelock

פאר v.
3) פֵּאֵר adorn
5) הִתְפָּאֵר boast

פְּאֵר; **פְּאֵרִים, פַּאֲרֵי-** n.m. a. glory
b. turban; headdress (root: פאר)

פֻּארָה (פֹּארָה); **פֹּארוֹת** n.f.
tree branch

פגע v.
1) פָּגַע a. touch
b. meet
c. strike; harm
d. beg; urge
6) הִפְגִּיעַ a. intervene
b. demand
c. bring about
d. visit upon

פֶּגֶר; **פְּגָרִים, פִּגְרֵי-** n.m. corpse

פגש v.
1) פָּגַשׁ meet
2) נִפְגַּשׁ meet
3) פִּגֵּשׁ encounter

פדה v.
1) פָּדָה a. redeem
b. rescue
פָּדוּי ransomed
2) נִפְדָּה be redeemed
6) הִפְדָּה redeem
7) הָפְדָּה be redeemed

פֶּה, פִּי-; **פִּיּוֹת** n.m. a. mouth
b. opening
c. twice פִּי-שְׁנַיִם
d. by the sword לְפִי חֶרֶב
(roots: פֶּה, חֶרֶב)

פֹּה (פוֹ) adv. a. here
b. from this side מִפֹּה (מִפּוֹ)

פוֹ see פֹּה

פוח v.
1) פָּח blow gently
6) הֵפִיחַ a. snort
b. blow
c. utter

פוץ v.
1) פָּץ spread; scatter
2) נָפוֹץ be scattered
6) הֵפִיץ scatter

פוק v.
1) פָּק stumble
6) הֵפִיק a. wobble
b. attain
c. provide
d. succeed

פוּר; **פּוּרִים** n.m. a. lot
b. Purim ("lots"), the festival of lots פּוּרִים

פָּז (פַּז) n.m. fine gold

פזר v.
2) נִפְזַר be scattered
3) פִּזֵּר scatter

פַּח, פַּח-; **פַּחִים, פַּחֵי-** n.m. a. trap
b. sheet of metal

פחד v.
1) פָּחַד fear
3) פִּחֵד fear
6) הִפְחִיד scare

פַּחַד, פַּחַד- ; **פְּחָדִים** n.m.
a. fear
b. anxiety (root: פחד)

פֶּחָה, פַּחַת- ; **פַּחוֹת, פַּחוֹת-** ; n.m.
governor; "pasha"

פַּחַת ; **פְּחָתִים** n.m.f.
a. pit
b. trap

פטר v.
1) פָּטַר a. release
b. set free
6) הִפְטִיר open wide

פֶּטֶר, פֶּטֶר- ; n.m. a. opening
b. first birth (root: פטר)

פִּי- see פֶּה

פִּיּוֹת n.m.pl. mouths (see פֶּה)

פִּילֶגֶשׁ, פִּילֶגֶשׁ- ; **פִּילַגְשִׁים,**
פִּילַגְשֵׁי- ; n.f. concubine

פלא v.
2) נִפְלָא a. be a marvel
b. be difficult
3) פִּלֵּא dedicate
6) הִפְלִיא a. cause to marvel
b. act marvelously
c. dedicate

פֶּלֶא ; **פְּלָאִים (פְּלָאוֹת)** n.m. a. marvel
b. wonder (root: פלא)

פֶּלֶג ; **פְּלָגִים, פַּלְגֵי-** ; n.m.
brook; stream

פלה v.
2) נִפְלָה a. be separate
b. be distinguished
6) הִפְלָה set apart

פלח v.
1) פָּלַח cleave; split
3) פִּלַּח pierce

פֶּלַח, פֶּלַח- ; n.m. slice; piece
(root: פלח)

פלט v.
1) פָּלַט escape
3) פִּלֵּט rescue; save
6) הִפְלִיט save

פָּלִיט ; **פְּלִיטֵי-** ; n.m. a. refugee
b. fugitive (root: פלט)

פְּלֵיטָה, פְּלֵיטַת- ; n.f. remnant;
remainder (root: פלט)

פֶּלֶךְ, פֶּלֶךְ- ; n.m. a. district
b. spindle
c. crutch

פלל v.
3) פִּלֵּל a. judge
b. expect
c. intervene
5) הִתְפַּלֵּל pray

פלס v.
3) פִּלֵּס level; smooth

פְּלֶשֶׁת pr.n.f. Philistia

פְּלִשְׁתִּי ; **פְּלִשְׁתִּים** adj., pr.n.m.
Philistine

פֶּן conj. a. lest
b. in order not to
c. perhaps

פנה v.
1) פָּנָה a. turn to; face
b. pay attention to

3) פִּנָּה remove; clear
6) הִפְנָה turn
7) הָפְנָה be turned

פִּנָּה, פִּנַּת-; פִּנּוֹת, פִּנּוֹת-; n.f.
a. corner
b. end

פָּנִים, פְּנֵי-; n.m.pl. a. face
b. front part
c. surface (root: פנה)
d. anger; ire
see under ל לִפְנֵי
see under מ מִפְּנֵי

פְּנִים n.m. inner area
inwardly פְּנִימָה

פְּנִימִי; פְּנִימִית; פְּנִמִיִּים; פְּנִימִיּוֹת
adj. internal

פְּנִינִים n.f.(?).pl. pearls

פסח v.
1) פָּסַח pass over
2) נִפְסַח limp
3) פִּסַּח skip

פֶּסַח n.m., pr.n.m.
a. Passover sacrifice in the Temple
b. the festival of unleavened bread ("Passover") (root: פסח)

פִּסֵּחַ n., adj.m. lame (root: פסח)

פסל v.
1) פָּסַל carve in stone

פֶּסֶל, פֶּסֶל-; פְּסִילִים, פְּסִילֵי-; n.m.
sculptured image; idol (root: פסל)

פעל v.
1) פָּעַל a. do
b. make
c. act
See also "Grammar", section 15.4

פֹּעַל, פֹּעַל-; פְּעָלִים n.m.
a. act; work
b. wages (root: פעל)

פְּעֻלָּה; פְּעֻלּוֹת-; n.f. a. act; work
b. wages (root: פעל)

פעם v.
1) פָּעַם strike
2) נִפְעַם a. be stricken
b. be moved; be troubled
5) הִתְפָּעֵם be moved

פַּעַם; פְּעָמִים, פַּעֲמֵי-; n.f.
a. time (once, twice, etc.)
b. step; pace (usually pl.)

פַּעֲמוֹן, פַּעֲמוֹן-; פַּעֲמוֹנִים, פַּעֲמוֹנֵי-;
n.m. bell (root: פעם)

פצה v.
2) פָּצָה a. open (mouth)
b. redeem; save

פָּצוּעַ adj.m. see v. פצע

פצח v.
1) פָּצַח open (mouth to sing)
3) פִּצַּח crack

פצע v.
1) פָּצַע injure; bruise
פָּצוּעַ injured

פֶּצַע; פְּצָעִים, פִּצְעֵי-; n.m. injury; wound (root: פצע)

פצר v.
1) פָּצַר urge; entreat

פקד v.
1) פָּקַד a. remember fondly
b. punish; take revenge
c. count; pass in review
d. order; command
e. appoint

f. visit
2) נִפְקַד — a. be absent; be missing
b. be counted
5) הִתְפַּקֵּד — be counted; be numbered
הָתְפַּקֵּד — be counted
(*a rare verbal stem: passive of* (5) הִתְפַּעֵל)
6) הִפְקִיד — a. appoint
b. deposit
c. trust
7) הֻפְקַד — be appointed

פְּקֻדָּה, פְּקֻדַּת-; פְּקֻדּוֹת, פְּקֻדּוֹת-; n.f.
a. duty; charge
b. clan
c. command
d. reward
e. punishment (root: פקד)

פְּקוּדִים, פְּקוּדֵי-; n.m.pl. census; enrollment (root: פקד)

פִּקּוּדִים, פִּקּוּדֵי-; n.m.pl.
commandments (root: פקד)

פקח v.
1) פָּקַח — open (eyes, ears)
2) נִפְקַח — be opened (eyes)

פָּקִיד, פְּקִיד-; פְּקִידִים n.m.
official; overseer (root: פקד)

פַּר (פָּר), פַּר-; פָּרִים n.m. bull

פֶּרֶא; פְּרָאִים n.m. wild ass

פרד v.
2) נִפְרַד — be divided; be separated
5) הִתְפָּרֵד — separate
6) הִפְרִיד — separate

פֶּרֶד; פְּרָדִים n.m. mule

פרה v.
1) פָּרָה — a. be fruitful; bear offspring
b. sprout; thrive
6) הִפְרָה — make fruitful

פָּרָה; פָּרוֹת, פָּרוֹת-; n.f. cow
(f. of פַּר)

פרח v.
1) פָּרַח — a. bloom
b. spread; break out
c. flourish
6) הִפְרִיחַ — cause to bloom

פֶּרַח, פֶּרַח-; פְּרָחִים n.m.
a. flower; blossom
b. flower-shaped ornament (root: פרח)

פְּרִי, פְּרִי-; n.m.
a. fruit
b. result
c. reward
d. offspring (root: פרה)

פָּרִיץ, פְּרִיץ-; פָּרִיצִים, פָּרִיצֵי-; n.m.
lawless man; thief (root: פרץ)

פֶּרֶךְ n.m. oppression

פָּרֹכֶת, פָּרֹכֶת-; n.f. curtain

פרס v.
1) פָּרַס — a. cut
b. break (bread)
6) הִפְרִיס — have hoofs (animal)

פָּרַס pr.n.f. Persia

פַּרְסָה; פְּרָסוֹת, פַּרְסוֹת-; n.f. hoof
(root: פרס)

פרע v.
1) פָּרַע — a. let go
b. reject
c. be disorderly
d. uncover (hair)
2) נִפְרַע — become disorderly
6) הִפְרִיעַ — distract; disturb

פַּרְעֹה pr.n.m. Pharaoh

פרץ v.

1) פָּרַץ a. break out
b. break into
c. destroy
d. spread out

פָּרוּץ ruined

2) נִפְרַץ be common

4) מְפֹרָץ destroyed; broken into

5) הִתְפָּרֵץ revolt

פֶּרֶץ, פֶּרֶץ־ ; פְּרָצִים (פְּרָצוֹת) n.m.
a. breach
b. affliction
c. breaking through (root: פרץ)

פרק v.

1) פָּרַק a. remove
b. break
c. rescue

3) פֵּרֵק a. break
b. remove

5) הִתְפָּרֵק a. break
b. remove from oneself

פרר v.

1) פּוֹר collapse (infinitive)

3) פּוֹרֵר shake

5) הִתְפּוֹרֵר collapse

6) הֵפִיר (הֵפֵר) a. annul
b. frustrate

7) הוּפַר be annulled

פרשׂ v.

1) פָּרַשׂ a. spread; extend
b. cut

פָּרוּשׂ spread out

2) נִפְרַשׂ scatter

3) פֵּרֵשׂ a. reach out
b. scatter

פרש v.

1) פָּרַש explain

2) נִפְרַש be separated

4) פֹּרַש be clarified; be explained

6) הִפְרִיש a. spit
b. emit

פֶּרֶשׁ n.m. excrement

פָּרָשׁ ; פָּרָשִׁים n.m. horseman

פְּרָת pr.n.m. Euphrates (the river)

פשׂה v.

1) פָּשָׂה spread

פשט v.

1) פָּשַׁט a. take off (garment)
b. attack (with בְּ־ ; אֶל ; עַל)

3) פִּשֵּׁט undress

6) הִפְשִׁיט a. undress (someone)
b. flay (hide)
c. remove

פשע v.

1) פָּשַׁע a. transgress; sin
b. revolt

פֶּשַׁע, פֶּשַׁע־ ; פְּשָׁעִים, פִּשְׁעֵי־ ; n.m.
transgression; sin (root: פשע)

פִּשְׁתָּה ; פִּשְׁתִּים, פִּשְׁתֵּי־ ; n.f. a. flax
b. linen

פַּת, פַּת־ ; פִּתִּים n.f. a. slice of bread
b. crumb

פִּתְאֹם adv. suddenly

פַּתְבַּג, פַּתְבַּג־ ; n.m. a. food
b. delicacy

פתה v.

1) פָּתָה be foolish

2) נִפְתָּה a. be fooled
b. be enticed

3) פִּתָּה a. entice
b. deceive
c. seduce

4) פֻּתָּה a. be seduced
b. be persuaded

6) הִפְתָּה enlarge

פָּתוּחַ see פתח

פִּתּוּחַ ; פִּתּוּחִים, פִּתּוּחֵי- ; n.m.
a. engraving
b. carved picture (root: פתח)

פתח v.
1) פָּתַח open
2) נִפְתַּח be opened
3) פִּתַּח a. untie
b. open
c. set free
d. carve; engrave
5) הִתְפַּתֵּחַ untie oneself

פֶּתַח, פֶּתַח- ; פְּתָחִים, פִּתְחֵי- ; n.m.
a. opening
b. doorway (root: פתח)

פֶּתִי ; פְּתָאִים (פְּתָיִים) n.m.
simpleton; fool (root: פתה)

פְּתִיל, פְּתִיל- ; פְּתִילִים n.m. thread; cord (root: פתל)

פתל v.
2) נִפְתַּל a. wrestle
b. be twisted
c. be perverted
5) הִתְפַּתֵּל be wily

פֶּתֶן ; פְּתָנִים n.m. viper

פֶּתַע adv. suddenly

פתר v.
1) פָּתַר a. solve
b. interpret (dreams)

פִּתְרוֹן, פִּתְרוֹן- ; פִּתְרוֹנִים n.m.
a. solution
b. interpretation (dreams) (root: פתר)

צ

צֹאן n.f.pl. a. sheep and goats
b. flock

צֶאֱצָאִים, צֶאֱצָאֵי- ; n.m.pl. offspring
(root: יצא)

צֵאת v. (construct) infinitive of יצא

צבא v.
1) צָבָא a. gather
b. wage war
6) הִצְבִּיא be in command

צָבָא, צְבָא- ; **צְבָאוֹת, צִבְאוֹת-** ; n.m.
a. army; host
b. service (military,etc.)
c. fixed time
d. the sun, moon and stars

צְבִי, צְבִי- ; **צְבָאִים** n.m. a. gazelle
b. glory
c. beauty

צבר v.
1) צָבַר amass; gather

צַד, צַד- ; **צִדִּים, צִדֵּי-** ; n.m. a. side
b. edge

צַדִּיק ; **צַדִּיקִים** n.,adj.m. a. righteous
b. just
c. honest
d. innocent
e. correct (root: צדק)

צדק v.
1) צָדַק a. be just
b. be in the right
c. be righteous
2) נִצְדַּק be justified
3) צִדֵּק acquit; clear
5) הִצְטַדֵּק apologize
6) הִצְדִּיק vindicate; justify

צֶדֶק n.m. justice; righteousness
(root: צדק)

צְדָקָה, צִדְקַת- ; **צְדָקוֹת, צִדְקוֹת-** ;
n.f. justice; righteousness
(root: צדק)

צִדְקִיָּה(וּ) pr.n.m. Zedekiah
("God's righteousness")
(roots: צֶדֶק, יָהּ)

צהל v.
1) צָהַל a. shout with joy
b. neigh

צָהֳרַיִם n.m.pl. noon

צַו n.m. command; order
(root: צוה)

צוֹאָה, צוֹאַת- ; n.f. excrement

צַוָּאר, צַוַּאר- ; **צַוְּארֵי-** ; n.m. neck

צוד v.
1) צָד a. trap
b. hunt
c. capture
3) צוֹדֵד capture

צוֹדֵד see צוד

צוה v.
3) צִוָּה a. command; instruct; order
b. appoint
c. make a will
4) צֻוָּה be instucted

צוֹם v.
1) צָם fast

צוֹם, צוֹם-; צוֹמוֹת n.m. fast
(root: צום)

צוֹפֶה see צפה

צוק v.
6) הֵצִיק appress; afflict

צור v.
1) צָר a. lay siege
b. tie; bind
c. shape; form
d. hate (see also צרר)
2) נָצוֹר be under siege

צוּר, צוּר-; צוּרִים, צוּרֵי-; n.m.
a. rock
b. shelter; fortress

צוֹר (צֹר) pr.n.f. (city of) Tyre

צוּרִישַׁדָּי pr.n.m. Zurishadai
("God is my fortress") (roots: צוּר, שַׁדַּי)

צוֹרֵף; צוֹרְפִים n.m.
silver (gold) smith (root: צרף)

צוֹרֵר; צוֹרְרִים, צוֹרְרֵי-; n.m. enemy
(root: צרר)

צְחִיחַ, צְחִיחַ-; צְחִיחִים n.m.
a. dryness
b. arid place

צחק v.
1) צָחַק laugh
3) צִחֵק a. mock
b. make merry
c. play

צִי; צִיִּים (צִים) n.m. a. ship; boat
b. desert animals (pl.)

צַיִד, צֵיד-; n.m. a. hunt
b. game
c. food (root: צוד)

צֵידָה n.f. food (root: צוד)

צִיָּה; צִיּוֹת n.f. a. dryness
b. desert

צִיּוֹן pr.n.f. Zion
a. fortress captured by David in Jerusalem
b. general name for Jerusalem and the land of Israel

ציץ v.
1) צָץ bloom
6) הֵצִיץ a. sprout flowers
b. look

צִיץ, צִיץ-; צִצִּים n.m.
a. blossom; flower
b. ornament shaped like a flower
(root: ציץ)

צִיר, צִיר-; צִירִים, צִירֵי-; n.m.
a. messenger
b. shape; form
c. door hinge
d. childbirth pains (pl.)

צֵל, צֵל-; צְלָלִים, צִלְלֵי-; n.m.
shadow (root: צלל)

צלח v.
1) צָלַח a. succeed
b. be fit
c. rest upon
d. cross; pass
6) הִצְלִיחַ a. succeed; prosper
b. make prosperous

צלל v.
1) צָלַל a. ring; tingle
b. sink; drown
c. be shadowed
6) הֵצֵל cast a shadow

צֶלֶם, צֶלֶם-; צַלְמֵי-; n.m. a. image; shape
b. idol

צַלְמָוֶת n.m. darkness
(roots: צֵל, מָוֶת ?)

צֵלָע, צֶלַע-; צְלָעוֹת, צַלְעוֹת-; n.f.
a. rib
b. side; edge
c. side room

צמא v.
1) צָמֵא be thirsty

צָמֵא; צְמֵאָה; צְמֵאִים adj. thirsty
(root: צמא)

צָמָא n.m. thirst (root: צמא)

צמד v.
2) נִצְמַד be joined
4) מְצֻמָּד joined; attached (present tense)
6) הִצְמִיד attach

צֶמֶד, צֶמֶד-; צְמָדִים, צִמְדֵּי-; n.m.
pair (root: צמד)

צמח v.
1) צָמַח grow; sprout
3) צִמֵּחַ grow; sprout
6) הִצְמִיחַ cause to grow

צֶמַח, צֶמַח-; n.m. plant; growth
(root: צמח)

צָמִיד; צְמִידִים n.m. a. bracelet
b. cover (root: צמד)

צֶמֶר n.m. wool

צמת v.
1) צָמַת a. oppress
b. destroy
2) נִצְמַת be destroyed
3) צִמֵּת a. oppress
b. destroy
6) הִצְמִית a. destroy
b. put an end to

צִנָּה; צִנּוֹת n.f. a. body armor; shield
b. cold
c. boat

צָנִיף, צְנִיף-; צְנִיפוֹת-; n.m.
headdress

צעד v.
1) צָעַד march; step
6) הִצְעִיד lead

צַעַד; צְעָדִים n.m. step; pace

צָעִיר; צְעִירָה; צְעִירִים; צְעִירֵי-;
n., adj. a. young; youngster
b. sherpherd's helper

צעק v.
1) צָעַק a. shout
צָעַק אֶל b. beg
2) נִצְעַק gather; be assembled
3) צִעֵק shout
6) הִצְעִיק gather; assemble

צְעָקָה, צַעֲקַת-; n.f. outcry; shout
(root: צעק)

צפה v.
1) צָפָה a. look out; observe
b. overlay; cover
3) צִפָּה a. wait
b. expect
c. overlay; cover
4) צֻפָּה be coated

צִפּוּי n.m. overlay; cover (root: צפה)

צָפוֹן, צְפוֹן-; n.m. north

צִפּוֹר, צִפּוֹר-; צִפֳּרִים n.f. bird; fowl

צַפַּחַת, צַפַּחַת-; n.f. flask

צפן v.
1) צָפַן hide
צָפוּן hidden
2) נִצְפַּן be hidden
6) הִצְפִּין conceal; hide

צְפַרְדֵּעַ ; צְפַרְדְּעִים n.f. frog

צֹר ; צוּרִים n.m. flint

צַר ; צָרָה adj., n.m.
a. narrow
b. oppressed; troubled
c. distress

צַר ; צָרִים, צָרֵי- ; n.m. enemy; oppressor (root: צרר)

צָרָה, צָרַת- ; צָרוֹת, צָרוֹת- ; n.f.
a. trouble
b. woe
c. rival wife

צְרוֹר, צְרוֹר- ; צְרוֹרוֹת n.m.
a. package (root: צרר)
b. pebble

צֳרִי n.m. balm

צָרַעַת, צָרַעַת- ; n.f. leprosy (root: צרע)

צרע v.
1) צָרוּעַ leper; leprous
4) מְצֹרָע leprous

צרף v.
1) צָרַף
a. smelt; refine metal
b. purify
see also צוֹרֵף
צָרוּף pure; clean
2) נִצְרַף be refined
3) צֵרֵף
a. smelt
b. purify

צרר v.
1) צָרַר
a. tie
b. bind
c. hate
צוֹרֵר enemy
צָרוּר bound
d. be narrow
3) יֵצַר be anxious (future tense)
4) מְצֹרָר tied; bound (present tense)
6) הֵצַר oppress

ק

קָאָת (קָאַת), קְאַת- ; n.f.
a. jackdaw (?)
b. cormorant (?)

קבב v.
1) קָבַב, קַב — curse

קְבוּרָה, קְבוּרַת- ; n.f.
a. burial
b. tomb (root: קבר)

קבל v.
3) קִבֵּל — a. receive
b. take
c. accept
6) הִקְבִּיל — correspond to; parallel

קבע v.
1) קָבַע — rob; despoil

קבץ v.
1) קָבַץ — gather; amass
2) נִקְבַּץ — be gathered
3) קִבֵּץ — gather
5) הִתְקַבֵּץ — gather; be assembled

קבר v.
1) קָבַר — bury
2) נִקְבַּר — be buried
3) קִבֵּר — bury
4) קֻבַּר — be buried

קֶבֶר, קֶבֶר- ; **קְבָרִים, קִבְרֵי-**
(קִבְרוֹת-) ; n.m. — tomb; grave

קדד v.
1) קָדַד, קַד — bow the head

קָדוֹשׁ, קְדוֹשׁ- ; **קְדוֹשִׁים** adj.m.
a. holy
b. saintly (root: קדש)

קדח v.
1) קָדַח — burn; kindle

קָדִים n.m. — a. east
b. hot eastern wind רוּחַ קָדִים

קדם v.
3) קִדֵּם — a. be early
b. hasten
c. greet
6) הִקְדִּים — a. be early
b. hasten

קֶדֶם n.m. — a. front side
b. east
c. ancient times (root: קדם)

קַדְמָה, קַדְמַת- ; n.f. — previous state; origin (root: קדם)

קַדְמוֹנִי ; **קַדְמוֹנִים** ; **קַדְמוֹנִיּוֹת** adj.
a. eastern
b. ancient (root: קדם)

קָדְקֹד, קָדְקֹד- ; n.m. — scalp

קדר v.
1) קָדַר — a. be dark
b. be gloomy
5) הִתְקַדֵּר — become dark
6) הִקְדִּיר — darken

קדש v.
1) קָדַשׁ — become holy
2) נִקְדַּשׁ — be sanctified
3) קִדֵּשׁ — a. sanctify; make holy
b. appoint; assign
c. dedicate
5) הִתְקַדֵּשׁ — be sanctified
6) הִקְדִּישׁ — a. consider holy
b. designate

קֹדֶשׁ, קֹדֶשׁ-; קֳדָשִׁים, קָדְשֵׁי- n.m.
a. holiness
b. holy place (root: קדש)

קָדֵשׁ; קְדֵשָׁה; קְדֵשִׁים; קְדֵשׁוֹת n.
cult prostitute

קהל v.
2) נִקְהַל be assembled; gather
6) הִקְהִיל gather; assemble

קָהָל, קְהַל- n.m. assembly; crowd
(root: קהל)

קֹהֶלֶת pr.n.m.
a. the Book of Ecclesiastes
b. King Solomon (?) (root: קהל?)

קָו, קַו- n.m. measuring line

קוה v.
1) קָוָה hope; expect
2) נִקְוָה be gathered
3) קִוָּה hope; expect

קוט v.
1) קָט be disgusted; loathe
2) נָקוֹט be disgusted
5) הִתְקוֹטֵט a. be disgusted
b. quarrel with

קוֹל, קוֹל-; קוֹלוֹת n.m. a. sound
b. voice
c. utterance

קום v.
1) קָם a. rise; stand up; stand
b. come true
c. be done
d. happen; occur
3) קוֹמֵם a. rebuild
b. erect
3) קִיֵּם fulfill
5) הִתְקוֹמֵם a. rise up
b. stand against
6) הֵקִים a. raise; erect
b. perform
c. fulfill
7) הוּקַם a. be raised
b. be fulfilled

קוֹמָה, קוֹמַת- n.f. height
(root: קום)

קוֹנֶה, קוֹנֵה- n., adj.m. buyer
(root: קנה)

קין v.
3) קוֹנֵן lament; mourn

קוֹסֵם; קוֹסְמִים n.m. sorcerer;
magician (root: קסם)

קוץ v.
1) קָץ loathe

קוֹץ; קוֹצִים, קוֹצֵי- n.m. thorn

קוֹרָה; קוֹרוֹת, קוֹרוֹת- n.f.
wooden beam (root: קרה)

קַח; קְחִי; קְחוּ v. לקח take!
(imperative of לָקַח (1))

קָטֹן (קָטָן); קְטַנָּה; קְטַנִּים; קְטַנּוֹת
a. young adj.
b. small
c. insignificant

קטף v.
1) קָטַף pluck; pick (fruit, etc.)

קטר v.
3) קִטֵּר burn ritual incense
6) הִקְטִיר burn ritual incense
7) הֻקְטַר be burned (incense)

קְטֹרֶת, קְטֹרֶת- n.f. ritual incense
(root: קטר)

קיא v.
1) קָא vomit
6) הֵקִיא vomit; spew out

קִיֵּם v. קום fulfill

קין v.
3) קוֹנֵן lament; mourn

קִינָה ; קִינוֹת (קִינִים) n.f. elegy;
lamentation (root: קין)

קיץ v.
6) הֵקִיץ a. awake
b. rouse to action

קַיִץ n.m. a. summer
b. ripe fruit

קִיקָיוֹן n.m. a. gourd
b. ricinus plant

קִיר, קִיר- ; קִירוֹת, קִירוֹת- ; n.m.
a. wall
b. fence

קַל קלל v. a. be slight
b. be swift

קַל ; קַלָּה ; קַלִּים adj. a. fast; swift
b. light (root: קלל)

קלה v.
1) קָלָה roast
קָלוּי roasted
2) נִקְלָה be disgraced

קָלוּי adj.m.s. roasted
(root: קלה)

קָלוֹן, קְלוֹן- ; n.m. disgrace
(root: קלה)

קָלִי (קָלִיא) n.m.
roasted corn or wheat
(root: קלה)

קלל v.
1) קַל (קָלַל) a. be light
b. be swift
2) נָקֵל a. be easy
b. be swift
3) קִלֵּל curse
4) קֻלַּל be cursed
6) הֵקֵל a. make light
b. ease
c. slight

קְלָלָה, קִלְלַת- ; קְלָלוֹת n.f. curse
(root: קלל)

קֶלֶס n.m. mockery

קלע v.
1) קָלַע a. sling; throw
b. twist; weave
3) קִלַּע hurl; sling

קֶלַע ; קְלָעִים, קַלְעֵי- ; n.m. a. sling
b. curtain (root: קלע)

קָמָה, קָמַת- ; קָמוֹת- ; n.f.
ripe crop (before the harvest)
(root: קום)

קֶמַח, קֶמַח- ; n.m. flour

קֵן, קַן- ; קִנִּים n.m. a. nest
b. home
c. compartment

קנא v.
3) קִנֵּא a. envy
b. be jealous
c. suspect infidelity
d. display passion
6) הִקְנִיא anger

קַנָּא adj.m. jealous
(one of God's attributes)
(root: קנא)

קִנְאָה, קִנְאַת- ; קְנָאוֹת n.f.
a. jealousy
b. suspicion of infidelity
c. anger (root: קנא)

קנה v.
1) קָנָה a. purchase

b. acquire; receive
c. create
2) נִקְנָה be purchased

קָנֶה, קְנֵה-; קָנִים, קְנֵי- n.m.
a. stalk
b. reed
c. measuring stick
d. beam of weight scales
e. arm of candelabrum
f. aromatic bush

קִנְיָן n.m. acquisition; property
(root: קנה)

קסם v.
1) קָסַם divine; portend

קֶסֶם; קְסָמִים n.m. magic; divination

קְעָרָה, קַעֲרַת-; קְעָרוֹת, קַעֲרוֹת- n.f.
bowl

קפץ v.
1) קָפַץ close; shut (mouth, hand)
2) נִקְפַּץ be shut
3) קִפֵּץ jump

קֵץ, קֵץ- n.m. end
at the end of מִקֵּץ

קָצֶה, קְצֵה-; קְצֵוֵי- n.m. a. end
b. edge; border

קֵצֶה n.m. end

קָצָה; קְצָווֹת, קְצוֹת- n.f.m. a. end
b. edge; border

קָצוּץ v. קצץ cut; trimmed

קָצִין, קְצִין-; קְצִינֵי- n.m.
leader; chief

קָצִיר, קְצִיר- n.m. a. harvest
b. harvested grain
c. harvest season
d. destruction
e. tree branch (root: קצר)

קצף v.
1) קָצַף be angry
5) הִתְקַצֵּף be angry
6) הִקְצִיף irritate; vex

קֶצֶף, קֶצֶף- n.m. anger; ire
(root: קצף)

קצץ v.
1) קָצַץ cut
קָצוּץ cut; trimmed; clipped
3) קִצֵּץ cut
4) קֻצַּץ be cut

קצר v.
1) קָצַר a. harvest; reap
b. be short
3) קִצֵּר shorten
6) הִקְצִיר shorten

קָצָר, קְצַר-; קִצְרֵי- adj.m. short
(root: קצר)

קרא v.
1) קָרָא a. call out; announce
b. read
c. proclaim
d. happen
e. name
f. invite
קָרוּא, קָרִיא invited
2) נִקְרָא a. be invited
b. be named
c. be read
d. happen to be
4) קֹרָא a. be read
b. be named

(קְרַאת) לִקְרַאת prep. against; towards (roots: ל, קרא)

קרב v.
1) קָרַב a. approach (in space or time)
b. copulate
2) נִקְרַב be brought
3) קֵרַב a. bring about
b. befriend
6) הִקְרִיב a. bring near
b. offer a sacrifice
c. come near

קֶרֶב, קֶרֶב- ; n.m. a. bowels
b. interior
inside; within בְּקֶרֶב
from amongst מִקֶּרֶב

קְרָב, קְרָב- ; **קְרָבוֹת** n.m. battle

קָרְבָּן, קָרְבַּן- ; n.m. sacrifice; offering (root: קרב)

קַרְדֹּם ; **קַרְדֻּמּוֹת (קַרְדֻּמִּים)** n.m.
axe

קרה v.
1) קָרָה a. happen; befall
b. meet
2) נִקְרָה a. meet
b. happen to be
3) קֵרָה install a roof; cover
6) הִקְרָה a. make happen
b. cause to meet

קָרָה n.f. cold

קָרוֹב ; **קְרוֹבָה** ; **קְרוֹבִים** ; **קְרוֹבוֹת**
n., adj. a. relative; friend
b. near (in space or time)
(root: קרב)

קרח v.
1) קָרַח shave smooth
2) נִקְרַח be shaved bald
6) הִקְרִיחַ shave smooth
7) הָקְרַח be shaved bald

קֶרַח n.m. ice

קָרְחָה n.f. baldness (root: קרח)

קֶרִי n.m. rebellion

קִרְיָה, קִרְיַת- ; n.f. city

קֶרֶן, קֶרֶן- ; **קַרְנַיִם (קְרָנַיִם), קַרְנֵי-** ;
קְרָנוֹת, קַרְנוֹת- ; n.f. a. horn
b. ram's horn (shofar)
c. container for oil
d. object shaped like a horn
e. corner
f. strength
g. beam of light

קֶרֶס ; **קְרָסִים, קַרְסֵי-** ; n.m. hook

קרע v.
1) קָרַע a. tear; cut off
b. remove forcefully
2) נִקְרַע a. be cut
b. be destroyed

קַרְקַע, קַרְקַע- ; n.f. a. ground; soil
b. bottom; basis

קֶרֶשׁ ; **קְרָשִׁים, קַרְשֵׁי-** ; n.m.
wooden board

קֶרֶת n.f. city

קַשׁ n.m. straw; chaff

קשב v.
1) קָשַׁב listen
6) הִקְשִׁיב listen

קשה v.
1) קָשָׁה a. be heavy
b. be difficult
3) קִשָּׁה have difficulty
make difficult;
6) הִקְשָׁה make hard

קָשֶׁה, קְשֵׁה- ; **קָשָׁה, קְשַׁת-** ; **קָשִׁים,**
קְשֵׁי- ; **קָשׁוֹת** adj. a. hard

b. heavy
c. stubborn
d. cruel (root: קשה)

קָשָׁה ; **קָשׁוֹת** n.f. harsh words

קָשׁוּר adj. tied; connected
(root: קשר)

קַשְׂקֶשֶׂת n.f. scale
(on fish or on armor)

קֶשֶׁר, קֶשֶׁר- ; n.m. conspiracy
(root: קשר)

קשר v.
1) קָשַׁר a. tie
b. conspire
קָשׁוּר tied; connected
2) נִקְשַׁר be tied
3) קִשֵּׁר tie
5) הִתְקַשֵּׁר conspire

קשש v.
1) קָשַׁשׁ gather
3) קוֹשֵׁשׁ gather

קֶשֶׁת, קֶשֶׁת- ; **קְשָׁתוֹת** n.f. a. bow
b. rainbow

ר

ראה v.
1) רָאָה a. see
b. perceive
c. choose
רְאֵה ; רְאִי ; רְאוּ behold! (imperative)
2) נִרְאָה a. be visible
b. appear
5) הִתְרָאָה see each other
6) הֶרְאָה a. show
b. cause to look
7) הָרְאָה be shown

רְאוּבֵן pr.n.m. Reuben
("behold, a son") (roots: ראה, בֵּן)

רְאֵם (רֵים) ; **רְאֵמִים** n.m. a. wild ox
b. Arabian oryx

רֵאשׁ see רִישׁ

רֹאשׁ, רֹאשׁ- ; **רָאשִׁים, רָאשֵׁי-** ; n.m.
a. head
b. top
c. leader; chief
d. part; section
e. beginning
f. sum
g. poisonous plant
h. venom
i. bitterness

רִאשׁוֹן ; **רִאשׁוֹנָה** ; **רִאשׁוֹנִים** ; **רִאשׁוֹנוֹת** adj. first
בָּרִאשׁוֹן on the first month
(root: רֹאשׁ)

רִאשׁוֹנָה adv. a. before
b. first (root: רֹאשׁ)

רֵאשִׁית, רֵאשִׁית- ; n.f. a. start; beginning; origin
b. first fruits
c. first born
d. choice; best part (root: רֹאשׁ)
The Book of Genesis בְּרֵאשִׁית
("Initially") (roots: בְּ, רֵאשִׁית)

רַב, רַב- ; **רַבָּה, רַבַּת-** ; **רַבִּים** ; **רַבּוֹת**
adj. a. much
b. large
c. mighty
d. abundant (root: רבה)

רַב adv. enough

רַב, רַב- ; **רַבֵּי-** ; n.m. a. chieftain; officer (root: רבה)
b. archer

רַב טַבָּחִים n.m. chief of guards

רֹב, רֹב- ; **רֻבֵּי-** ; n.m. a. abundance
b. majority
greatly לָרֹב

רבב v.
1) רָבַב, רַב a. be great
b. be numerous
c. shoot

רְבָבָה ; **רְבָבוֹת, רִבְבוֹת-** ; n.f.
ten thousand

רבה v.
1) רָבָה a. increase
(in number, size, difficulty)
b. shoot
3) רִבָּה increase in number
6) הִרְבָּה a. increase
b. extend
c. do more

רִבּוֹ (רִבּוֹא) ; רִבּוֹת n.f. ten thousand

רָבוּעַ ; רְבוּעָה ; רְבוּעִים adj. square
(root: רבע)

רְבִיבִים n.m.pl. rain

רְבִיעִי ; רְבִיעִית ; רְבִיעִים adj. fourth
See "Grammar", section 14

רְבִיעִית, רְבִיעִית n.f. one-fourth

רבע v.
1) רָבַע mate (an animal)
4) מְרֻבָּע square (present tense)
6) הִרְבִּיעַ mate (an animal)

רֶבַע ; רְבָעִים n.m. a. one-fourth
b. side of a square

רבץ v.
1) רָבַץ lie down (animal)
6) הִרְבִּיץ a. cause to lie down
b. set (precious stones)

רגז v.
1) רָגַז a. shudder
b. be excited
5) הִתְרַגֵּז a. be enraged
b. be excited
6) הִרְגִּיז a. make shudder
b. disturb

רֹגֶז, רֹגֶז- ; n.m. a. anger
b. trouble; agitation (root: רגז)

רגל v.
1) רָגַל slander
3) רִגֵּל a. spy
b. slander

רֶגֶל, רֶגֶל- ; רַגְלַיִם, רַגְלֵי- ; n.f.
a. foot; leg
b. base
c. support
לְרֶגֶל ...because of...; on account of

רֶגֶל ; רְגָלִים n.f. time
(once, twice, etc.)
the "three times" of pilgrimage (festivals) to Jerusalem
שָׁלֹשׁ רְגָלִים : פֶּסַח, שָׁבוּעוֹת, סֻכּוֹת

רַגְלִי ; רַגְלִים adj.m. walking; on foot
(root: רֶגֶל)

רגם v.
1) רָגַם stone to death

רגן v.
1) רָגַן complain
2) נִרְגַּן complain

רגע v.
1) רָגַע disturb; stir up
2) נִרְגַּע be calmed
6) הִרְגִּיעַ calm; give rest

רֶגַע ; רְגָעִים n.m. instant; moment

רדה v.
1) רָדָה a. rule; dominate
b. scoop out; scrape
3) רִדָּה subjugate; overpower
6) הִרְדָּה subdue; dominate

רדם v.
2) נִרְדַּם fall asleep

רדף v.
1) רָדַף a. pursue; chase
b. persecute
2) נִרְדַּף be pursued
3) רִדֵּף pursue hotly
4) רֻדַּף be pursued
6) הִרְדִּיף pursue; chase

רַהַב ; רְהָבִים n.m. a. sea deity
b. arrogance

רוֹאֶה ; רוֹאִים n.m. seer; prophet
(root: ראה)

רוה v.
1) רָוָה drink thirstily
3) רִוָּה water; drench
6) הִרְוָה a. water
b. make drink
c. rain

רוֹזֵן ; רוֹזְנִים n.m. prince; ruler

רוּחַ, רוּחַ- ; רוּחוֹת, רוּחוֹת- ; n.m.f.
a. wind
b. soul; spirit
c. nil
d. side; direction

רוֹכֵל ; רוֹכְלִים, רוֹכְלֵי- ; n.m.
merchant; trader (root: רכל)

רום v.
1) רָם a. rise
b. be high
c. be exalted
2) נָרוֹם elevate oneself
3) רוֹמֵם a. elevate
b. raise (children)
c. praise
4) רוֹמַם be elevated
5) הִתְרוֹמֵם a. exalt oneself
b. raise oneself
6) הֵרִים a. lift; raise
b. remove
c. offer (as a gift)
7) הוּרַם a. be lifted
b. be offered

רוּם (רוֹם), רוּם- ; n.m. a. height
b. pride; haughtiness (root: רום)

רוֹמֵם רום v. a. elevate
b. raise (children)
c. praise

רוע v.
4) רוֹעַע be shouted
5) הִתְרוֹעֵעַ shout
6) הֵרִיעַ a. shout
b. blow a trumpet or a shofar

רוֹעֶה ; רוֹעִים, רוֹעֵי- ; n.m.
a. shepherd
b. leader (root: רעה)

רוץ v.
1) רָץ run
3) רוֹצֵץ run
5) הִתְרוֹצֵץ run back and forth
6) הֵרִיץ a. cause to run
b. rush

רוֹצֵחַ n.m. a. slayer
b. murderer (root: רצח)

רוּת pr.n.f. Ruth

רחב v.
1) רָחַב spread; grow wide
6) הִרְחִיב a. make wide; increase in size
b. relieve from distress

רֹחַב, רֹחַב- ; n.m. a. width
b. plenty (root: רחב)

רָחָב, רְחַב- ; רְחָבָה, רַחֲבַת- ; רַחֲבֵי- ;
adj. wide (root: רחב)

רְחוֹב, רְחוֹב- ; רְחוֹבוֹת, רְחוֹבוֹת- ;
n.m. city square; plaza (root: רחב)

רַחוּם adj.m. merciful
(one of God's attributes) (root: רחם)

רָחוֹק ; רְחוֹקָה ; רְחוֹקִים ; רְחוֹקוֹת
adj. far; distant (root: רחק)

רֵחַיִם n.m.pl. handmill

רָחֵל ; רְחֵלִים n.f. ewe

רָחֵל pr.n.f. Rachel ("ewe")

רחם v.
3) רִחֵם a. pity; have compassion
b. love
4) רֻחַם be shown compassion

רֶחֶם (רַחַם), רֶחֶם- ; n.m. womb

רַחֲמִים, רַחֲמֵי- ; n.m.pl. pity; compassion (root: רחם)

רחץ v.
1) רָחַץ wash; bathe
4) רֻחַץ be washed
5) הִתְרַחֵץ wash oneself

רחק v.
1) רָחַק be far; be remote; be removed from...
6) הִרְחִיק a. remove; put far away
b. go far away
הַרְחֵק far away

רטש v.
3) רִטֵּשׁ dash
4) רֻטַּשׁ be dashed

ריב v.
1) רָב quarrel with; strive

רִב, רִיב- ; **רִיבוֹת, רִיבוֹת-** ; **רִיבֵי-** ; n.m. contention; dispute (root: ריב)

ריח v.
6) הֵרִיחַ smell

רֵיחַ, רֵיחַ- ; n.m. smell; scent; odor (root: ריח)

ריק v.
6) הֵרִיק a. empty
b. pour out
7) הוּרַק be emptied

רֵיק ; **רֵיקָה** ; **רֵיקִים** ; **רֵיקוֹת** adj.
a. empty
b. worthless
c. idle (root: ריק)

רִיק n.m. void; emptiness (root: ריק)

רֵיקָם adv. a. in vain
b. emptily (root: ריק)

רִישׁ (רֵישׁ, רֵאשׁ) n.m. poverty

רַךְ ; **רַכָּה** ; **רַכִּים** ; **רַכּוֹת** adj. a. young
b. soft; tender
c. timid (root: רכך)

רכב v.
1) רָכַב ride (on a vehicle or an animal)
6) הִרְכִּיב cause to ride; put on a vehicle or an animal

רֶכֶב, רֶכֶב- ; n.m. a. chariot
b. the top millstone (root: רכב)

רְכוּשׁ, רְכוּשׁ- ; n.m. property; possessions (root: רכש)

רָכִיל n.m. slander; gossip

רכך v.
1) רָכַךְ, רַךְ become soft or weak
4) רֻכַּךְ be softened

רכש v.
1) רָכַשׁ acquire

רֶכֶשׁ n.m. steeds; war horses

רָם ; **רָמָה** ; **רָמִים, רָמֵי-** ; **רָמוֹת** adj.
a. high
b. lofty; supreme (root רום)

רמה v.
1) רָמָה a. cast
b. shoot
3) רִמָּה a. deceive
b. betray

רִמָּה n.f. worms

רִמּוֹן ; **רִמּוֹנִים, רִמּוֹנֵי-** ; n.m. pomegranate

רֹמַח ; רְמָחִים n.m. spear

רְמִיָּה n.f. deceit (root: רמה)

רמס v.
1) רָמַס tread on; trample

רמשׂ v.
1) רָמַשׂ creep; crawl

רֶמֶשׂ, רֶמֶשׂ- ; n.m.
creeping invertebrates (root: רמשׂ)

רִנָּה n.f.
a. song
b. prayer song (root: רנן)

רנן v.
1) רָנַן, רָן sing
3) רִנֵּן sing
4) רֻנַּן be sung
6) הִרְנִין a. rejoice
b. sing

רַע (רָע) ; רָעָה ; רָעִים ; רָעוֹת adj.
a. bad; evil; wicked
b. dangerous
c. destructive
(see also רעע)

רַע (רָע), רַע- ; n.m.
a. wickedness; evil
b. trouble; calamity

רֹעַ, רֹעַ- ; n.m. evil; wickedness

רֵעַ ; רֵעִים, רֵעֵי- ; n.m.
a. friend
b. intention
c. noise

רעב v.
1) רָעֵב be hungry
6) הִרְעִיב starve (someone)

רָעֵב ; רְעֵבָה ; רְעֵבִים adj. hungry (root: רעב)

רָעָב n.m. hunger (root: רעב)

רעה v.
1) רָעָה a. tend (livestock)
b. graze
c. lead; guide
d. befriend; keep company

רָעָה, רָעַת- ; רָעוֹת, רָעוֹת- ; n.f.
a. trouble; misery
b. evil; wickedness
c. harm (root: רעע)

רְעוּת, רְעוּת- ; n.f.
a. woman friend
b. friendship (root: רעה)

רַעְיָה, רַעְיַת- ; n.f.
a. wife
b. beloved woman

רעם v.
1) רָעַם a. thunder
b. roar; rage
6) הִרְעִים thunder; roar

רַעֲנָן ; רַעֲנָנָה ; רַעֲנַנִּים adj.
a. fresh
b. flourishing

רעע v.
1) רַע a. be evil; be bad
b. crush; break
c. be broken
2) נָרַע be broken
6) הֵרַע a. cause harm
b. do evil

רעף v.
1) רָעַף drip
6) הִרְעִיף cause to drip

רעשׁ v.
1) רָעַשׁ a. quake; shake
b. rage
6) הִרְעִישׁ cause to quake; shake

רַעַשׁ n.m.
a. noise
b. quake
c. rage (root: רעשׁ)

רפא v.
1) רָפָא cure; heal
2) נִרְפָּא a. be cured
b. be repaired
3) רִפֵּא a. cure; heal
b. repair
5) הִתְרַפֵּא recover; be healed

רְפָאִים n.m.pl. a. the dead
b. ghosts

רְפָאִים pr.n.m. Rephaim,
a tribe of giants

רפה v.
1) רָפָה a. weaken
b. sink; drop
2) נִרְפָּה be lax
3) רִפָּה weaken
5) הִתְרַפָּה be lax
6) הִרְפָּה let go; slacken

רָץ ; רָצִים n.m. messenger
(root: רוץ)

רצה v.
1) רָצָה a. want
b. accept favorably
c. like
2) נִרְצָה a. be accepted
b. be forgiven
3) רִצָּה appease
5) הִתְרַצָּה reconcile
6) הִרְצָה accept favorably

רָצוֹן, רְצוֹן- ; n.m. a. wish; desire
b. goodwill
c. acceptance
d. grace
e. blessing (root: רצה)

רצח v.
1) רָצַח murder
2) נִרְצַח be murdered
3) רִצַּח murder

רִצְפָּה, רִצְפַּת- ; n.f. paved floor

רצץ v.
1) רָצַץ crush; oppress
רָצוּץ oppressed
2) נָרוֹץ be broken
3) רִצֵּץ, רוֹצֵץ crush; smash
5) הִתְרוֹצֵץ struggle with each other
6) הֵרַץ crush

רַק adv. a. only
b. except; nothing but

רָקָב, רְקַב- ; n.m. decay; rot

רקד v.
1) רָקַד a. dance
b. jump
3) רִקֵּד a. jump
b. dance
6) הִרְקִיד cause to jump

רַקָּה n.f. temple
(side of the human forehead)

רקח v.
1) רָקַח compound (mix) spices

רָקִיעַ, רְקִיעַ- ; n.m. a. firmament
b. expanse (root: רקע)

רָקִיק, רְקִיק- ; **רְקִיקִים, רְקִיקֵי-** ;
n.m. wafer

רקם v.
1) רָקַם embroider

רִקְמָה ; **רְקָמוֹת** n.f.
embroidered clothing

רקע v.
1) רָקַע a. stamp; kick
b. spread out
c. hammer
3) רִקַּע a. spread out
b. overlay

6) הִרְקִיעַ a. spread out
b. soar sky-high

רָשׁ (רָאשׁ) ; **רָשִׁים** adj., n.m.
poor; beggar

רשע v.
1) רָשַׁע a. sin; do evil
b. be found guilty
6) הִרְשִׁיעַ a. find guilty
b. do evil

רָשָׁע ; **רְשָׁעִים, רִשְׁעֵי-** n., adj.m.
a. wicked; evil
b. sinner
c. guilty (root:רשע)

רֶשַׁע n.m. a. wickedness; evil
b. iniquity (root: רשע)

רִשְׁעָה, רִשְׁעַת- ; n.f. evil; wickedness
(root: רשע)

רֶשֶׁף ; **רְשָׁפִים, רִשְׁפֵי- (רִשְׁפֵּי-)** ; n.m.
a. spark
b. plague; destruction

רֶשֶׁת n.f. a. net; snare
b. meshwork

Note: In this dictionary, only the letter שׂ carries the upperleft dot. The letter שׁ carries no dot and appears as ש.

שֶׁ-, שַׁ-, שָׁ-, שְׁ- ; pron. particle
a. that; who; whom
b. which; what
c. since; because
See also "Grammar", section 6.5

שאב v.
1) שָׁאַב draw (water); pump

שאג v.
1) שָׁאַג a. roar (lion)
b. shout; cry

שְׁאָגָה, שַׁאֲגַת- ; n.f. roar; cry
(root: שאג)

שאה v.
1) שָׁאָה be in ruins
2) נִשְׁאָה a. be desolate
b. rage; make noise
5) הִשְׁתָּאָה wonder
6) הִשְׁאָה destroy

שֹׁאָה see שׁוֹאָה

שְׁאוֹל n.m.f. "Sheol",
the nether world; grave

שָׁאוּל pr.n.m. Saul
("requested", "borrowed") (root: שאל)

שָׁאוֹן, שְׁאוֹן- ; n.m. noise; uproar

שְׂאוֹר n.m. leaven

שאל v.
1) שָׁאַל a. ask; inquire
b. seek; search
c. borrow
2) נִשְׁאַל ask permission
3) שִׁאֵל a. inquire
b. beg
6) הִשְׁאִיל lend

שְׁאֵלָה, שְׁאֵלַת- ; n.f. request
(root: שאל)

שַׁאֲנָן ; שַׁאֲנַנִּים ; שַׁאֲנַנּוֹת adj. a. calm
b. secure

שאף v.
1) שָׁאַף a. gasp
b. long for
c. trample; stomp on

שאר v.
1) שָׁאַר remain
2) נִשְׁאַר remain; be left behind
6) הִשְׁאִיר leave; spare

שְׁאָר, שְׁאָר- ; n.m. remnant; rest
(root: שאר)

שְׁאֵר, שְׁאֵר- ; n.m. a. flesh; food
b. blood relative

שְׁאֵרִית, שְׁאֵרִית- ; n.f. remainder;
rest (root: שאר)

שְׂאֵת, שְׂאֵת- ; n.f. a. majesty
b. skin swelling
c. infinitive (construct) of נשׂא

שבה v.
1) שָׁבָה capture; take prisoner
2) נִשְׁבָּה be captured;
be taken prisoner

שָׁבוּעַ ; שָׁבוּעִים (שָׁבוּעוֹת) n.m.
a. week

b. seven years (root: שֶׁבַע)

שְׁבוּעָה, שְׁבוּעַת- ; **שְׁבוּעוֹת, שְׁבוּעֵי-** ; n.f.
a. oath
b. curse (root: שבע)

שָׁבוּר adj. see v. שבר

שְׁבוּת, שְׁבוּת- ; n.f. return
(to previous condition); recovery
(root: שוב)

שבח v.
3) שִׁבַּח a. praise; glorify
b. calm
5) הִשְׁתַּבֵּחַ boast
6) הִשְׁבִּיחַ calm; soothe

שֵׁבֶט, שֵׁבֶט- ; **שְׁבָטִים, שִׁבְטֵי-** ; n.m.
a. rod; stick
b. scepter
c. tribe

שְׁבִי, שְׁבִי- ; n.m. a. captivity
b. prisoners; captives (root: שבה)

שִׁבְיָה n.f. a. captivity
b. captives (root: שבה)

שְׁבִיעִי ; **שְׁבִיעִית** adj. seventh
See also "Grammar", section 14.2

שְׁבִית, שְׁבִית- ; n.f. captivity
(root: שבה)

שְׂבָכָה ; **שְׂבָכִים (שְׂבָכוֹת)** n.f.
a. latticework
b. trellis

שִׁבֹּלֶת ; **שִׁבֳּלִים, שִׁבֳּלֵי-** ; n.f.
a. ear of corn
b. top of a branch
c. stream of water

שׂבע v.
1) שָׂבַע a. be sated; be full
b. be fulfilled
c. be satisfied
3) שִׂבַּע feed to fullness
6) הִשְׂבִּיעַ feed to fullness; satisfy

שָׂבֵעַ, שְׂבַע- ; **שְׂבֵעָה** ; **שְׂבֵעִים** adj.
sated; full; satisfied

שָׂבָע n.m. abundance (root: שׂבע)

שֹׂבַע, שֹׂבַע- ; n.m. satiety; fill
(root: שׂבע)

שׁבע v.
2) נִשְׁבַּע take an oath
6) הִשְׁבִּיעַ cause to take an oath

שֶׁבַע, שְׁבַע- ; adj., n.f. seven
See also "Grammar", section 14.1

שִׁבְעָה, שִׁבְעַת- ; adj., n.m. seven
See also "Grammar", section 14.1

שִׁבְעִים adj., n.m.f. seventy
See also "Grammar", section 14.1

שִׁבְעָתַיִם n.m. sevenfold (root: שֶׁבַע)

שׂבר v.
1) שָׂבַר see; observe
3) שִׂבֵּר expect; hope

שׁבר v.
1) שָׁבַר a. break; destroy
b. overcome
c. buy food
d. sell food
2) נִשְׁבַּר be broken; be destroyed
3) שִׁבֵּר smash; shatter
6) הִשְׁבִּיר sell food

שֶׁבֶר, שֶׁבֶר- ; **שְׁבָרִים** n.m. a. breach
b. disaster
c. corn; grain
d. interpretation (of a dream)
(root: שבר)

שֶׁבֶת ישב .v
1) יָשַׁב infinitive (construct) of

שבת .v
1) שָׁבַת a. cease
b. stop working
2) נִשְׁבַּת stop; cease
6) הִשְׁבִּית a. cause to cease
b. destroy; put an end to

שַׁבָּת, שַׁבַּת-; שַׁבָּתוֹת, שַׁבְּתוֹת-; n.m.f.
a. Sabbath, the seventh day of the week
b. seventh year, sabbatical
c. week
d. period of seven years (root: שבת)

שַׁבָּתוֹן n.m. complete rest (root: שבת)

שגב .v
1) שָׂגַב be too high or too mighty
2) נִשְׂגַּב be high; be exalted
3) שִׂגֵּב a. keep on high
b. keep safe

שְׁגָגָה n.f. a. error
b. unintentional sin (root: שגה)

שגה .v
1) שָׁגָה a. err; sin unintentionally
b. be infatuated
6) הִשְׁגָּה mislead; lead astray

שגע .v
4) מְשֻׁגָּע mad; madman (present tense)
5) הִשְׁתַּגֵּעַ go mad

שֶׁגֶר, שְׁגַר-; n.m. offspring (of animals)

שַׁד; שָׁדַיִם, שְׁדֵי-; n.f.
breast (female)

שֹׁד, שֹׁד-; n.m. a. violence (root: שדד)
b. female breast

שדד .v
1) שָׁדַד a. rob
b. ravage
c. overpower
3) שִׁדֵּד a. destroy
b. rob
4) שֻׁדַּד be destroyed
7) הוּשַׁד be destroyed

שָׂדֶה, שְׂדֵה-, שְׂדֵי-; שָׂדוֹת, שְׂדוֹת-; שָׂדָי; n.m.
a. field
b. land

שָׁדוּד adj. a. slain
b. overpowered (root: שדד)

שָׂדָי see שָׂדֶה

שַׁדַּי n., adj.m. Almighty (one of God's descriptions)

שְׁדֵמָה; שְׁדֵמוֹת, שַׁדְמוֹת-; n.f.
a. wheat field
b. vine field

שֶׂה, שֵׂה-; n.m.f. young sheep; lamb

שֹׁהַם n.m. onyx

שָׁוְא n.m. a. vanity
b. vain
c. naught
לַשָּׁוְא in vain; for naught

שׁוֹאָה, שׁוֹאַת-; n.f. destruction; devastation

שׁוב .v
1) שָׁב a. return
b. turn back
c. go back
d. repeat an action
e. repent
f. regret
3) שׁוֹבֵב a. return
b. go back
c. lead astray

6) הֵשִׁיב a. return; give back
b. reply
c. cancel; revoke
d. forgive
7) הוּשַׁב be returned

שׁוֹבָב see שוב

שׁוֹדֵד ; שׁוֹדְדִים, שׁוֹדְדֵי- ; n.m.
robber (root: שדד)

שוה v.
1) שָׁוָה a. be worth
b. be equal
c. be fit
3) שִׁוָּה a. imagine
b. smooth (a surface)
5) הִשְׁתַּוָּה be equal
6) הִשְׁוָה make like; liken

שׁוּחָה n.f. pit

שׁוֹחֵחַ see שיח

שוט v.
1) שָׁט a. roam; wander
b. row (boat)
3) שׁוֹטֵט wander

שׁוֹט, שׁוֹט- ; שׁוֹטִים n.m. whip

שׁוֹטֵט see שוט

שׁוֹטֵר ; שׁוֹטְרִים, שׁוֹטְרֵי- ; n.m.
a. officer
b. official

שׁוּלַיִם, שׁוּלֵי- ; n.m.pl. hem;
border (of a garment or a cloth)

שׁוּם see שִׁים

שׁוֹמֵם ; שׁוֹמֵמִים ; שׁוֹמֵמוֹת
(שׁוֹמְמוֹת) adj. a. desolate; empty
b. lonely (root: שמם)

שׁוֹמֵם see v. שמם

שׁוֹמֵר, שׁוֹמֵר-, שׁוֹמְרִים, שׁוֹמְרֵי- ;
n.m. guard; watchman (root: שמר)

שֹׁמְרוֹן (שֹׁמְרוֹן) pr.n.f. Samaria
(root: שמר)

שׂוֹנֵא n.m. enemy (see also שָׂנֵא)

שוע v.
3) שִׁוַּע cry out for help

שַׁוְעָה, שַׁוְעַת- ; n.f. cry for help
(root: שוע)

שׁוּעָל ; שׁוּעָלִים n.m. fox

שׁוֹעֵר ; שׁוֹעֲרִים, שׁוֹעֲרֵי- ; n.m.
gatekeeper (root: שַׁעַר)

שׁוֹפֵט, שׁוֹפֵט- ; שׁוֹפְטִים, שׁוֹפְטֵי- ;
n.m. a. judge
b. leader (root: שפט)
The Book of Judges שׁוֹפְטִים

שׁוֹפָר, שׁוֹפַר- ; שׁוֹפָרוֹת, שׁוֹפְרוֹת- ;
n.m. a. ram's horn ("shofar")
b. trumpet

שׁוֹק, שׁוֹק- ; שׁוֹקַיִם, שׁוֹקֵי- ; n.f.
thigh

שור v.
1) שָׁר look; observe
3) שׁוֹרֵר observe; watch

שׁוּר n.m.f., pr.n.m. a. enemy (m.)
b. wall (f.)
c. Shur (name of a desert)

שׁוֹר, שׁוֹר- ; שְׁוָרִים n.m. ox; bull

שׁוֹרֵר see v. שיר, שור

שׁוֹשׁ see v. שׂישׂ

שׁוֹשָׁן ; שׁוֹשַׁנִּים n.m. a. lily

b. lily-shaped decoration
c. ancient musical instrument

שׁוֹשַׁנָּה, שׁוֹשַׁנַּת- ; n.f. lily

שות see v. שית

שזר v.
7) מָשְׁזָר interwoven (present tense)

שֹׁחַד n.m. bribe

שחה v.
1) שָׁחָה bow down
5) הִשְׁתַּחֲוָה bow down; prostrate oneself
6) הִשְׁחָה cause to bow down

שְׂחוֹק, שְׂחוֹק- ; n.m. a. laughter
b. mockery

שָׁחוֹר (שָׁחֹר) ; שְׁחוֹרָה ; שְׁחֹרִים ; שְׁחֹרוֹת adj. black

שחח v.
1) שָׁחַח (שַׁח) bow down
2) נָשַׁח be bowed down; be humiliated
5) הִשְׁתּוֹחֵחַ be downcast
6) הֵשַׁח lay low

שחט v.
1) שָׁחַט a. slaughter (animal)
b. kill (person)
שָׁחוּט hammered (metal)
2) נִשְׁחַט be slaughtered

שְׁחִין, שְׁחִין- ; n.m. boils (skin disease)

שַׁחַל n.m. lion

שחק v.
1) שָׂחַק a. laugh
b. mock
2) שִׂחֵק jest; make sport
6) הִשְׂחִיק mock

שַׁחַק ; שְׁחָקִים n.m. a. fine dust
b. cloud
c. sky

שחר v.
1) שָׁחַר a. seek diligently
b. darken
3) שִׁחֵר seek eagerly

שַׁחַר n.m. a. dawn
b. meaning

שָׁחֹר see שָׁחוֹר

שחת v.
2) נִשְׁחַת a. be destroyed
b. be spoiled
3) שִׁחֵת a. destroy; obliterate
b. corrupt (morally)
6) הִשְׁחִית a. spoil; ruin
b. corrupt
7) מָשְׁחָת ruined; spoiled (present tense)

שַׁחַת, שַׁחַת- ; n.f. a. pit
b. grave (root: שוח)

שטה v.
1) שָׂטָה a. veer
b. go astray

שִׁטָּה ; שִׁטִּים n.f. acacia

שָׂטָן n.m. a. adversary
b. Satan, the accusing angel

שטף v.
1) שָׁטַף a. rinse
b. flow
c. sweep away
2) נִשְׁטַף a. be rinsed
b. be swept away
4) שֻׁטַּף be rinsed

שֶׁטֶף n.m. flow (root: שטף)

שֵׂיבָה, שֵׂיבַת- ; n.f.
a. gray hair
b. old age

שׂיח v.
1) שָׂח a. tell
b. converse
3) שׂוֹחֵחַ a. speak
b. tell

שִׂיחַ, שִׂיחַ- ; שִׂחִים n.m.
a. talk
b. meditation (root: שׂיח)
c. bush; shrub

שׂים v.
1) שָׂם a. put; place; set
b. cause; make
c. appoint
d. establish
e. arrange
6) הֵשִׂים make; cause
7) הוּשַׂם be placed

שׁיר v.
1) שָׁר sing
3) שׁוֹרֵר sing
7) הוּשַׁר be sung

שִׁיר, שִׁיר- ; שִׁירִים, שִׁירֵי- ; n.m.
a. song
b. hymn
c. poem (root: שׁיר)
The Song of Songs; The Song of Solomon שִׁיר הַשִּׁירִים

שִׁירָה, שִׁירַת- ; שִׁירוֹת ; n.f.
a. song
b. hymn (root: שׁיר)

שׂישׂ v.
1) שָׂשׂ rejoice

שׁית v.
1) שָׁת a. set; place; establish
b. cause; make
c. appoint
7) הוּשַׁת be set; be made

שַׁיִת n.m.
thornbush

שׁכב v.
1) שָׁכַב a. lie down
b. lie with; have sex
2) נִשְׁכְּבָה she was raped (f.)
4) שֻׁכְּבָה she was raped (f.)
6) הִשְׁכִּיב cause to lie down
7) הָשְׁכַּב be caused to lie down

שִׁכְבָה, שִׁכְבַת- ; n.f.
layer
(root: שׁכב)

שַׁכּוּל ; שַׁכֻּלָה ; שַׁכֻּלוֹת adj.
bereaved of children (root: שׁכל)

שִׁכּוֹר ; שִׁכּוֹרִים, שִׁכּוֹרֵי- ; adj., n.m.
drunk; drunkard (root: שׁכר)

שָׁכוּר n., adj.m.
drunkard; drunk
(root: שׁכר)

שׁכח v.
1) שָׁכַח forget
2) נִשְׁכַּח be forgotten
3) שִׁכַּח a. end
b. cause to be forgotten
5) הִשְׁתַּכֵּחַ be forgotten
6) הִשְׁכִּיחַ cause to forget

שָׂכִיר, שְׂכִיר- ; שְׂכִירִים n.m.
a. hired worker
b. mercenary (root: שׂכר)

שׂכל v.
1) שָׂכַל behave wisely
3) שִׂכֵּל place crosswise
6) הִשְׂכִּיל a. act wisely
b. observe
c. teach

שֶׂכֶל (שֵׂכֶל), שֵׂכֶל- ; n.m.
a. wisdom
b. understanding (root: שׂכל)

שׁכל v.
1) שָׁכַל be bereaved of children
3) שִׁכֵּל a. bereave of children
b. destroy
6) הִשְׁכִּיל bereave of children

שכם v.
6) הִשְׁכִּים rise early
הַשְׁכֵּם וְ- (do) repeatedly

שֶׁכֶם (שְׁכֶם), שְׁכֶם- ; n.m. shoulder

שְׁכֶם pr.n. a. Shechem (m.)
b. Nablus (city) (f.)

שכן v.
1) שָׁכַן a. reside; dwell
b. be a resident
3) שִׁכֵּן cause to dwell; settle
6) הִשְׁכִּין cause to dwell; establish

שָׁכֵן, שְׁכַן- ; **שְׁכֵנָה** ; **שְׁכֵנִים** n., adj.
neighbor (root: שכן)

שׂכר v.
1) שָׂכַר hire
2) נִשְׂכַּר be hired
5) הִשְׂתַּכֵּר earn wages

שָׂכָר, שְׂכַר- ; n.m. a. wage; salary
b. cost
c. reward (root: שׂכר)

שכר v.
1) שָׁכַר be drunk
שָׁכוּר drunkard
3) שִׁכֵּר make (someone) drunk
5) הִשְׁתַּכֵּר become drunk
6) הִשְׁכִּיר cause to be drunk

שֵׁכָר n.m. liquor; intoxicating drink
(root: שכר)

שֶׁל prep. a. of (belonging to)
b. made of
(see also שֶׁ-)

שֶׁלֶג, שֶׁלֶג- ; n.m. snow

שלה v.
1) שָׁלָה be at ease
2) נִשְׁלָה be at ease
6) הִשְׁלָה deceive

שָׁלֵו ; **שְׁלֵוָה** ; **שַׁלְוֵי-** ; adj. calm
(root: שלה)

שַׁלְוָה, שַׁלְוַת- ; n.f. calmness
(root: שלה)

שָׁלוֹם, שְׁלוֹם- ; **שְׁלוֹמִים** n.m.
a. calmness
b. safety; security
c. peace
d. condition; standing
question about the health or condition of someone הֲשָׁלוֹם

שָׁלוֹשׁ ; **שְׁלוֹשָׁה** ; **שְׁלוֹשִׁים**
see שָׁלֹשׁ ; שְׁלֹשָׁה ; שְׁלֹשִׁים

שלח v.
1) שָׁלַח a. send
b. send by messenger
c. extend; stretch out
d. expel
2) נִשְׁלַח be sent
3) שִׁלַּח a. dismiss; send away
b. release
c. expel
d. divorce
e. send forth
f. stretch out
4) שֻׁלַּח a. be dismissed
b. be expelled
c. be abandoned
d. be sent
6) הִשְׁלִיחַ a. send
b. bring about

שֶׁלַח n.m. a. sword
b. irrigation ditch

שֻׁלְחָן, שֻׁלְחַן- ; **שֻׁלְחָנוֹת, שֻׁלְחֲנוֹת-** ;
n.m. table

שלט v.
1) שָׁלַט rule; govern
6) הִשְׁלִיט make a ruler

שֶׁלֶט ; **שְׁלָטִים, שִׁלְטֵי-** ; n.m. shield

שַׁלִּיט ; שַׁלֶּטֶת ; שַׁלִּיטִים n., adj.
ruler; master (root: שלט)

שָׁלִישׁ ; שָׁלִישִׁים n.m.
a. military officer
b. measure of volume
c. musical instrument

שְׁלִישִׁי ; שְׁלִישִׁית ; שְׁלִישִׁים adj.
third
See also "Grammar", section 14.2

שְׁלִישִׁית, שְׁלִישִׁית- ; n.f. one third

שלך v.
6) הִשְׁלִיךְ a. throw; cast
b. remove; drive away
7) הָשְׁלַךְ be thrown

שלל v.
1) שָׁלַל a. loot; plunder
b. pull out
5) הִשְׁתּוֹלֵל be despoiled

שָׁלָל, שְׁלַל- ; n.m. booty; loot
(root: שלל)

שלם v.
1) שָׁלֵם a. be completed
b. be safe
3) שִׁלֵּם a. complete
b. restore
c. pay a debt
d. fulfill an obligation
4) שֻׁלַּם be paid (a debt)
6) הִשְׁלִים a. finish; complete
b. make peace
7) הָשְׁלַם be made (peace)

שָׁלֵם ; שְׁלֵמָה ; שְׁלֵמִים ; שְׁלֵמוֹת adj.
a. unharmed
b. whole
c. perfect
d. faithful (root: שלם)

שָׁלֵם pr.n.f. Jerusalem's former name

שֶׁלֶם ; שְׁלָמִים, שַׁלְמֵי- ; n.m.
offering of well-being (to God)
(root: שלם)

שַׂלְמָה, שַׂלְמַת- ; שְׂלָמוֹת, שַׂלְמוֹת- ;
n.f. garment; robe

שְׁלֹמֹה pr.n.m. Solomon
(roots: שָׁלוֹם, שָׁלֵם)

שלף v.
1) שָׁלַף a. draw out (a sword)
b. remove

שלש v.
3) שִׁלֵּשׁ a. divide into three parts
b. do on the third day
c. do a third time
4) מְשֻׁלָּשׁ a. 3-years old
b. woven of three threads
c. of three floors

שָׁלֹשׁ (שָׁלוֹשׁ), שְׁלֹשׁ- ; adj., n.f.
three
See also "Grammar", section 14.1

שְׁלֹשָׁה (שְׁלוֹשָׁה), שְׁלֹשֶׁת- ; adj., n.m.
three
See also "Grammar", section 14.1

שִׁלְשׁוֹם adv. the day before yesterday

שְׁלֹשִׁים adj., n.m.f. thirty
See also "Grammar", section 14.1

שֵׁם, שֵׁם- ; שֵׁמוֹת, שְׁמוֹת- ; n.m.
a. name; designation
b. designation of God
c. fame; reputation
in the name of...; בְּשֵׁם-
by the authority of...

שֵׁם pr.n.m. Shem ("name")

שָׁם adv. a. there
b. thereto
thereto שָׁמָּה

שְׂמֹאל n.m.f. a. left side
b. left hand

שְׂמָאלִי ; שְׂמָאלִית adj. left;
left-handed

שמד v.
2) נִשְׁמַד a. be destroyed
b. be exterminated
6) הִשְׁמִיד a. destroy
b. exterminate

שָׁמָּה adv. a. there
b. thereto

שַׁמָּה ; שַׁמּוֹת n.f. a. desolation;
destruction
b. consternation
c. horror

שְׁמוּאֵל pr.n.m. Samuel
("requested from God")
(roots: שָׁאוּל, מֵ, אֵל)

שְׁמוֹנָה (שְׁמֹנָה), שְׁמוֹנַת- ; n.m.
eight
See also "Grammar", section 14.1

שְׁמוֹנֶה (שְׁמֹנֶה) n.f. eight
See also "Grammar", section 14.1

שְׁמוֹנִים (שְׁמֹנִים) n.m.f. eighty
See also "Grammar", section 14.1

שְׁמוּעָה, שְׁמוּעַת- ; שְׁמוּעוֹת n.f. news;
information; report (root: שמע)

שְׁמוֹת The Book of Exodus
"the names of..."

שמח v.
1) שָׂמַח rejoice
3) שִׂמַּח cause to rejoice
6) הִשְׂמִיחַ cause to rejoice

שָׂמֵחַ ; שְׂמֵחָה ; שְׂמֵחִים, שְׂמֵחֵי-,
שְׂמֵחוֹת- ; adj. glad; happy
(root: שׂמח)

שִׂמְחָה, שִׂמְחַת- ; שְׂמָחוֹת n.f. joy
(root: שׂמח)

שמט v.
1) שָׁמַט a. abandon
b. detach
c. let go; drop
d. slip
e. fall
2) נִשְׁמַט a. be moved
b. be dropped
6) הִשְׁמִיט cause to drop

שְׁמִטָּה n.f. remission
(of debts, every 7 years) (root: שמט)

שָׁמַיִם, שְׁמֵי- ; n.m.pl. a. heavens; sky
b. Heavens

שְׁמִינִי ; שְׁמִינִית adj. eighth
See also "Grammar", section 14.2

שָׁמִיר n.m. a. thorny bush; thistle
b. adamant, hard substance

שִׂמְלָה, שִׂמְלַת- ; שְׂמָלוֹת, שִׂמְלוֹת- ;
n.f. robe; garment

שמם v.
1) שָׁמַם a. be desolate; be deserted
b. be appalled
2) נָשַׁם a. be destroyed
b. be appalled
3) שׁוֹמֵם a. cause horror
b. be horrified
5) הִשְׁתּוֹמֵם a. be amazed
b. be horrified
6) הִשְׁמִים, הֵשַׁם a. destroy
b. horrify
7) הָשַׁם be horrified

שָׁמֵם ; שְׁמֵמָה adj. desolate
(root: שמם)

שְׁמָמָה ; שְׁמָמוֹת, שִׁמְמוֹת- ; n.f.
a. desolation
b. anxiety; horror (root: שמם)

שמן v.
1) שָׁמַן be fat; grow fat
6) הִשְׁמִין a. be fat
b. fatten

שָׁמֵן ; שְׁמֵנָה adj. a. fat
b. stout
c. robust (root: שמן)

שֶׁמֶן, שֶׁמֶן- ; שְׁמָנִים n.m. a. oil
b. fat (root: שמן)

שְׁמֹנָה ; שְׁמֹנֶה ; שְׁמֹנִים
see שְׁמוֹנָה ; שְׁמוֹנֶה ; שְׁמוֹנִים

שמע v.
1) שָׁמַע a. hear
b. listen
c. obey
d. know
e. understand
f. recognize
2) נִשְׁמַע a. be heard
b. be accepted
c. obey
3) שִׁמַּע summon
6) הִשְׁמִיעַ a. announce
b. summon

שֵׁמַע, שֵׁמַע- ; n.m. a. report
b. hearing (root: שמע)

שֹׁמַע n.m. fame (root: שמע)

שִׁמְעוֹן pr.n.m. Simeon ("heard" ?)
(root: שמע)

שְׁמַעְיָה(וּ) pr.n.m. Shemaiah
("hear, o Lord") (roots: שמע, יָהּ)

שמר v.
1) שָׁמַר a. guard
b. watch over
c. keep
d. heed
2) נִשְׁמַר be careful; heed
3) שִׁמֵּר cling to
5) הִשְׁתַּמֵּר a. be careful
b. be guarded

שְׁמָרִים n.m.pl. dregs; sediment; lees

שֶׁמֶשׁ, שֶׁמֶשׁ- ; שְׁמָשׁוֹת- ; n.m.f. sun

שִׁמְשׁוֹן pr.n.m. Samson
(root: שֶׁמֶשׁ ?)

שֵׁן, שֵׁן-, שֶׁן- ; שִׁנַּיִם, שִׁנֵּי- ; n.f.
a. tooth
b. ivory
c. peak; crag

שׂנא v.
1) שָׂנֵא hate
שָׂנוּא unloved
2) נִשְׂנָא be unloved
3) מְשַׂנֵּא enemy (present tense)

שִׂנְאָה, שִׂנְאַת- ; n.f. a. hatred
b. enmity (root: שׂנא)

שנה v.
1) שָׁנָה a. change
b. repeat
2) נִשְׁנָה be repeated
3) שִׁנָּה alter
4) שֻׁנָּה be altered
5) הִשְׁתַּנָּה disguise oneself

שָׁנָה, שְׁנַת- ; שָׁנִים, שְׁנֵי-, שְׁנוֹת- ;
n.f. year
this year הַשָּׁנָה

שֵׁנָה, שְׁנַת- ; שֵׁנוֹת n.f. sleep
(root: ישן)

שָׁנוּן v. שנן sharp

שָׁנִי n.m. a. scarlet
b. crimson thread
c. crimson cloth

שֵׁנִי ; שֵׁנִית ; שְׁנִיִּים adj. second
See also "Grammar", section 14.2

שְׁנַיִם, שְׁנֵים-, שְׁנֵי- ; adj., n.m.
two
See also "Grammar", section 14.1

שֵׁנִית adv.
again;
for the second time (root: שֵׁנִי)

שנן v.
1) שָׁנַן sharpen
שָׁנוּן sharp
3) שִׁנֵּן teach diligently

שִׁנְעָר pr.n.f. Shinar
(alternate name of Babylon)

שסה v.
1) שָׁסָה plunder
שָׁסוּי plundered
3) שׁוֹסָה, שׁוֹשָׁה a. plunder
b. destroy

שסס v.
1) שָׁסַס plunder
2) נָשַׁס be plundered

שסע v.
1) שָׁסַע split
3) שִׁסַּע a. split; rent
b. interrupt someone

שעה v.
1) שָׁעָה a. look at
b. turn to (אֶל, לְ)
c. run away from (מִן)
5) הִשְׁתָּעָה look at each other
6) הִשְׁעָה a. remove
b. seal

שְׂעוֹרָה, שְׂעוֹרִים n.f. barley

שָׂעִיר, שְׂעִיר-; שְׂעִירִים, שְׂעִירֵי- ; n.m.
a. demon
b. he-goat

שֵׂעִיר pr.n.m.f. Seir
a. Edom, the son of Esau
b. the land of Edom (root: שֵׂעָר ?)

שען v.
2) נִשְׁעַן a. lean
b. trust
c. be near

שער v.
1) שָׂעַר a. stir fear
b. shudder
2) נִשְׂעַר be stormy
3) שֵׂעֵר carry away
5) הִשְׂתָּעֵר attack; storm

שֵׂעָר, שַׂעַר-, שְׂעַר- ; n.m. hair

שַׁעַר, שַׁעַר-; שְׁעָרִים, שַׁעֲרֵי- ; n.m.
a. gate
b. measure

שַׂעֲרָה, שַׂעֲרַת-; שַׂעֲרוֹת n.f.
single hair (root: שֵׂעָר)

שַׁעֲשׁוּעִים n.m.pl. pleasure; delight
(root: שעשע)

שעשע v.
3) שִׁעֲשַׁע be delighted; have pleasure
4) שֻׁעֲשַׁע be delighted
5) הִשְׁתַּעֲשַׁע a. be delighted
b. be amazed

שָׂפָה, שְׂפַת-; שְׂפָתַיִם, שִׂפְתֵי-, שִׂפְתוֹת- ; n.f.
a. edge; rim
b. shore
c. lip
d. speech; language

שִׁפְחָה, שִׁפְחַת-; שְׁפָחוֹת, שִׁפְחוֹת- ; n.f.
maid; handmaid

שפט v.
1) שָׁפַט a. judge
b. rule
c. punish
d. condemn
2) נִשְׁפַּט a. be judged
b. plead
c. punish

שְׁפָטִים n.m.pl.
a. judgement
b. punishment (root: שפט)

שְׁפִי ; שְׁפָיִים n.m.
hill

שפך v.
1) שָׁפַךְ a. pour; spill
b. throw
2) נִשְׁפַּךְ a. be poured
b. be thrown
4) שֻׁפַּךְ a. be poured
b. be thrown
5) הִשְׁתַּפֵּךְ a. be spilled
b. run out

שפל v.
1) שָׁפַל a. become low
b. be weak
6) הִשְׁפִּיל a. lower
b. humiliate

שָׁפָל, שְׁפַל- ; שְׁפָלָה, שִׁפְלַת- ; שְׁפָלִים adj.
a. low
b. deep
c. modest; meek
d. mean (root: שפל)

שְׁפֵלָה n.f.
a. lowland
b. the coastal plain of Israel

שָׂפָם n.m.
moustache
(root: שָׂפָה)

שָׁפָן ; שְׁפַנִּים n.m.
a. daman; cony; pika; rabbit
b. Shaffan (pr.n.m.)

שִׁפְעָה, שִׁפְעַת- ; n.f.
abundance

שפת v.
1) שָׁפַת a. establish
b. set (a pot, etc.) over a fire

שַׂק ; שַׂקִּים n.m.
a. sack; bag
b. sackcloth

שקד v.
1) שָׁקַד a. keep watch
b. be eager
4) מְשֻׁקָּד almond-shaped (present tense)

שָׁקֵד ; שְׁקֵדִים n.m.
a. almond tree
b. almond

שקה v.
6) הִשְׁקָה a. give a drink
b. water

שִׁקּוּץ, שִׁקּוּץ- ; שִׁקּוּצִים, שִׁקּוּצֵי- ; n.m.
a. abomination
b. idol (root: שקץ)

שקט v.
1) שָׁקַט rest; be quiet
6) הִשְׁקִיט give rest; calm; pacify

שקל v.
1) שָׁקַל a. weigh
b. pay
2) נִשְׁקַל a. be weighed
b. be paid

שֶׁקֶל, שֶׁקֶל- ; שְׁקָלִים, שִׁקְלֵי- ; n.m.
Biblical weight and coin
(= twenty גֵּרָה) (root: שקל)

שִׁקְמָה ; שִׁקְמִים n.f.
sycamore

שקע v.
1) שָׁקַע sink; go down
2) נִשְׁקַע sink
6) הִשְׁקִיעַ cause to sink

שקף v.
2) נִשְׁקַף a. be seen
b. look
6) הִשְׁקִיף look

שקץ v.
3) שִׁקֵּץ detest

שֶׁקֶץ n.m.
a. abomination
b. ritually unclean animal
(root: שקץ)

שׁקר v.
1) שָׁקַר lie
3) שִׁקֵּר lie

שֶׁקֶר ; שְׁקָרִים n.m. lie
in vain לַשֶּׁקֶר

שַׂר, שַׂר- ; שָׂרִים, שָׂרֵי- ; n.m.
a. leader
b. ruler
c. captain
d. prince (root: שׂרר)

שַׁרְבִיט n.m. scepter

שׂרה v.
1) שָׂרָה fight; contend

שָׂרָה ; שָׂרוֹת n.f. a. princess
b. Sarah ("princess") pr.n.f. (root: שׂרר)

שָׁרוֹן pr.n.m. Sharon,
the northern seacoast region of Israel

שׂרט v.
1) שָׂרַט a. scratch
b. tattoo

שָׂרִיד ; שְׂרִידִים, שְׂרִידֵי- ; n.m.
a. survivor
b. refugee

שִׁרְיוֹן ; שִׁרְיוֹנוֹת, שִׁרְיוֹנִים n.m.
armored breastplate

שְׁרִירוּת-לֵב n.f. stubbornness
("hardness of the heart")

שׂרף v.
1) שָׂרַף burn; set fire to
2) נִשְׂרַף be burned

שָׂרָף ; שְׂרָפִים n.m. a. serpent
b. fiery angel ("seraph") (root: שׂרף)

שְׂרֵפָה, שְׂרֵפַת- ; n.f. fire; burning
(root: שׂרף)

שׁרץ v.
1) שָׁרַץ a. swarm; teem
b. crawl; creep
c. breed (insects, snakes, etc.)

שֶׁרֶץ, שֶׁרֶץ- ; n.m.
creeping, crawling or swarming
creatures (insects, snakes, etc.)
(root: שׁרץ)

שׁרק v.
1) שָׁרַק a. whistle
b. whistle with amazement or derision

שְׁרֵקָה n.f. derisive whistle or hiss
(root: שׁרק)

שׂרר v.
1) שָׂרַר rule over
5) הִשְׂתָּרֵר become ruler; dominate
6) הֵשִׂיר make king
(see also שַׂר)

שׁרשׁ v.
3) שֵׁרֵשׁ uproot
4) שֹׁרַשׁ a. be uprooted
b. take root
6) הִשְׁרִישׁ a. strike root
b. thrive

שֹׁרֶשׁ, שֹׁרֶשׁ- ; שָׁרָשֵׁי- ; n.m. a. root
b. source
c. basis; origin (root: שׁרשׁ)

שַׁרְשֶׁרֶת ; שַׁרְשְׁרוֹת, שַׁרְשְׁרוֹת- ; n.f.
chain

שׁרת v.
3) שֵׁרֵת a. serve
b. officiate at the Temple (serve God)
c. worship idols
(see also מְשָׁרֵת)

שֵׁשׁ n.m. a. fine linen
b. white marble

שֵׁשׁ, שֶׁשׁ- ; adj., n.f. six
See "Grammar", section 14.1

שִׁשָּׁה, שֵׁשֶׁת- ; adj., n.m. six
See "Grammar", section 14.1

שָׂשׂוֹן, שְׂשׂוֹן- ;n.m. joy (root: שׂישׂ)

שִׁשִּׁי ; **שִׁשִּׁית** adj. sixth
See "Grammar", section 14.2

שִׁשִּׁים n.m.f. sixty
See "Grammar", section 14.1

שֵׁשֶׁת see שִׁשָּׁה

שֵׁת ; **שֵׁתוֹת** n.m. a. buttocks
b. Seth (pr.n.m.)

שתה v.
1) שָׁתָה drink
2) נִשְׁתָּה be drunk

שְׁתִי n.m. a. warp (in weaving)
b. drinking (root: שתה)

שְׁתַּיִם, שְׁתֵּים-, שְׁתֵּי- ; adj., n.f.
two
See "Grammar", section 14.1

שתל v.
1) שָׁתַל plant

שתן v.
6) הִשְׁתִּין urinate

ת

תָּא, תָּא- ; **תָּאִים, תָּאֵי-**; n.m.
a. compartment
b. room

תַּאֲוָה, תַּאֲוַת- ; n.f.
a. desire (root: אוה)
b. border

תְּאוֹמִים, תְּאוֹמֵי- ; n.m.pl.
twins

תְּאֵנָה ; **תְּאֵנִים, תְּאֵנֵי-** ; n.f.
fig (tree or fruit)

תאר v.
1) תָּאַר surround
3) תֵּאֵר draw (a line)
4) תֹּאַר be drawn (a line)

תֵּבָה, תֵּבַת- ; n.f.
a. ark
b. box

תְּבוּאָה, תְּבוּאַת- ; **תְּבוּאוֹת, תְּבוּאוֹת-** ; n.f.
a. yield of the field; harvest
b. produce (root: בוא)

תְּבוּנָה ; **תְּבוּנוֹת** n.f.
a. understanding
b. wisdom (root: בין)

תֵּבֵל n.f.
world

תֶּבֶן n.m.
straw

תַּבְנִית, תַּבְנִית- ; n.f.
pattern; shape (root: בנה)

תֹּהוּ n.m.
a. void; emptiness
b. vanity
c. worthlessness
d. in vain (adv.)

תְּהוֹם ; **תְּהוֹמוֹת, תְּהוֹמוֹת-** ; n.m.f.
a. primeval water
b. deep underground water
c. abyss

תְּהִלָּה, תְּהִלַּת- ; **תְּהִלּוֹת-** ; n.f.
a. praise
b. fame (root: הלל)

תְּהִלִּים, תְּהִלִּים n.m.pl.
the Book of Psalms ("praises")
(root: הלל)

תַּהְפּוּכָה ; **תַּהְפּוּכוֹת** n.f.
treachery; duplicity
(root: הפך)

תּוֹדָה, תּוֹדַת- ; **תּוֹדוֹת-** ; n.f.
a. thanksgiving
b. sacrifice of thanksgiving
c. thanksgiving choir
(root: ידה)

תּוֹחֶלֶת, תּוֹחֶלֶת- ; n.f.
hope (root: יחל)

תָּוֶךְ, תּוֹךְ- ; n.m.
middle
בְּתוֹךְ among; inside
מִתּוֹךְ from among

תּוֹכַחַת, תּוֹכַחַת- ; **תּוֹכָחוֹת, תּוֹכְחוֹת-** ; n.f.
reproof; chiding
(root: יכח)

תּוֹלָדוֹת, תּוֹלְדוֹת- ; n.f.pl.
a. generations; offspring (root: ילד)
b. history; annals

תּוֹלַעַת, תּוֹלַעַת- ; **תּוֹלָעִים** n.f.
a. worm
b. crimson (color and cloth)

תּוֹעֵבָה, תּוֹעֲבַת-; תּוֹעֵבוֹת, תּוֹעֲבוֹת-; n.f.
abomination
(root: תעב)

תּוֹצָאָה; תּוֹצָאוֹת, תּוֹצְאוֹת-; n.f.
a. escape
b. edge; extremity
(root: יצא)

תור v.
1) תָּר a. explore; scout
b. probe
6) הֵתִיר explore

תּוֹר, תּוֹר-; תּוֹרִים, תּוֹרֵי-; n.m.
a. appointed time
b. plaited wreath
c. turtledove

תּוֹרָה, תּוֹרַת-; תּוֹרוֹת, תּוֹרוֹת-; n.f.
a. teaching; instruction
b. Torah, the Five Books of Moses, the first division of the Bible ("teaching")
See also "The Books of the Bible"

תּוֹשָׁב, תּוֹשַׁב-; תּוֹשָׁבִים, תּוֹשָׁבֵי-; n.m.
resident; settler
(root: ישב)

תּוּשִׁיָּה n.f.
a. wisdom
b. advice

תַּזְנוּת n.f.
a. lust
b. fornication (root: זנה)

תַּחְבּוּלָה; תַּחְבּוּלוֹת, תַּחְבּוּלוֹת-; n.f.
a. strategy
b. counsel

תְּחִלָּה, תְּחִלַּת-; n.f.
a. beginning
b. inception (root: חלל)

תַּחֲלוּאִים, תַּחֲלוּאֵי-; n.m.pl.
diseases (root: חלה)

תְּחִנָּה, תְּחִנַּת-; תְּחִנּוֹת n.f.
a. prayer
b. mercy (root: חנן)

תַּחֲנוּנִים, תַּחֲנוּנֵי-; n.m.pl.
supplications; prayers
(root: חנן)

תַּחַשׁ; תְּחָשִׁים n.m.
a. dolphin (?)
b. badger (?)

תַּחַת prep.
a. under; below
b. instead of; for
because תַּחַת אֲשֶׁר, תַּחַת כִּי

תַּחְתּוֹן; תַּחְתּוֹנָה; תַּחְתּוֹנוֹת adj.
lower (root: תַּחַת)

תַּחְתִּי; תַּחְתִּיָּה, תַּחְתִּית; תַּחְתִּיִּים; תַּחְתִּיּוֹת adj.
lower
(root: תַּחַת)

תַּחְתִּית; תַּחְתִּיּוֹת n.f.
bottom;
lowest part (root: תַּחַת)

תִּיכוֹן; תִּיכוֹנָה; תִּיכוֹנוֹת adj.
center; middle (root: תּוֹךְ)

תִּימֹרָה; תִּימֹרִים, תִּימֹרוֹת n.f.
ornament shaped like a palm tree
(root: תָּמָר)

תֵּימָן n.m., pr.n.f.m.
a. south
b. city and region in Edom (pr.n.f.)
c. Teiman (pr.n.m.)

תִּירוֹשׁ n.m.
new unfermented wine

תַּיִשׁ; תְּיָשִׁים n.m.
he-goat

תַּכְלִית, תַּכְלִית-; n.f.
a. end
b. edge (root: כלה)

תְּכֵלֶת n.f.
blue dye

תכן v.
1) תָּכַן a. measure
b. examine
2) נִתְכַּן a. be measured
b. be examined
3) תִּכֵּן set measure to...
4) תֻּכַּן a. be measured
b. be calculated

תֵּל, תֵּל- ; n.m. a. mound
b. heap of rubble

תלה v.
1) תָּלָה a. hang
b. suspend
תָּלוּי hanged; hung
2) נִתְלָה be hanged
3) תִּלָּה hang up

תלל v.
6) הֵתֵל a. mock
b. deceive
7) הֻתַּל be mocked

תֶּלֶם, תֶּלֶם- ; **תַּלְמֵי-** ; n.m. furrow

תְּלֻנָּה ; **תְּלֻנּוֹת** n.f. complaint
(root: לון)

תָּם ; **תַּמָּה** ; **תַּמִּים** adj.
a. complete; perfect
b. fitting; matching

תֹּם, תֹּם-, תֻּם- ; n.m. a. honesty
b. innocence
c. perfection (root: תמם)

תֻּמָּה, תֻּמַּת- ; n.f. a. honesty
b. innocence
c. integrity (root: תמם)

תמה v.
1) תָּמַהּ a. wonder
b. be astonished
5) הִתַּמְהַהּ be astonished

תְּמוֹל adv. yesterday

תְּמוּנָה, תְּמוּנַת- ; n.f.
image; likeness

תְּמוּרָה n.f. exchange
(root: מור)

תָּמִיד adv., n.m. a. always
b. continuity; eternity
c. short form for עוֹלַת-תָּמִיד, a daily offering at the Temple

תָּמִים, תְּמִים- ; **תְּמִימָה** ; **תְּמִימִים, תְּמִימֵי-** ; **תְּמִימוֹת** adj.
a. whole
b. unblemished
c. honest
d. perfect
e. honesty (n.m.s.) (root: תמם)

תֻּמִּים n.m.pl.
objects on the breastplate of the High Priest (always together with אוּרִים)

תמך v.
1) תָּמַךְ a. support; hold up
b. help
2) נִתְמַךְ be held up; be supported

תמם v.
1) תָּמַם, תַּם a. be completed; come to an end
b. be destroyed
2) נִתַּם be destroyed
5) הִתַּמֵּם behave honestly
6) הֵתֵם a. complete
b. destroy

תָּמָר, תֹּמֶר ; **תְּמָרִים** n.m., pr.n.f.
a. palm tree
b. Tamar

תֵּן ; **תְּנִי** ; **תְּנוּ** נתן v. give!
(imperative tense)

1) קַל (פָּעַל) 2) נִפְעַל 3) פִּעֵל 4) פֻּעַל 5) הִתְפַּעֵל 6) הִפְעִיל 7) הָפְעַל

jackal n.m. תַּן ; תַּנִּים, תַּנּוֹת

תְּנוּבָה, תְּנוּבַת- ; תְּנוּבוֹת- ; n.f.
produce; fruit (root: נוב)

lobe (of the ear) n.m. תְּנוּךְ, תְּנוּךְ- ;

sleep; slumber n.f. תְּנוּמָה ; תְּנוּמוֹת
(root: נום)

תְּנוּפָה, תְּנוּפַת- ; תְּנוּפוֹת- ; n.f.
a. wave offering
b. waving (root: נוף)

תַּנּוּר, תַּנּוּר- ; תַּנּוּרִים n.m.
oven; furnace

תַּנְחוּמִים, תַּנְחוּמוֹת- ; n.m.pl.
condolences (root: נחם)

a. sea monster n.m. תַּנִּין ; תַּנִּינִים
b. dragon
c. serpent

תעב v.
be abhorred 2) נִתְעַב
a. abhor 3) תִּעֵב
b. defile
behave abhorrently 6) הִתְעִיב

תעה v.
a. stray 1) תָּעָה
b. go astray (morally)
c. be confused
be led astray 2) נִתְעָה
lead astray 6) הִתְעָה

תְּעָלָה, תְּעָלַת- ; תְּעָלוֹת n.f.
a. trench; canal
b. remedy; recovery

תַּעֲנוּג ; תַּעֲנוּגִים, תַּעֲנוּגוֹת- ; n.m.
pleasure (root: ענג)

a. razor n.m. תַּעַר, תַּעַר- ;
b. sheath (of a sword)

drum n.m. תֹּף ; תֻּפִּים

a. glory n.f. תִּפְאֶרֶת, תִּפְאֶרֶת- ;
b. beauty (root: פאר)

תַּפּוּחַ ; תַּפּוּחִים, תַּפּוּחֵי- ; n.m.
a. apple (tree or fruit)
b. Tapuach (pr.n.m.)

a. tasteless adj., n.m.s. תָּפֵל
b. plaster (?)

תְּפִלָּה, תְּפִלַּת- ; תְּפִלּוֹת- ; n.f.
prayer; supplication
(root: פלל)

תפש v.
a. hold; grab 1) תָּפַשׂ
b. capture; seize
be captured; be caught 2) נִתְפַּשׂ
seize; hold 3) תִּפֵּשׂ

a. fire n.m. תֹּפֶת
b. site of child sacrifices to the idol Molech

a. hope n.f. תִּקְוָה, תִּקְוַת- ;
b. cord (root: קוה)
c. Tikvah ("hope") (pr.n.f.)

תקע v.
a. drive into; push 1) תָּקַע
b. fix
c. blow a ram's horn
d. clap (hands)
guarantee תָּקַע כַּף
be blown (ram's horn) 2) נִתְקַע

deep sleep n.f. תַּרְדֵּמָה, תַּרְדֵּמַת- ;
(root: רדם)

תְּרוּמָה, תְּרוּמַת- ; תְּרוּמוֹת,
a. donation n.f. תְּרוּמוֹת- ;
(to priests, or the Temple)

b. gift (root: רום)

תְּרוּעָה, תְּרוּעַת- ; n.f.
a. blast (of a trumpet or a ram's horn)
b. shout (root: רוע)

תַּרְמִית, תַּרְמִית- ; n.f. deceit
(root: רמה)

תְּרָפִים n.m.pl. household idols

תַּרְשִׁישׁ n.m.
a. precious stone; beryl (?)
b. Tarshish (pr.n.m.)
c. Mediterranean port city (pr.n.f.)

תִּשְׁבִּי adj.m. of the town of תִּשְׁבֶּה
(describing Elijah the prophet)

תְּשׁוּבָה, תְּשׁוּבַת- ; **תְּשׁוּבוֹת** n.f.
a. cycle; period
b. return
c. reply (root: שוב)

תְּשׁוּעָה, תְּשׁוּעַת- ; n.f. a. help
b. deliverance (root: ישע)

תְּשִׁיעִי ; **תְּשִׁיעִית** adj. ninth
See also "Grammar", section 14.2

תֵּשַׁע, תְּשַׁע- ; adj., n.f. nine
See also "Grammar" section 14.1

תִּשְׁעָה, תִּשְׁעַת- ; adj., n.m. nine
See also "Grammar" section 14.1

תִּשְׁעִים n.m.f. ninety
See also "Grammar" section 14.1

תֵּת נתן v.
1) נָתַן infinitive (construct) of

1) קַל (פָּעַל) 2) נִפְעַל 3) פִּעֵל 4) פֻּעַל 5) הִתְפַּעֵל 6) הִפְעִיל 7) הָפְעַל

GRAMMAR

The Names of God

The Books of the Bible

GRAMMAR

1. THE HEBREW ALPHABET

	Name	Printed
1.	אָלֶף	א
2.	בֵּית, בֵית	ב
3.	גִּימֶל	ג
4.	דָּלֶת	ד
5.	הֵא	ה
6.	וָו	ו
7.	זַיִן	ז
8.	חֵית	ח
9.	טֵית	ט
10.	יוֹד (יוּד)	י
11.	כַּף, כַף	כּ, כ, ך
12.	לָמֶד	ל
13.	מֵם	מ, ם
14.	נוּן	נ, ן
15.	סָמֶךְ	ס
16.	עַיִן	ע
17.	פֵּא, פֵא	פּ, פ, ף
18.	צָדִי(ק)	צ, ץ
19.	קוֹף, קוּף	ק
20.	רֵישׁ	ר
21.	שִׁין, שִׂין	שׁ, שׂ
22.	תָּו, תָו	תּ, ת

Note: In this dictionary, only the letter שׂ carries the upper-left dot. The letter שׁ carries no dot and appears as ש.

2. THE VOWEL POINTS נִקּוּד

Vowel Point	Name
◌ָ	קָמַץ גָּדוֹל
◌ֵ	צֵירֶה
◌ִי	חִירִיק גָּדוֹל
וֹ	חוֹלָם מָלֵא
וּ	שׁוּרֶק
◌ַ	פַּתָּח
◌ֶ	סֶגּוֹל
◌ִ	חִירִיק קָטָן

Vowel Point	Name
◌ֹ	חוֹלָם חָסֵר
◌ָ	קָמַץ קָטָן
◌ֻ	קֻבּוּץ
◌ֲ	חֲטַף-פַּתָּח
◌ֱ	חֲטַף-סֶגּוֹל
◌ֳ	חֲטַף-קָמַץ
◌ְ	שְׁוָא

Notes:
1. Vowel points appear below the letters, except for the חוֹלָם חָסֵר, חוֹלָם מָלֵא and שׁוּרֶק.
2. Strictly, the שְׁוָא is not a vowel point; rather, it marks a consonant without a vowel.

3. DIGGING UP THE ROOT

Consider, in English, the words “going”, “goes”, “bygone”, and “went”; they are all *patterns* of the *root* letters “go”. Suffixes like “ing”, “es” and "ne" and prefixes like “by” are attached to the root letters “go”. “Went” is extreme: it does not retain any of the root letters “go”; still, its root is “go”. Similarly, “am”, “is”, “was”, “been”, and “were” are patterns of the root “be”. A good dictionary will list “went” and “is” as separate entries and cross-reference them with the entries “go” and “be”, respectively.

In Hebrew, the situation is similar: most words are patterned after their root letters. Root letters are normally three (rarely four). Unlike English, no extreme patterns occur; at least two, and often all three of the root letters are found in the patterns. It is easier, therefore, to dig up the root of a word. The other side of the coin is that a full one-half of the Hebrew alphabet, specifically, א, ב, ה, ו, י, כ, ל, מ, נ, ש, ת may be used as suffixes, prefixes, or infixes – as well as being root letters themselves. But that is where the fun and excitement begin.

Let us look at two examples:

a. they were counted הִתְפָּקְדוּ
is the third person plural (they), past tense, of the verbal stem הִתְפָּעֵל for the root פקד. The prefix הִתְ is typical of this stem, and the suffix וּ is typical of the third person plural in the past tense. Such an entry is found in this dictionary both under the root פקד as well as under הִתְפַּקֵּד, third person, masculine singular (he), past tense. More details are found in section 13.

b. and the prophets וְהַנְּבִיאִים
has the prefixes “and” וְ; “the” הַ; and the suffix ים, common for masculine plural. Strip these, and under the entry נָבִיא, we find “prophet”, which, in itself, has the root letters נבא, and is listed there, too.

In summary, finding the root of a word is both educational and exciting. It provides a deeper insight into Hebrew. This section explains the basic ideas and methods of identifying and learning the common patterns of root letters.

4. THE FUNDAMENTAL RULE OF GRAMMAR

Rule: Every rule has its exceptions.
Exceptions: None

This rule, known affectionately as The F.R.O.G., is invoked from time to time in Hebrew, as it is in any other language. The good news is that it is done so much less than, say, in English. Just think of the rule of pronouncing "ough" at the end of a word, and of all the exceptions there!

5. THE PREFIX ה

5.1 The definite article

There is no indefinite article ("a", "an") in Hebrew. So, אִישׁ means "man", or "a man".

The definite article "the" is formed with the prefix הַ or its variations הֶ, הָ.

For example:

covenant = בְּרִית	the covenant = הַבְּרִית
woman = אִשָּׁה	the woman = הָאִשָּׁה
mountains = הָרִים	the mountains = הֶהָרִים

5.2 The interrogative ה

The prefix הֲ or its variations הֶ, הַ, may serve to introduce a question.

For example:

I am my brother's keeper = שֹׁמֵר אָחִי אָנֹכִי

Am I my brother's keeper? (Gen. 4:9) הֲשֹׁמֵר אָחִי אָנֹכִי (בראשית ד 9)

You (m.s.) will build = אַתָּה תִּבְנֶה

Will you build? (II Samuel 7:5) הַאַתָּה תִּבְנֶה (שמואל ב׳ ז 5)

I conceived = אָנֹכִי הָרִיתִי

Did I conceive? (Numbers 11:12) הֶאָנֹכִי הָרִיתִי (במדבר יא 12)

5.3 The directional suffix ה

This suffix is the same as the English suffix "-ward", or "-wards", thus:

North = צָפוֹן	Northward, to the north = צָפוֹנָה

6. THE PREFIXES ב- כ- ל- מ- ש-

6.1 The preposition ב

The preposition ב "in", "with", "by", "at", "among", "for" is prefixed as בְּ, בִּ to indefinite words, as:

in a town בְּעִיר, with words בִּדְבָרִים

and as בַּ, בָּ to definite words, as:

in the town בָּעִיר (instead of בְּהָעִיר)

with the words בַּדְּבָרִים (instead of בְּהַדְּבָרִים)

The declension of בְּ is:

בִּי, בְּךָ, בָּךְ, בּוֹ, בָּהּ, בָּנוּ, בָּכֶם, בָּכֶן, בָּהֶם (בָּם), בָּהֶן (בָּהֵנָּה)

in me, in you (m.s.),in you (f.s.), in him, in her, in us, in you (m.pl.),in you (f.pl.), in them (m.), in them (f.)

The abbreviations m., f., s. and pl., are explained on page 8.

6.2 The preposition כ

The preposition כ "as", "like", "after", "when" is prefixed like ב:

as a man כְּאִישׁ, as the man כָּאִישׁ (instead of כְּהָאִישׁ)

6.3 The preposition ל

The preposition ל "to", "for", "near", "about" follows the same rules as the preposition ב. For its declension, see the entry ל in the dictionary.

6.4 The preposition מ

The preposition מ "from", "of", "more than", "because of" is just a contraction of the separate preposition מִן. Its prefix patterns are מֵ, מִ for an indefinite word, as in:

from a prophet מִנָּבִיא, from a woman מֵאִשָּׁה

However, the definite article ה remains here with definite words:

from the prophet מֵהַנָּבִיא, from the woman מֵהָאִשָּׁה

The declension of מ uses the full and separate preposition מִן as follows:

מִמֶּנִּי, מִמְּךָ, מִמֵּךְ, מִמֶּנּוּ, מִמֶּנָּה, מִמֶּנּוּ, מִכֶּם, מֵהֶם (מֵהֵמָּה), מֵהֶן (מֵהֵנָּה)

from me, from you (m.s.), from you (f.s.), from him, from her, from us, from you (m.pl.), from them (m.), from them (f.)

6.5 The prefix ש

See the entry ש in the dictionary.

7. THE PREFIX ו

The conjunction "and" is the prefix וְ and its variants וֵ, וֶ, וָ, וַ, וּ
Here are several examples:
- and the man וְהָאִישׁ
- fat and blood חֵלֶב וָדָם
- and slaves וַעֲבָדִים

Before the vowel point ְ and before the letters פ, מ, ו, ב, the conjunction ו becomes וּ, as in:
- and words וּדְבָרִים
- and tomorrow וּמָחָר

For additional meanings, see the entry ו in the dictionary.

Note: A special meaning takes place when ו is prefixed to a verb. See section 15.7.

8. GENDER

There is no neuter gender ("it") in Hebrew, only masculine and feminine. In this dictionary, they are indicated by m. and f.
For example:

eye n.f. עַיִן	candle n.m. נֵר	house n.m. בַּיִת
handsome adj.m. יָפֶה	service n.f. עֲבוֹדָה	

where n. stands for "noun" and adj. for "adjective".
See the complete list of abbreviations on page 8.
A common ending of the feminine singular is ָה , or ת.
For example:
- woman, wife n.f. אִשָּׁה   covenant n.f. בְּרִית

but remember the F.R.O.G. Similarly, but not always, a typical ending of the masculine singular is ֶה , as in
- seer n.m. רוֹאֶה.

9. NUMBER

9.1 Masculine plural (m.pl.)

To form this plural, we usually add to the singular the suffix ים

horse סוּס	horses סוּסִים
seer רוֹאֶה	seers רוֹאִים

9.2 Feminine plural (f.pl.)

This plural is formed by usually replacing the singular ending ה with the suffix וֹת, as in:

war מִלְחָמָה wars מִלְחָמוֹת

Note: The F.R.O.G. is very evident in forming such exceptional plurals as:

father (m.s.) אָב fathers (m.pl.) אָבוֹת

year (f.s.) שָׁנָה years (f.pl.) שָׁנִים

9.3 The dual plural

Body parts and nouns that are pairs have a special form of plural, with the suffix ַיִם .

For example:

hand (n.f.) יָד hands (f.pl.) יָדַיִם

wing (n.f.) כָּנָף wings (f.pl.) כְּנָפַיִם

day (n.m.) יוֹם two days (m.pl.) יוֹמַיִם

shoe (n.f.) נַעַל shoes (f.pl.) נַעֲלַיִם

Note: The F.R.O.G. hits נַעַל twice: the plural נְעָלִים is also found in the Bible – and it is a regular m.pl. ending to נַעַל which is f.s.!

9.4 Only plural

Several nouns have only the plural form; examples include:

pity (n.m.pl.) רַחֲמִים water (m.pl.) מַיִם

face (n.m.pl.) פָּנִים heaven (n.m.pl.) שָׁמַיִם

handmill (n.m.pl.) רֵחַיִם life (n.m.pl.) חַיִּים

10. THE CONSTRUCT FORM

When two words are dependent on each other, we use in English the form "of" or "s", as in "the son of Noah", or "Noah's son". In Hebrew, this *construct form* puts the two words together, usually hyphenated, and the first word is slightly changed. In our example, we have:

son בֵּן, son of בֶּן son of Noah (or Noah's son) בֶּן-נֹחַ

More examples:

life חַיִּים Sarah's life חַיֵּי שָׂרָה

man אָדָם, hand יָד a man's hand יַד-אָדָם

Rule: In the construct form, the definite article "the" ה is always prefixed to the second word, *never* to the first one. So:

the man’s hand יַד הָאָדָם (not הַיַּד אָדָם).

In this dictionary, the construct form is listed after the singular and after the plural, for example:
hand, hand of; hands, hands of יָד, יַד- ; יָדַיִם, יְדֵי-

11. PRONOUN SUFFIXES

In English, possession is expressed by separate pronouns, “my”, “your”, “his”, etc. before the noun. In Hebrew we use suffixes.

Here are a few examples:

1. horse (n.m.s.) סוּס
   סוּסִי, סוּסְךָ, סוּסֵךְ, סוּסוֹ, סוּסָהּ, סוּסֵנוּ, סוּסְכֶם, סוּסְכֶן, סוּסָם, סוּסָן
   my horse, your (m.s.) horse, your (f.s.) horse, his horse, her horse, our horse, your (m.pl.) horse, your (f.pl.) horse, their (m.pl.) horse, their (f.pl.) horse

2. wall (n.f.s.) חוֹמָה
   חוֹמָתִי, חוֹמָתְךָ, חוֹמָתֵךְ, חוֹמָתוֹ, חוֹמָתָהּ, חוֹמָתֵנוּ, חוֹמַתְכֶם, חוֹמַתְכֶן, חוֹמָתָם, חוֹמָתָן
   my wall, your (m.s.) wall, your (f.s.) wall, his wall, her wall, our wall, your (m.pl.) wall, your (f.pl.) wall, their (m.pl.) wall, their (f.pl.) wall

3. horses (n.m.pl.) סוּסִים
   סוּסַי, סוּסֶיךָ, סוּסַיִךְ, סוּסָיו, סוּסֶיהָ, סוּסֵינוּ, סוּסֵיכֶם, סוּסֵיכֶן, סוּסֵיהֶם, סוּסֵיהֶן
   my horses, your (m.s.) horses, your (f.s.) horses, his horses, her horses, our horses, your (m.pl.) horses, your (f.pl.) horses, their (m.pl.) horses, their (f.pl.) horses

4. walls (n.f.pl.) חוֹמוֹת
   חוֹמוֹתַי, חוֹמוֹתֶיךָ, חוֹמוֹתַיִךְ, חוֹמוֹתָיו, חוֹמוֹתֶיהָ, חוֹמוֹתֵינוּ, חוֹמוֹתֵיכֶם, חוֹמוֹתֵיכֶן, חוֹמוֹתֵיהֶם, חוֹמוֹתֵיהֶן
   my walls, your (m.s.) walls, your (f.s.) walls, his walls, her walls, our walls, your (m.pl.) walls, your (f.pl.) walls, their (m.pl.) walls, their (f.pl.) walls

The general pattern of the pronoun suffixes is evident from these examples. Exceptions may occur in the vowel points of the root letters, not the suffixes.

Examples:

child (n.m.s) יֶלֶד — יַלְדִּי, יַלְדְּךָ, יַלְדֵּךְ, ...
soul (n.f.s.) נְשָׁמָה — נִשְׁמָתִי, נִשְׁמָתְךָ, נִשְׁמָתֵךְ, ...
house (n.m.s.) בַּיִת — בֵּיתִי, בֵּיתְךָ, בֵּיתֵךְ, ...

12. ADJECTIVES

The adjective follows the noun and agrees in gender and number. If the noun is definite, the adjective is prefixed with the definite article ה.

Examples:

a good man אִישׁ טוֹב	the good man הָאִישׁ הַטּוֹב
a good woman אִשָּׁה טוֹבָה	the good woman הָאִשָּׁה הַטּוֹבָה
good words דְּבָרִים טוֹבִים	the good words הַדְּבָרִים הַטּוֹבִים
good years שָׁנִים טוֹבוֹת	the good years הַשָּׁנִים הַטּוֹבוֹת

However, הָאִישׁ טוֹב is a complete sentence, "the man is good".
The verb "to be" היה does not have an explicit form in the present tense; it is simply implied by the context.
Sometimes, an adjective appears in the construct form. For example, the two words:

eyes עֵינַיִם
fair, handsome (adj.m.s.) יָפֶה

become an adjective in the construct form

bright-eyed (adj.m.s.) יְפֵה-עֵינַיִם

13. PERSONAL PRONOUNS

13.1 Subject

אָנֹכִי (אֲנִי), אַתָּה, אַתְּ, הוּא, הִיא, אֲנַחְנוּ, אַתֶּם, אַתֶּן, הֵם (הֵמָּה), הֵן (הֵנָּה)

I, you or thou (m.s.), you or thou (f.s.), he, she, we, you (m.pl.), you (f.pl.), they (m.), they (f.)

13.2 Object

אֹתִי, אֹתְךָ, אֹתָךְ, אֹתוֹ, אֹתָהּ, אֹתָנוּ, אֶתְכֶם, אֶתְכֶן, אֹתָם (אֶתְהֶם), אֹתָן (אֶתְהֶן)

Me, you or thee (m.s.), you or thee (f.s.), him, her, us, you (m.pl.), you (f.pl.), them (m.), them (f.).

14. NUMBERS

14.1 Cardinal numbers

Cardinal numbers (“one”, “two”, “three”...) are used in the absolute form or the construct form, masculine or feminine.

Masculine			Feminine	
Absolute	Construct		Absolute	Construct
אֶחָד	אַחַד	1	אַחַת	אַחַת
שְׁנַיִם	שְׁנֵי	2	שְׁתַּיִם	שְׁתֵּי
שְׁלֹשָׁה	שְׁלֹשֶׁת	3	שָׁלֹשׁ	שְׁלֹשׁ (שְׁלָשׁ)
אַרְבָּעָה	אַרְבַּעַת	4	אַרְבַּע	אַרְבַּע
חֲמִשָּׁה	חֲמֵשֶׁת	5	חָמֵשׁ	חֲמֵשׁ
שִׁשָּׁה	שֵׁשֶׁת	6	שֵׁשׁ	שֵׁשׁ
שִׁבְעָה	שִׁבְעַת	7	שֶׁבַע	שְׁבַע
שְׁמֹנָה	שְׁמֹנַת	8	שְׁמֹנֶה	שְׁמֹנֶה
תִּשְׁעָה	תִּשְׁעַת	9	תֵּשַׁע	תְּשַׁע
עֲשָׂרָה	עֲשֶׂרֶת	10	עֶשֶׂר	עֶשֶׂר
אַחַד עָשָׂר		11	אַחַת עֶשְׂרֵה	
שְׁנֵים עָשָׂר		12	שְׁתֵּים עֶשְׂרֵה	
שְׁלֹשָׁה עָשָׂר		13	שְׁלֹשׁ עֶשְׂרֵה	
....		....	....	
עֶשְׂרִים		20	עֶשְׂרִים	
שְׁלֹשִׁים		30	שְׁלֹשִׁים	
אַרְבָּעִים		40	אַרְבָּעִים	
חֲמִשִּׁים		50	חֲמִשִּׁים	
שִׁשִּׁים		60	שִׁשִּׁים	
שִׁבְעִים		70	שִׁבְעִים	
שְׁמֹנִים		80	שְׁמֹנִים	
תִּשְׁעִים		90	תִּשְׁעִים	
מֵאָה		100	מֵאָה	
מָאתַיִם		200	מָאתַיִם	
שְׁלֹשׁ מֵאוֹת		300	שְׁלֹשׁ מֵאוֹת	
אַרְבַּע מֵאוֹת		400	אַרְבַּע מֵאוֹת	
חֲמֵשׁ מֵאוֹת		500	חֲמֵשׁ מֵאוֹת	
שֵׁשׁ מֵאוֹת		600	שֵׁשׁ מֵאוֹת	
שְׁבַע מֵאוֹת		700	שְׁבַע מֵאוֹת	

....	....	....
אֶלֶף	1,000	אֶלֶף
אַלְפַּיִם	2,000	אַלְפַּיִם
שְׁלֹשֶׁת אֲלָפִים	3,000	שְׁלֹשֶׁת אֲלָפִים
אַרְבַּעַת אֲלָפִים	4,000	אַרְבַּעַת אֲלָפִים
חֲמֵשֶׁת אֲלָפִים	5,000	חֲמֵשֶׁת אֲלָפִים
רְבָבָה	10,000	רְבָבָה

Notes:

1. "One" follows the noun, as in: one man אִישׁ אֶחָד, one year שָׁנָה אַחַת
   In the construct form it reads: one of the sons אַחַד הַבָּנִים
2. "Two" precedes the noun in a construct form: two bulls שְׁנֵי פָּרִים
   or follows the noun in the absolute form פָּרִים שְׁנַיִם
3. Other cardinal numbers either precede or follow the noun:
   three fathers שְׁלֹשָׁה אָבוֹת, אָבוֹת שְׁלֹשָׁה
   four mothers אַרְבַּע אִמָּהוֹת, אִמָּהוֹת אַרְבַּע
4. Between "two" and "ten", the noun is always in the plural:
   seven days שִׁבְעָה יָמִים
   From "eleven" on, the noun may be in the plural or the singular:
   forty years אַרְבָּעִים שָׁנָה, אַרְבָּעִים שָׁנִים
5. Tens and units are connected with "and" וְ, וּ:
   thirty-four (f.) שְׁלֹשִׁים וְאַרְבַּע, אַרְבַּע וּשְׁלֹשִׁים
   twenty-two (m.) שְׁנַיִם וְעֶשְׂרִים, עֶשְׂרִים וּשְׁנַיִם
6. From "thirty" on, tens are formed by the plural of the units, e.g., 30 שְׁלֹשִׁים, 40 אַרְבָּעִים, 50 חֲמִשִּׁים, 60 שִׁשִּׁים ...

14.2 Ordinal numbers

	f.	m.		f.	m.
first	רִאשׁוֹנָה	רִאשׁוֹן	sixth	שִׁשִּׁית	שִׁשִּׁי
second	שֵׁנִית	שֵׁנִי	seventh	שְׁבִיעִית	שְׁבִיעִי
third	שְׁלִישִׁית	שְׁלִישִׁי	eighth	שְׁמִינִית	שְׁמִינִי
fourth	רְבִיעִית	רְבִיעִי	ninth	תְּשִׁיעִית	תְּשִׁיעִי
fifth	חֲמִישִׁית	חֲמִישִׁי	tenth	עֲשִׂירִית	עֲשִׂירִי

Notes:

1. From "first" to "tenth", the ordinal numbers are adjectives. As such, they follow the noun and agree with its gender. Examples:
   on the third day בַּיּוֹם הַשְּׁלִישִׁי
   the sixth year הַשָּׁנָה הַשִּׁשִּׁית
2. From "eleventh", ordinal numbers are replaced by cardinals:
   בְּאַרְבָּעָה עָשָׂר לַחֹדֶשׁ (עזרא ו 19)
   On the fourteen of the month (Ezra 6:19)

15. THE VERB

15.1 Tenses

In Hebrew, unlike in English, the tenses are few and quite simple: a) past, b) present (participle), c) future, d) imperative (command).

a) The past tense designates a completed action. English variations like "he remembered", "he has remembered", "he had remembered", are all expressed in Hebrew as the past פָּקַד. In this dictionary, a verb is given in the past tense, third person, masculine singular ("he"). This pattern is the simplest, with the least prefixes or suffixes; in many cases, it retains all three root letters. For example, the previous verb is listed as
v. פקד פָּקַד
with the root letters פקד, unvowelled, marking it as a verb.

b) The present tense designates an action that is happening now, and also a continued action.
Examples:
שׁוֹמֵר מִצְוָה (קהלת ח 5) is translated as
He who obeys a commandment (Eccles. 8:5)
וְעֵלִי שֹׁמֵר (שמואל א' א 12) is translated as
And Eli is watching (I Sam. 1:12)

The present tense may also serve as a verbal adjective, or as a participle.
More examples:
הָאֹכְלִים אֵת פַּת-בַּג הַמֶּלֶךְ (דניאל א 13) is translated as
(Those) eating the king's food (Dan. 1:13)

שֹׁמֵר הַבְּרִית (דברים ז 9) is translated as
He keeps the covenant (Deut. 7:9),
or as The keeper of the covenant
in the construct form.

In the passive form, the present participle is an adjective.
For example, the verb
v. כתב כָּתַב
is used as the passive participle in
כָּתוּב בְּתוֹרַת מֹשֶׁה (דניאל ט 13)
is written in the teaching of Moses (Dan. 9:13)

c) The future tense designates an uncompleted, yet to be done, action. So, “he will guard”, *or* “he will be guarding” becomes in Hebrew יִשְׁמֹר (הוּא) where the pronoun הוּא ("he") is optional.

d) The imperative (command) takes on a short form of the future, without the prefix. For example, שְׁמֹר is translated as “keep!” or “guard!” (masculine, singular) and is a short form of the future יִשְׁמֹר without the prefix יִ.
Negative commands (“You shall not...”, “Thou shalt not...”) are formed with the future tense preceded by לֹא for a *permanent* prohibition, and by אַל for an *immediate, short-term* prohibition.
Examples:
לֹא תִּגְנֹב (שמות כ 13, דברים ה 17)
reads
You shall not steal *or* Thou shalt not steal
(Ex.20:13, Deut. 5:17)
אַל תִּשְׁלַח יָדְךָ אֶל הַנַּעַר (בראשית כב 12)
means
Do not raise your hand against the boy (Gen. 22:12)

15.2 The infinitive

The infinitive is a gerund (verbal noun) with the suffix “ing”, as in the English expression “Stealing is a sin.” In Hebrew there are two infinitives:

a) The infinitive absolute, a basic pattern of the verb without a tense, a pronoun, a gender, or a number. For example,

Fall	v. נפל	נָפוֹל
Guard, keep	v. שמר	שָׁמוֹר

This pattern is used mostly for emphasis, as in
שָׁמוֹר תִּשְׁמְרוּן (דברים ו 17)
Be sure to keep, *or* You shall diligently keep (Deut. 6:17)

b) The infinitive construct,

v. נפל	נְפֹל
v. שמר	

With the prefixes ב, כ, ל, מ (see section 6), they express:

while falling	בִּנְפֹל
as guarding	כִּשְׁמֹר
to fall	לִנְפֹּל
from guarding	מִשְּׁמֹר

15.3 Sound and weak verbs

A *sound* verb retains all its three root letters in all its patterns. These letters are: ב, ג, ד, ז, ח, ט, כ, ל, מ, ס, ע, פ, צ, ק, ר, ש, ת
Examples of sound verbs are:
ברך, גמר, דבר, זרע, פקד, צחק, רחץ, שמע
A *weak* verb has in its root letters one (or more) of the letters א, ה, ו, י, נ which may disappear in some of the patterns of that verb. (That is why it is called "weak"!)
Some examples of weak verbs are: בנה, ישב, נפל, קום, קרא

15.4 The generic name for a verb

The letters פעל are used as the generic root letters for any verb. Coincidentally, the true verb
to do, to act פָּעַל
reminds us of the meaning of a verb. Also, in modern Hebrew, the word for "verb" is פֹּעַל.
So, in the previous examples:

1. In שמר, ש is the פ root letter; מ is the ע root letter, and ר is the ל root letter.
2. In ישב, י is the פ root letter, ש the ע root letter, ב the ל root letter. It is a weak פ״י verb, the first letter being י.
3. In קום, ק is the פ, ו the ע, and ם the ל root letter, respectively. It is a weak ע״ו verb, the second letter being ו.
4. In בנה, ב is the פ, נ is the ע, and ה is the ל root letter, respectively. It is a weak ל״ה verb.

Such classifications are useful, and are presented in the following sections.

15.5 Verbal stems

There are seven verbal stems (patterns) in which a verb can be conjugated. Using the generic letters פעל, these stems are:

1) פָּעַל (קַל) Simple (light)
   This stem denotes a simple, active form of the verb. For example:
   break (v. שבר) שָׁבַר

2) נִפְעַל The passive form of פָּעַל. In our example:
   be broken (v. שבר) נִשְׁבַּר

3) פִּעֵל Usually denotes a stronger action than פָּעַל. In our example:
smash, shatter (v. שבר) שִׁבֵּר

4) פֻּעַל The passive form of פִּעֵל. For example:
attach (v. חבר) חִבֵּר
be attached (v. חבר) חֻבַּר

5) הִתְפַּעֵל Denotes generally a reflexive (self) action. For example:
wash (v. רחץ) רָחַץ
wash oneself, bathe הִתְרַחֵץ
strengthen (v. חזק) חִזֵּק
grow strong הִתְחַזֵּק

6) הִפְעִיל Denotes generally a causative action, making someone do something.
For example:
wear (v. לבש) לָבַשׁ
dress someone (cause someone to wear) הִלְבִּישׁ
become low (v. שפל) שָׁפַל
lower (make low); humiliate הִשְׁפִּיל

7) הֻפְעַל ,הָפְעַל This is the passive form of הִפְעִיל. For example:
shame, offend (v. כלם) הִכְלִים
be shamed הָכְלַם
deposit (v. פקד) הִפְקִיד
be deposited הָפְקַד

Notes:

1. In practice, not all verbs have meaningful conjugations in all seven stems. This dictionary lists, by their respective numbers, 1), 2), 3),...7), *only verbs that have meanings* in these specific stems. In addition, they are cross-listed; so, for example, the word נִשְׁבַּר is listed under the letter נ, as follows:

   be broken, be destroyed v. שבר **נִשְׁבַּר**

   showing its root letters שבר (unvowelled), and it is also listed under the letter ש as:

   v. **שבר**

   be broken, be destroyed 2) נִשְׁבַּר
2. Not all stems have these stated meanings (the F.R.O.G. in action). For example,
   inform; tell (v. נגד) הִגִּיד is in the stem הִפְעִיל, though there is no causative action here.

This dictionary gives the different meanings for such entries.

3. Verbs whose first root letter (פ) is one of ד, ז, ט, ס, צ, ש, ת are modified slightly in the stem הִתְפַּעֵל, in order to make the pronunciation easy.
For example:

(instead of הִתְדַּבֵּר)	v. דבר	הִדַּבֵּר
(instead of הִתְזַכָּה)	v. זכה	הִזַּכָּה
(instead of הִתְטַמָּא)	v. טמא	הִטַּמָּא
(instead of הִתְסַתֵּר)	v. סתר	הִסְתַּתֵּר
(instead of הִתְצַדֵּק)	v. צדק	הִצְטַדֵּק
(instead of הִתְשַׁגֵּעַ)	v. שגעה	הִשְׁתַּגֵּעַ
(instead of הִתְתַּמֵּם)	v. תמם	הִתַּמֵּם

15.6 Sample Verb Conjugations

Notes:

1. The sound verb פקד is given in all seven stems. In the weak verbs, samples are given from the various groups, and they are listed at the beginning of each stem as פ״י, פ״נ, ע״ו, ל״ה.
2. In all the following listings, the order for the past tense and the future tense is:
אֲנִי, אַתָּה, אַתְּ, הוּא, הִיא, אֲנַחְנוּ, אַתֶּם, אַתֶּן, הֵם, הֵן
I, you (m.s.), you (f.s.), he, she, we, you (m.pl.), you (f.pl.), they (m.), they (f.).
For the present and the imperative, the order is: m.s., f.s., m.pl., f.pl.

A) Sound verb פקד

1) פָּעַל:

Past tense:

פָּקַדְתִּי, פָּקַדְתָּ, פָּקַדְתְּ, פָּקַד, פָּקְדָה, פָּקַדְנוּ, פְּקַדְתֶּם, פְּקַדְתֶּן, פָּקְדוּ, פָּקְדוּ

Present tense (active participle):

פּוֹקֵד, פּוֹקֶדֶת (פּוֹקְדָה), פּוֹקְדִים, פּוֹקְדוֹת

Present tense (passive participle):

פָּקוּד, פְּקוּדָה, פְּקוּדִים, פְּקוּדוֹת

Future tense:

אֶפְקֹד, תִּפְקֹד, תִּפְקְדִי, יִפְקֹד, תִּפְקֹד, נִפְקֹד, תִּפְקְדוּ, תִּפְקֹדְנָה, יִפְקְדוּ, תִּפְקֹדְנָה

Some verbs follow the pattern:

אֶלְמַד, תִּלְמַד, תִּלְמְדִי,...

A long pattern exists:

אֶפְקְדָה, אֶלְמְדָה, נִפְקְדָה, נִלְמְדָה

Imperative tense:

פְּקֹד, פִּקְדִי, פִּקְדוּ, פְּקֹדְנָה

2) נִפְעַל:

Past tense:

נִפְקַדְתִּי, נִפְקַדְתָּ, נִפְקַדְתְּ, נִפְקַד, נִפְקְדָה, נִפְקַדְנוּ, נִפְקַדְתֶּם, נִפְקַדְתֶּן, נִפְקְדוּ, נִפְקְדוּ

Present tense:

נִפְקָד, נִפְקֶדֶת, נִפְקָדִים, נִפְקָדוֹת

Future tense:

אֶפָּקֵד, תִּפָּקֵד, תִּפָּקְדִי, יִפָּקֵד, תִּפָּקֵד, נִפָּקֵד, תִּפָּקְדוּ, תִּפָּקַדְנָה, יִפָּקְדוּ, תִּפָּקַדְנָה

Imperative tense:

הִפָּקֵד, הִפָּקְדִי, הִפָּקְדוּ, הִפָּקַדְנָה

3) פִּעֵל:

Past tense:

פִּקַּדְתִּי, פִּקַּדְתָּ, פִּקַּדְתְּ, פִּקֵּד, פִּקְּדָה, פִּקַּדְנוּ, פִּקַּדְתֶּם, פִּקַּדְתֶּן, פִּקְּדוּ

Present tense:

מְפַקֵּד, מְפַקֶּדֶת, מְפַקְּדִים, מְפַקְּדוֹת

Future tense:

אֲפַקֵּד, תְּפַקֵּד, תְּפַקְּדִי, יְפַקֵּד, תְּפַקֵּד, נְפַקֵּד, תְּפַקְּדוּ, תְּפַקֵּדְנָה, יְפַקְּדוּ, תְּפַקֵּדְנָה

Imperative tense:

פַּקֵּד, פַּקְּדִי, פַּקְּדוּ, פַּקֵּדְנָה

4) פֻּעַל:

Past tense:

פֻּקַּדְתִּי, פֻּקַּדְתָּ, ..., פֻּקַּדְנוּ, פֻּקַּדְתֶּם, ...

Present tense:

מְפֻקָּד, מְפֻקֶּדֶת, מְפֻקָּדִים, מְפֻקָּדוֹת

Future tense:

אֲפֻקַּד, תְּפֻקַּד, ...

Imperative tense: none

5) הִתְפַּעֵל:

Past tense:

הִתְפַּקַּדְתִּי, הִתְפַּקַּדְתָּ, הִתְפַּקַּדְתְּ, הִתְפַּקֵּד, הִתְפַּקְּדָה, הִתְפַּקַּדְנוּ, הִתְפַּקַּדְתֶּם, הִתְפַּקַּדְתֶּן, הִתְפַּקְּדוּ

Present tense:

מִתְפַּקֵּד, מִתְפַּקֶּדֶת, מִתְפַּקְּדִים, מִתְפַּקְּדוֹת

Future tense:

אֶתְפַּקֵד, תִּתְפַּקֵד, תִּתְפַּקְדִי, יִתְפַּקֵד, תִּתְפַּקֵד, נִתְפַּקֵד, תִּתְפַּקְדוּ, תִּתְפַּקֵדְנָה, יִתְפַּקְדוּ, תִּתְפַּקֵדְנָה

Imperative tense:

הִתְפַּקֵד, הִתְפַּקְדִי, הִתְפַּקְדוּ, הִתְפַּקֵדְנָה

6) הִפְעִיל:

Past tense:

הִפְקַדְתִּי, הִפְקַדְתָּ, הִפְקַדְתְּ, הִפְקִיד, הִפְקִידָה, הִפְקַדְנוּ, הִפְקַדְתֶּם, הִפְקַדְתֶּן, הִפְקִידוּ

Present tense:

מַפְקִיד, מַפְקִידָה, מַפְקִידִים, מַפְקִידוֹת

Future tense:

אַפְקִיד, תַּפְקִיד, תַּפְקִידִי, יַפְקִיד, תַּפְקִיד, נַפְקִיד, תַּפְקִידוּ, תַּפְקֵדְנָה, יַפְקִידוּ, תַּפְקֵדְנָה

A long pattern exists:

אַפְקִידָה, ...

Imperative tense:

הַפְקֵד, הַפְקִידִי, הַפְקִידוּ, הַפְקֵדְנָה

7) הֻפְעַל, הָפְעַל:

Past tense:

הָ/הֻפְקַדְתִּי, הָ/הֻפְקַדְתָּ, הָ/הֻפְקַדְתְּ, הָ/הֻפְקַד, הָ/הֻפְקְדָה, הָ/הֻפְקַדְנוּ, הָ/הֻפְקַדְתֶּם, הָ/הֻפְקַדְתֶּן, הָ/הֻפְקְדוּ

Present tense:

מָ/מֻפְקָד, מָ/מֻפְקֶדֶת, מָ/מֻפְקָדִים, מָ/מֻפְקָדוֹת

Future tense:

אָפְקַד (אֻפְקַד), תָּפְקַד, ..., נָפְקַד (נֻפְקַד), תָּפְקְדוּ, ...

Imperative tense: none

B) Weak verbs

1) פָּעַל

ישב (פ״י), נפל (פ״נ), אכל (פ״א), קום (ע״ו), בנה (ל״ה)

Past tense:

יָשַׁבְתִּי, נָפַלְתִּי, אָכַלְתִּי, קַמְתִּי, בָּנִיתִי

Present tense:

יוֹשֵׁב, יוֹשֶׁבֶת, נוֹפֵל, נוֹפֶלֶת, אוֹכֵל, אוֹכֶלֶת, קָם, קָמָה, בּוֹנֶה, בּוֹנָה

Future tense:

אֵשֵׁב, יֵשֵׁב, אֶפֹּל, יִפֹּל, אֹכַל, יֹאכַל, אָקוּם, יָקוּם, אֶבְנֶה, יִבְנֶה

Short and long patterns exist:

יִבֶן, אָקוּמָה

Imperative tense:

שֵׁב, שְׁבוּ, נְפֹל, נִפְלוּ, אֱכֹל, אִכְלוּ, קוּם, קוּמוּ, בְּנֵה, בְּנוּ

2) נִפְעַל:

ישב (פ״י), נצל (פ״נ), אכל (פ״א), כון (ע״ו) בנה (ל״ה)

Past tense:

נוֹשַׁבְתִּי, נִצַּלְתִּי, נֶאֱכַלְתִּי, נְכוּנוֹתִי, נִבְנֵיתִי

Present tense:

נוֹשָׁב, נוֹשֶׁבֶת, נִצָּל, נִצֶּלֶת, נֶאֱכָל, נֶאֱכֶלֶת, נָכוֹן, נְכוֹנָה, נִבְנֶה, נִבְנֵית

Future tense:

אִוָּשֵׁב, יִוָּשֵׁב, אִנָּצֵל, יִנָּצֵל, אֵאָכֵל, יֵאָכֵל, אִכּוֹן, יִכּוֹן, אֶבָּנֶה, יִבָּנֶה

Imperative tense:

הִוָּשֵׁב, הִוָּשְׁבִי, הִנָּצֵל, הִנָּצְלִי, הֵאָכֵל, הֵאָכְלִי, הִכּוֹן, הִכּוֹנִי, הִבָּנֵה, הִבָּנִי

3) פִּעֵל

Past tense:

יִשַּׁבְתִּי, נִצַּלְתִּי, אִכַּלְתִּי, כּוֹנַנְתִּי, בִּנִּיתִי

Present tense:

מְיַשֵּׁב, מְיַשֶּׁבֶת, מְנַצֵּל, מְנַצֶּלֶת, מְאַכֵּל, מְאַכֶּלֶת, מְכוֹנֵן, מְכוֹנֶנֶת, מְבַנֶּה, מְבַנָּה

Future tense:

אֲיַשֵּׁב, יְיַשֵּׁב, אֲנַצֵּל, יְנַצֵּל, אֲאַכֵּל, יְאַכֵּל, אֲכוֹנֵן, יְכוֹנֵן, אֲבַנֶּה, יְבַנֶּה

Imperative tense:

יַשֵּׁב, יַשְּׁבִי, נַצֵּל, נַצְּלִי, אַכֵּל, אַכְּלִי, כּוֹנֵן, כּוֹנְנִי, בַּנֵּה, בַּנִּי

4) פֻּעַל:

Past tense:

יֻשַּׁבְתִּי, נֻצַּלְתִּי, אֻכַּלְתִּי, כּוֹנַנְתִּי, בֻּנֵּיתִי

Present tense:

מְיֻשָּׁב, מְיֻשֶּׁבֶת, מְנֻצָּל, מְנֻצֶּלֶת, מְאֻכָּל, מְאֻכֶּלֶת, מְכוֹנָן, מְכוֹנֶנֶת, מְבֻנֶּה, מְבֻנָּה

Future tense:

אֲיֻשַּׁב, יְיֻשַּׁב, אֲנֻצַּל, יְנֻצַּל, אֲאֻכַּל, יְאֻכַּל, אֲכוֹנַן, יְכוֹנַן, אֲבֻנֶּה, יְבֻנֶּה

Imperative tense: none

5) הִתְפַּעֵל:

ישב (פ״י), נצל (פ״נ), אכל (פ״א), בין (ע״י), עלה (ל״ה)

Past tense:

הִתְיַשַּׁבְתִּי, הִתְנַצַּלְתִּי, הִתְאַכַּלְתִּי, הִתְבּוֹנַנְתִּי, הִתְעַלֵּיתִי

Present tense:

מִתְיַשֵּׁב, מִתְיַשֶּׁבֶת, מִתְנַצֵּל, מִתְנַצֶּלֶת, מִתְאַכֵּל, מִתְאַכֶּלֶת, מִתְבּוֹנֵן, מִתְבּוֹנֶנֶת, מִתְעַלֶּה, מִתְעַלָּה

Future tense:

אֶתְיַשֵּׁב, יִתְיַשֵּׁב, אֶתְנַצֵּל, יִתְנַצֵּל, אֶתְאַכֵּל, יִתְאַכֵּל, אֶתְבּוֹנֵן, יִתְבּוֹנֵן, אֶתְעַלֶּה, יִתְעַלֶּה

Imperative tense:

הִתְיַשֵּׁב, הִתְנַצֵּל, הִתְאַכֵּל, הִתְבּוֹנֵן, הִתְעַלֵּה

6) הִפְעִיל:

Past tense:

הוֹשַׁבְתִּי, הִצַּלְתִּי, הֶאֱכַלְתִּי, הֵבַנְתִּי (הֲבִינוֹתִי), הֶעֱלֵיתִי

Present tense:

מוֹשִׁיב, מוֹשִׁיבָה, מַצִּיל, מַצִּילָה (מַצֶּלֶת), מַאֲכִיל, מַאֲכִילָה, מֵבִין, מְבִינָה, מַעֲלֶה, מַעֲלָה

Future tense:

אוֹשִׁיב, יוֹשִׁיב, אַצִּיל, יַצִּיל, אַאֲכִיל, יַאֲכִיל, אָבִין, יָבִין, אַעֲלֶה, יַעֲלֶה

Imperative tense:

הוֹשֵׁב, הוֹשִׁיבִי, הַצֵּל, הַצִּילִי, הַאֲכֵל, הַאֲכִילִי, הָבֵן, הָבִינִי, הַעֲלֵה, הַעֲלִי

7) הֻפְעַל, הָפְעַל:

Past tense:

הוּשַׁבְתִּי, הֻצַּלְתִּי, הָאֳכַלְתִּי, הוּבַנְתִּי, הָעֳלֵיתִי

Present tense:

מוּשָׁב, מוּשָׁבָה, מֻצָּל, מֻצָּלָה, מָאֳכָל, מָאֳכֶלֶת, מוּבָן, מוּבֶנֶת, מָעֳלֶה, מָעֳלָה

Future tense:

אוּשַׁב, יוּשַׁב, אֻצַּל, יֻצַּל, אָאֳכַל, יָאֳכַל, אוּבַן, יוּבַן, אָעֳלֶה, יָעֳלֶה

Imperative tense: none

C) Weak verb: be היה

while being, to be, from being בִּהְיוֹת, לִהְיוֹת, מִהְיוֹת

1) פָּעַל:

Past tense:

הָיִיתִי, הָיִיתָ, הָיִית, הָיָה (הָוָה), הָיְתָה, הָיִינוּ, הֱיִיתֶם, הָיוּ, הָיוּ

Present tense (rare):

הֹוֶה, הוֹיָה

Future tense:

אֶהְיֶה (אֱהִי), תִּהְיֶה (תְּהִי), תִּהְיִי, יִהְיֶה (יְהִי), תִּהְיֶה (תְּהִי), נִהְיֶה,
תִּהְיוּ, יִהְיוּ, תִּהְיֶינָה (תִּהְיֶיןָ)

Imperative tense:

הֱיֵה, הֲיִי, הֱיוּ

2) נִפְעַל:

Past tense:

נִהְיֵיתִי, נִהְיֵיתָ, נִהְיָה, נִהְיְתָה

All other patterns and stems do not exist in the Bible.

15.7 The prefix ו marking the past; marking the future

A unique and very common use of the prefix ו is found in the Bible: when in front of a verb in the future, it changes the meaning to the past; when in front of a verb in the past – to the future. Examples:

1. Moses spoke וַיְדַבֵּר מֹשֶׁה
2. וְשָׁמְרוּ בְנֵי יִשְׂרָאֵל אֶת הַשַּׁבָּת (שמות לא 16)
   The children of Israel shall keep the Sabbath (Ex. 31:16)
3. But in
   וְיַעֲקֹב הָלַךְ לְדַרְכּוֹ (בראשית לב 1)
   And Jacob went on his way (Gen. 32:1)
   the prefix ו is in front of a noun and serves as the usual "and".

In many cases, the short form of the future is used. For example:

He struck	וַיַּךְ	instead of	וַיַּכֶּה
I appeared	וָאֵרָא	instead of	וָאֵרָאֶה
He saw	וַיַּרְא	instead of	וַיִּרְאֶה

Rule: A verb with this prefixed ו *always* precedes its subject. So, Moses said וַיֹּאמֶר מֹשֶׁה (never מֹשֶׁה וַיֹּאמֶר). However, a verb without this ו may precede or follow its subject: מֹשֶׁה אָמַר or אָמַר מֹשֶׁה is correct for Moses said.

15.8 Verbal suffixes

Instead of a personal pronoun as a direct object, a proper suffix is attached to the verb.

To illustrate, “I remembered him” is פָּקַדְתִּי אֹתוֹ with the personal pronoun, or פְּקַדְתִּיו with the suffix for “him”.

The following lists give the typical verbal suffixes which are easily recognizable:

פְּקַדְתִּיךָ, פְּקַדְתִּיךְ, פְּקַדְתִּיו (פְּקַדְתִּיהוּ), פְּקַדְתִּיהָ

I remembered you (m.s.),...(f.s.),...him,...her

פְּקַדְתִּיכֶם, פְּקַדְתִּיכֶן, פְּקַדְתִּים, פְּקַדְתִּין

I remembered you (m.pl.),...you (f.pl.),...them (m.pl.), them (f.pl.)

פְּקַדְתַּנִי, פְּקַדְתּוֹ (פְּקַדְתָּהוּ), פְּקַדְתָּהּ

You (m.s.) remembered me,...him,...her

פְּקַדְתָּנוּ, פְּקַדְתָּם, פְּקַדְתָּן

You (m.s.) remembered us,...them (m.),...them (f.)

פְּקַדְתִּינִי, פְּקַדְתִּיהוּ, פְּקַדְתִּיהָ

You (f.s.) remembered me,...him,...her

פְּקַדְתִּינוּ, פְּקַדְתִּים, פְּקַדְתִּין

You (f.s.) remembered us,...them (m.),...them (f.)

פְּקָדַנִי, פְּקָדְךָ, פְּקָדֵךְ, פְּקָדוֹ (פְּקָדָהוּ), פְּקָדָהּ

He remembered me,...you (m.s.),...you (f.s.),...him,...her

פְּקָדָנוּ, פְּקָדָם, פְּקָדָן

He remembered us,...them (m.),...them (f.)

פְּקָדַתְנִי, פְּקָדַתְךָ, פְּקָדָתֶךְ, פְּקָדַתְהוּ, פְּקָדַתָּהּ

She remembered me,...you (m.s.),...you (f.s.),...him,...her

פְּקָדַתְנוּ, פְּקָדָתַם, פְּקָדָתַן

She remembered us,...them (m.),...them (f.)

פְּקַדְנוּךָ

We remembered you (m.s.),...etc., with the same suffixes as in “he remembered”.

פְּקַדְתּוּנִי

You (m.pl., f.pl.) remembered me,...etc., with the same suffixes as in “he remembered”.

פְּקָדוּנִי, פְּקָדוּךָ, פְּקָדוּךְ, פְּקָדוּהוּ, פְּקָדוּהָ

They (m., f.) remembered me,...you (m.s.),...you (f.s.),...him,...her

פְּקָדוּנוּ, פְּקָדוּם, פְּקָדוּן

They (m., f.) remembered us,...them (m.),...them (f.)

15.9 Transitive and intransitive verbs; the particle אֶת (אֵת)

A transitive verb is accompanied by a direct object. For example, in the sentence, "we read a book," "read" is a transitive verb and "book" is a direct, indefinite object. In "we read the book," the verb "read" is transitive, and "book" is a direct, *definite* object.
An intransitive verb has no direct object. Examples of intransitive verbs are: sleep, come, sit, go, live.
To distinguish a direct, definite object, Hebrew inserts the particle אֶת or אֵת in front of that object.
Examples:

בְּרֵאשִׁית בָּרָא אֱלֹהִים אֵת הַשָּׁמַיִם (בראשית א 1)
Initially, God created the heaven (Gen. 1:1)
Here, "create" is a transitive verb, "heaven" is its direct object and it is definite because of the הַ. Therefore, use אֵת before הַשָּׁמַיִם.

קָנִיתִי עֲבָדִים (קהלת ב 7) I have acquired slaves (Eccl. 2:7)
Here, "slaves" is, in fact, a direct object of the transitive verb "acquire". But "slaves" is indefinite, hence no אֶת.

וַיִּשְׁמַע הַמֶּלֶךְ The king heard
Here, הַמֶּלֶךְ is the definite *subject.*
וַיִּשְׁמַע אֶת הַמֶּלֶךְ He heard the king
Here, הַמֶּלֶךְ is the direct, definite object of the transitive verb "heard", as is clear from the particle-אֶת.

וַיִּשְׁמַע מֶלֶךְ is ambiguous, it can be "a king heard", or "he heard a king". The exact meaning must be understood from the context.

Notes:

1. The F.R.O.G. is very active here; in many instances, the particle אֵת is missing when really needed:
   גָּרֵשׁ הָאָמָה הַזֹּאת וְאֶת בְּנָהּ (בראשית כא 10)
   Expel this maid servant and her son (Gen. 21:10).
   Quite obviously, one אֶת is missing in front of הָאָמָה.
2. Do not confuse this use of אֵת with its other meaning "with", as in:
   אֶת הָאֱלֹהִים הִתְהַלֶּךְ נֹחַ (בראשית ו 9)
   Noah walked with God (Gen. 6:9).
   In the following example, both usages of אֶת are seen:
   וְאֶת בְּרִיתִי אָקִים אֶת יִצְחָק (בראשית יז 21)
   And my covenant I will maintain with Isaac (Gen. 17:21).

THE NAMES OF GOD

There are many names of God in the Bible. The more common are:

1. **אֲדֹנָי**
The plural majestic ("my Lords"), to be read "my Lord".

2. **אֶהְיֶה**
Literally, I shall be (see the verb היה, section 15.6c, above). It is from Exodus 3:14, (שמות ג 14) אֶהְיֶה אֲשֶׁר אֶהְיֶה "I shall be what I shall be".

3. **אֵל**
The usual translation is "God". In the plural, **אֵלִים** is translated as "gods", or "celestials". A common suffix in proper names.

4. **אֱלֹהִים**
When referring to God, it has the majestic plural ending, but verbs and adjectives are in the m.s. (rarely, in the m.pl.). Out of reverence, pious Jews pronounce it אֱלֹקִים in secular use. As the plural of **אֱלוֹהַּ**, meaning "gods", "angels", or "judges", the accompanying verbs and adjectives are, of course, in the plural.

5. **אֱלוֹהַּ**

6. **יְהֹוָה**
Transliterated as "Jehovah", "Yahweh", or "YHWH". It is the Tetragrammaton, standing for the ineffable name of God. It is pronounced **אֲדֹנָי** (see 1 above). Pious Jews don't even do so, unless in prayer. For secular purposes, they prefer The Name **הַשֵּׁם** or Ado-Name **אֲדֹשֵׁם**. The root and the true meaning of the Tetragrammaton are not known.

7. **יָהּ**
This is a short version of 6. The suffixes יָהּ and יָהוּ are common in proper names.

8. **יְיָ**
Another form of the Tetragrammaton, also pronounced **אֲדֹנָי**.

9. **שַׁדַּי**
"Almighty", or "Provider".

10. **אֲדֹנָי יֱהֹוִה**
This combination is pronounced **אֲדֹנָי אֱלֹהִים**.

THE BOOKS OF THE BIBLE

The Hebrew Bible consists of 25 books arranged in three major divisions:

1. **תּוֹרָה** ("Teaching"), known also as the Torah, The Five Books of Moses, or the Pentateuch (from the Greek for "five books").
2. **נְבִיאִים** ("Prophets").
3. **כְּתוּבִים** ("Writings").

The acronym תַּנַ״ךְ is formed from the first letters of these names, is often used for the Hebrew Bible. Within the תַּנַ״ךְ, the books are arranged in the following order:

Torah	**תּוֹרָה**
1. Genesis	בְּרֵאשִׁית
2. Exodus	שְׁמוֹת
3. Leviticus	וַיִּקְרָא
4. Numbers	בְּמִדְבַּר
5. Deuteronomy	דְּבָרִים

Prophets - Former	**נְבִיאִים רִאשׁוֹנִים**
6. Joshua	יְהוֹשֻׁעַ
7. Judges	שׁוֹפְטִים
8. Samuel I, II	שְׁמוּאֵל א׳, ב׳
9. Kings I, II	מְלָכִים א׳, ב׳

Prophets - Latter	**נְבִיאִים אַחֲרוֹנִים**
10. Isaiah	יְשַׁעְיָהוּ
11. Jeremiah	יִרְמְיָהוּ
12. Ezekiel	יְחֶזְקֵאל
13.The Twelve (minor prophets)	תְּרֵי עָשָׂר
i. Hosea	הוֹשֵׁעַ
ii. Joel	יוֹאֵל
iii. Amos	עָמוֹס
iv. Obadiah	עֹבַדְיָה
v. Jonah	יוֹנָה
vi. Micah	מִיכָה
vii. Nahum	נַחוּם
viii. Habakkuk	חֲבַקּוּק
ix. Zephaniah	צְפַנְיָה
x. Haggai	חַגַּי
xi. Zechariah	זְכַרְיָה
xii. Malachi	מַלְאָכִי

Writings	**כְּתוּבִים**
14. Psalms	תְּהִילִים
15. Proverbs	מִשְׁלֵי
16. Job	אִיּוֹב
17. Song of Songs	שִׁיר הַשִּׁירִים
18. Ruth	רוּת
19. Lamentations	אֵיכָה
20. Ecclesiastes	קֹהֶלֶת
21. Esther	אֶסְתֵּר
22. Daniel	דָּנִיֵּאל
23. Ezra	עֶזְרָא
24. Nehemiah	נְחֶמְיָה
25. Chronicles I,II	דִּבְרֵי הַיָּמִים א׳, ב׳

Note: For the meaning of the Hebrew name of a book, see the appropriate entry in this dictionary.